Moira Walshe has spent 30 years researching her maternal grandfather's family. She has a lifelong passion for history and has a BA (Hons) degree in Humanities with Art History and Classical Studies following six years of part-time study with the Open University. She lives in Suffolk.

I am bound to them,
though I cannot look into their eyes or hear their voices,
I honour their history.
I cherish their lives,
I will tell their story,
I will remember them.

Author unknown

THE CLARKS OF CROFTON HALL

The Rise of a Victorian Family

MOIRA WALSHE

Matador
Unit E2 Airfield Business Park,
Harrison Road, Market Harborough,
Leicestershire. LE16 7UL
Tel: 0116 2792299
Email: books@troubador.co.uk
Web: www.troubador.co.uk/matador
Twitter: @matadorbooks

ISBN 978 1803131 702

British Library Cataloguing in Publication Data.
A catalogue record for this book is available from the British Library.

Printed and bound in the UK by TJ Books Ltd, Padstow, Cornwall
Typeset in 12pt Minion Pro by Troubador Publishing Ltd, Leicester, UK

Matador is an imprint of Troubador Publishing Ltd

In memory of my mother,
Marjorie (1926-2020)

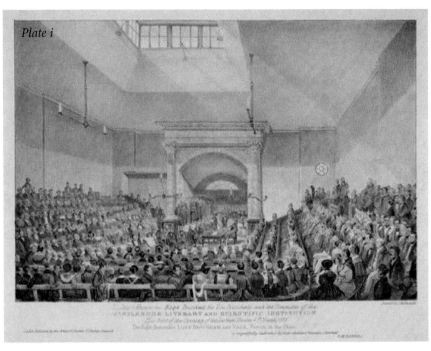

Plate i

Plate ii

Plate iii

Plate iv

CONTENTS

PART ONE – THOMAS CLARK 1819-1895

LIST OF ILLUSTRATIONS

PART ONE – THOMAS CLARK 1819-1895

1. Newington map 1862 © Michael McEvoy
2. Mary Ann Westfield c. 1840s
3. George Aldridge c. 1854 *State Library of South Australia*, B53485
4. Percy Aldridge Grainger (the composer) 1882-1961 with his mother Rose (née Aldridge) Bergen Public Library, Norway <https://www.flickr.com/photos/37381115@N04/3482046579>
5. The Great Exhibition in the Crystal Palace, Hyde Park, London: the transept looking north. Steel engraving by W. Lacey after J.E. Mayall, 1851. This work is licensed under the Creative Commons Public Domain Mark 1.0 License. To view a copy of this license, visit http://creativecommons.org/publicdomain/mark/1.0/ or send a letter to Creative Commons, PO Box 1866, Mountain View, CA 94042, USA.
6. Thomas Clark, Freedom of the City of London certificate, 1853
7. Thomas Clark, admittance to be a broker, 1854
8. A pestilent suburban cottage, Old Kent Road 1854. This work is licensed under the Creative Commons Public Domain Mark 1.0 License. To view a copy of this license, visit http://creativecommons.org/publicdomain/mark/1.0/ or send a letter to Creative Commons, PO Box 1866, Mountain View, CA 94042, USA.
9. Mrs W.K. Clifford (née Miss Lucy Lane) © National Portrait Gallery
10. Crofton Hall, Orpington Kent – rear view c. 1863
11. Crofton Hall, Orpington Kent – front view c. 1863
12. Anerley Road and Crystal Palace, Sydenham c. 1900
13. Matilda Hephzibah Clark

PART TWO – THOMAS CLARK 1841-1927

PART 3 – THE CHILDREN OF THOMAS CLARK 1841-1927

Thomas William Francis

Ernest Percival Frederick (Percy)

Herbert Lionel Alexander

COLOUR PLATES

ACKNOWLEDGEMENTS

There are several people and organisations that I wish to thank for their support, assistance and encouragement in the completing of this book.

Firstly, I was greatly inspired and guided by John Titford's publication *Writing Up Your Family History*. John was very helpful following my contact and I wish to thank him wholeheartedly for his interest in this project and for his contribution by way of the Foreword he has supplied.

A special thanks to Jeremy Gordon-Smith, together with his father, Bruce. They supplied the copy of the diary written by Matilda Bawtree which has been invaluable in illuminating family life. Jeremy has supplied several of the images contained within these pages and digitally restored some of my own torn photographs as well as helping with reading and supplying valuable feedback.

I wish to thank Anthony Foreman for the use of his computer and scanner in compiling my manuscript.

Michael McEvoy, a local resident, was very useful to have at hand as he is a genealogist with a special collection of old maps.

Tonia Hart, secretary of the Ongar Millennium History Society (OMHS), has been extremely helpful in tracking down images of Ongar Grammar School as well as arranging permission for the use of Chapter 14 of *Aspects of the History of Ongar* which I have used extensively to reconstruct the school lives of my great-uncles', Thomas W.F. Clark and Ernest P.F. Clark.

Likewise, thanks to Abby Matthews from Sutton Local Studies and Archives who assisted in tracking down a couple of images from their collections.

I wish to thank Robert Randell-Clark, for providing copies of photographs from his own collection.

I must also mention John Loveday, a former resident of Old Buckenham, Norfolk, for his support and interest in my publication. As he was born the same year as my Mum, the link with him has been very poignant.

During the final stages of the publication process, Jill de Laat has provided invaluable assistance in proof-reading. Thank you Jill for all your work.

A big thank you to the team at Troubador Publishing for taking on my manuscript and all the help and support along the journey. I wish to give a special mention to Joe Shillito, Senior Production Controller and to Hannah Dakin who dealt with my initial enquiry.

Finally, my thanks to everyone else whom I may not have named here but who has provided stories, anecdotes or photographs over the years which appear in this work.

FOREWORD

Writing a history of your own family is a devilishly difficult task to undertake. You would certainly wish to write as a 'proper' historian, yet the material you present is so personal to you, that at times it can be difficult to stand back and to be suitably objective.

In this present family history, Moira Walshe has steered her way through the story she has to tell with commendable skill and expertise; she is both a historian and an enthusiast, and tells a fascinating tale with admirable professionalism.

She says – and how true it is! – that her family history 'is much more than a collection of names, places and dates. Everything contained in these pages is based on solid sometimes painstaking research as well as the verbal and written testimonies of more recent generations'.

Moira had no grandparents to talk to about family matters, yet – adopting the Clark family motto of *Nil Desparandum* – she has turned a fascination with family history, a 'life's mission', into a fascinating and readable saga of the highest order. In at least one way Moira succeeds where so many budding writers of a family history fail – that is, her story is expertly ordered and organized, and her sources are identified with great thoroughness, numbers in the text relating to source details by way of endnotes. Appendices and a bibliography complete the work.

And all those wonderful illustrations, incorporated into the text and each given a clear and precise title! A sheer joy. Who could resist a book which contained an illustration entitled "Frances with cat"? The human touch is everywhere in evidence.

I have no hesitation in commending this book to one and all; it will delight and entertain you, offering up a tale of everyday folk, all of whom are ordinary in their way, yet somehow extraordinary at the same time.

John Titford MA FSA
Trustee and Chairman of Examiners,
Institute of Heraldic and Genealogical Studies.

PREFACE

I can hear my mother's voice through the years informing me of an important occasion in my early life which concerned a visit to my father's former landlady, Miss Georgianna Germany – one which I was far too young to remember. It was the mid-1960s and on observing me running around the lawn at her home, next door to my grandfather's former home in Old Buckenham, the old lady had exclaimed "Humph, she's a Westfield!" This was indeed confirmation that I belonged firmly in this side of my family.

In 1970, I moved with my family from Attleborough, Norfolk, to the neighbouring county of Suffolk. My father had employment in Stowmarket and so this town came to be my home from that time as I was growing up.

My mother was sad to leave behind the area in Norfolk where she had lived all her life and throughout the 1970s my parents made frequent journeys back to Norfolk at weekends to visit her step-mother. On many occasions we faithfully stopped at the churchyard of All Saints', Old Buckenham, which is a short distance from the former family home at Attleborough. Old Buckenham was where my mother was born, grew up and met my father. In the churchyard of the village known for its massive green, lies interred the remains of my grandfather, Herbert Clark-Westfield, his brother Ernest Percival Clark (known as Percy) who lived next door to him and mother's half-brother, Raymond, who died at just 18 months of age.

Unlike most of my contemporaries, I lacked grandparents to visit, talk with and get to know. My father's parents were in Ireland, a place I had never been and as a child seemed a very remote location indeed. So instead, there was a void in which getting to know my close relatives involved the ritual of tending the grave of my long-deceased grandfather. What seemed to be each Saturday but perhaps was not so frequent, we left our alien Suffolk town equipped with flowers, jam jars and shears for a journey lasting about an hour. Restless children in the back seat of my father's car would ask if we were nearly there it was such a long way. Arriving at the churchyard, my parents told me and my younger siblings that if we ran seven times around a railed box tomb near the entrance to the churchyard, we could make something remarkable occur – the church bells would ring! This would be attempted many times but of course, the bells remained silent. If only I could have achieved this, perhaps I could conjure up my lost relatives too.

After the churchyard visit was completed the car journey continued onwards to Attleborough and the home which Grandpa shared with his wife after his retirement from his working life in Old Buckenham in the early 1950s. At the bottom of the large garden here, his workshop contained his tools and looked just as it must have done 20 years previously at the time he had died. The workshop had a distinct musty smell and seemed a magical place.

Having a deceased grandparent whom my mother was very attached to and spent time discussing in great detail with her very inquisitive daughter, made a significant impact. For not only was her father cruelly unknown to me but his sister and brothers too, several of whom my mother knew and recalled with great affection. As I was growing up, I heard stories and anecdotal information about my impressive relations. Increasingly, I felt that I had to find out about the past and its inhabitants to understand and appreciate how and what I shared in character with my relatives.

The main character I heard about from my mother was my great-grandpa, Thomas Clark Westfield. My mother had not known her own grandpa either as he had died when she was a few months old. In the family, we had copies of two books he had published in the 1860s and he wrote the preface from a mysterious place called Crofton Hall. We did not know where Crofton Hall had been at all but someone said that a race horse recently had been heard of bearing that name. Mum declared she was going to Somerset House in London to find out about this elusive and enigmatic place and discover the relationship it had with her family. She never did. There was also a sepia photograph of my creative ancestor inside the cover which showed a bearded man, looking very erect and superior inside a sumptuous interior with a backdrop of a bookcase and heavy velvet curtains with a tassel. I imagined that this photo was taken at Crofton Hall and my ancestors were aristocrats, adding to their special aura.

As a young adult, visits were made in the early to mid-1980s to mum's elderly cousin in Ilford and she passed on many photographs to me of the Clark family knowing that they would be in safe hands. For the first time, I saw the likeness of my great-grandmother, Miss Frances or Fanny Bailey. I felt overwhelmed for the picture of her around 20 years of age, the same age as I then was, was like looking at myself. I made a copy of the photograph which afterwards adorned the hallway at home. Visitors asked about the identity of the lady who looked just like me.

Within a few years, I embarked on a life's mission to find out all I could about my maternal grandfather's family starting with interviewing the elderly relatives left, especially my mother's half-sister Doris who was born in 1900, to construct a basic family tree. The project gathered momentum in the early 1990s when I made my first exciting visits to the London archives in the days before research could be conducted online. In the years that have followed, I have built up a remarkable view into the lives of my ancestors which has led me to write this book. My aim has always been to reconstruct lives and give my relatives immortality which will resonate through the ages for posterity. I believe I have succeeded in this work.

Just as most of the material was written, my mother passed away after a long illness. As I look back, the link we share with past generations of relations seems to become even more accentuated and a vital part of honouring her memory.

INTRODUCTION

This family story is much more than a collection of names, places and dates. Everything contained in these pages is based on solid, sometimes painstaking, research as well as the verbal and written testimonies of more recent generations. As we escort the Clark family through time, we will walk with them through the weather they experienced on the day they married or on another significant event in their lives. We will step with them over the threshold to experience their homes and family life and all the drama that often entailed!

We also meet their neighbours, friends and business associates. When able, we can take an intimate view of life at school, the food they enjoyed and take an in-depth look at their innermost thoughts, beliefs and psyche.

Everything that is recorded in these pages is seen through the eyes of the people who felt what was happening in the time and place.

It has taken over two years to write this history and thirty years of research, as time has allowed. The exercise of writing a historical work has been approached and researched as if the characters lived influential lives, as they indeed were. You or I would certainly like to think that we will be remembered for generations to come in some way. I was amazed that so much material has come to light during the last two years that perhaps would have otherwise been overlooked without this project.

Harsh realities had to be confronted such as the world of 19th century trading – elephant and hippopotamus ivory, feathers from exotic birds, to name some of the most prominent. Reading details of the sales that took place in The Commercial Sale Rooms of Mincing Lane in the daily trade paper made for unpalatable reading as well as a fair amount of research to discover what the produce actually was. However, they were part of an era which accepted this largely, it would appear, without questions. As we pass through these years accompanying them, we observe how this age passes away.

It is a family in spite of this, whose identity blended in with what was in many ways the greatest cultural epoch of music, literature, scientific discovery, architectural greatness, technology and learning. This family engaged with all of this – they were fortunate in being in a position to do so when so many people lived lives in poverty.

This book is called 'The Clarks of Crofton Hall' but it wasn't a family seat, instead it was the place that we always knew was their home and at the time we knew of no other. It was an important place; there is only one other Crofton Hall in the country and that is in Cumbria. The Clarks only lived at Crofton Hall, Orpington for a few years and now it has vanished without trace having been demolished in the 1930s to make way for a modern estate. It then entered the realms of mythology.

TREE A

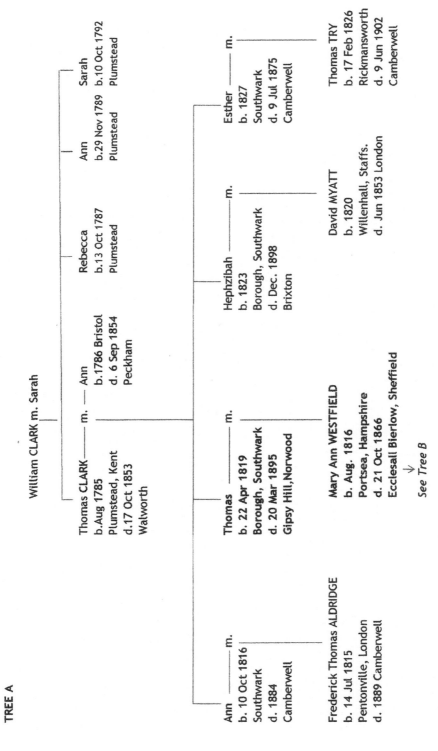

William CLARK m. Sarah

Thomas CLARK ———— m. ———— Ann
b.Aug 1785   b.1786 Bristol
Plumstead, Kent   d. 6 Sep 1854
d.17 Oct 1853   Peckham
Walworth

Rebecca
b.13 Oct 1787
Plumstead

Ann
b.29 Nov 1789
Plumstead

Sarah
b.10 Oct 1792
Plumstead

Ann ———— m.
b. 10 Oct 1816
Southwark
d. 1884
Camberwell

Frederick Thomas ALDRIDGE
b. 14 Jul 1815
Pentonville, London
d. 1889 Camberwell

Thomas ———— m. ———— Mary Ann WESTFIELD
b. 22 Apr 1819   b. Aug. 1816
Borough, Southwark   Portsea, Hampshire
d. 20 Mar 1895   d. 21 Oct 1866
Gipsy Hill, Norwood   Ecclesall Bierlow, Sheffield
                                                    ↓
                                              See Tree B

Hephzibah ———— m. ———— David MYATT
b. 1823   b. 1820
Borough, Southwark   Willenhall, Staffs.
d. Dec. 1898   d. Jun 1853 London
Brixton

Esther ———— m. ———— Thomas TRY
b. 1827   b. 17 Feb 1826
Southwark   Rickmansworth
d. 9 Jul 1875   d. 9 Jun 1902
Camberwell   Camberwell

TREE B

Thomas CLARK
b. 22 Apr 1819
Borough, Southwark
d. 20 Mar 1895
Gipsy Hill, Norwood

m. 1839

1. Mary Ann WESTFIELD
b. Aug 1816
Portsea, Hampshire
d. 21 Oct 1866
Ecclesall Bierlow

m. 2 1867 — Frances COLEBATCH
b. 30 Oct 1825
Aldgate, London
d. 2 Jul 1916
Islington, London

Thomas
b. 9 Dec 1841
Newington
d. 31 Jan 1927
Leytonstone
m. Frances Charlotte BAILEY
b. 9 Jun 1846
Camberwell
d. 31 Oct 1904
Bowers Gifford

SEE TREE C →

Frederick Henry
b. 23 Apr 1843
Milton, Gravesend
d. 28 Jan 1893
Brixton, Surrey
m. Annie POTTER
b. 1838 Westminster
d. 1926 Kensington

Mary Ann Esther (Polly)
b. 31 Oct 1844
Peckham
d. 18 Sep 1930
Epsom

James
b. 1846
Peckham

Emma Ann
b. 4 Mar 1848
Peckham
d. 4 Feb 1927
Cheam
m. Arthur William HILL b. 1849
Bourton, Glos.
d. 28 Sep 1916
Haywards Heath

Alfred
Dec 49 P'ham
18 Feb 1850

Matilda Hephzibah
b. 26 Dec 1850
Peckham
d. 17 Sep 1932
Sutton, Surrey
m. Alfred BAWTREE
b. 5 Dec 1846
Stoke Newington
d. 18 Nov 1929
Sutton, Surrey

Melina Elizabeth (Milly)
b. 31 Oct 1852
Peckham
d. 25 May 1937
Sutton, Surrey
m. Edmund Howe LILLEY
b. 20 Mar 1851
Camberwell
d. Oct. 1903
Tooting, London

Eliza (Lizzie)
b. 16 Sep 54
Peckham
30 May 1913
Adelaide
S. Australia
m. Frederick Albert FIELD
b. 1 Nov 1853
Islington
d. 31 Oct 1890
Adelaide

Amelia Seagrave
b. 1856 Shooters Hill
d. 21 Jun 1863
Cudham, Kent

Alice Mary
b. 1858 Shooters Hill
d. 1 Aug 1917
Bowers Gifford
m. Edward Alexander TROUP b. Mar 1864
Halstead, Essex

Florence Ada
b. 30 Oct 1860
Shooters Hill
d. 20 Mar 1938
Hove, Sussex
m. Thomas Alfred PAGE
b. 19 Feb 1869
Lambeth.
d. 9 Dec 1908
Streatham

TREE C

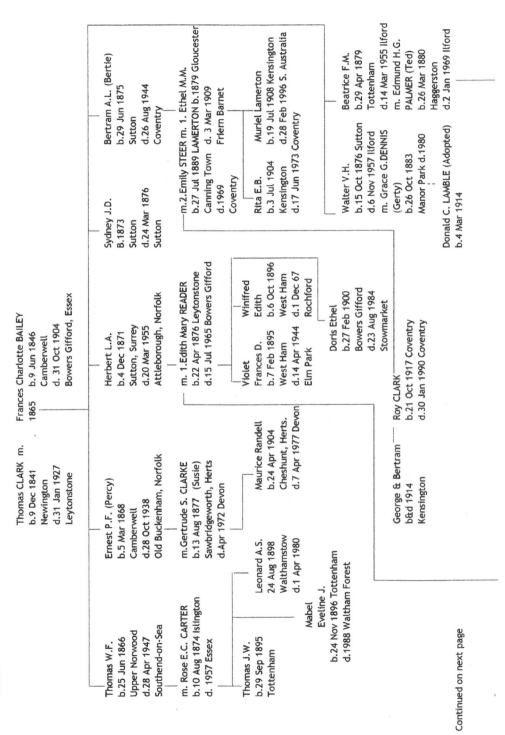

Thomas CLARK m.
b.9 Dec 1841
Newington
d.31 Jan 1927
Leytonstone

Frances Charlotte BAILEY
1865   b.9 Jun 1846
Camberwell
d. 31 Oct 1904
Bowers Gifford, Essex

Thomas W.F.
b.25 Jun 1866
Upper Norwood
d.28 Apr 1947
Southend-on-Sea

m. Rose E.C. CARTER
b.10 Aug 1874 Islington
d. 1957 Essex

Ernest P.F. (Percy)
b.5 Mar 1868
Camberwell
d.28 Oct 1938
Old Buckenham, Norfolk

m.Gertrude S. CLARKE
b.13 Aug 1877   (Susie)
Sawbridgeworth, Herts
d.Apr 1972 Devon

Herbert L.A.
b.4 Dec 1871
Sutton, Surrey
d.20 Mar 1955
Attleborough, Norfolk

m. 1.Edith Mary READER
b.22 Apr 1876 Leytonstone
d.15 Jul 1965 Bowers Gifford

Sydney J.D.
B.1873
Sutton
d.24 Mar 1876
Sutton

Bertram A.L. (Bertie)
b.29 Jun 1875
Sutton
d.26 Aug 1944
Coventry

m.2.Emily STEER m. 1. Ethel M.M.
b.27 Jul 1889 LAMERTON b.1879 Gloucester
Canning Town   d. 3 Mar 1909
d.1969   Friern Barnet
Coventry

Muriel Lamerton
b.19 Jul 1908 Kensington
d.28 Feb 1996 S. Australia

Rita E.B.
b.3 Jul 1904
Kensington
d.17 Jun 1973 Coventry

Walter V.H.
b.15 Oct 1876 Sutton
d.6 Nov 1957 Ilford
m. Grace G.DENNIS
(Gerty)
b.26 Oct 1883
Manor Park d.1980

Beatrice F.M.
b.29 Apr 1879
Tottenham
d.14 Mar 1955 Ilford
m. Edmund H.G.
PALMER (Ted)
b.26 Mar 1880
Haggerston
d.2 Jan 1969 Ilford

Donald C. LAMBLE (Adopted)
b.4 Mar 1914

Leonard A.S.
24 Aug 1898
Walthamstow
d.1 Apr 1980

Maurice Randell
b.24 Apr 1904
Cheshunt, Herts.
d.7 Apr 1977 Devon

Violet
Frances D.
b.7 Feb 1895
West Ham
d.14 Apr 1944
Elm Park

Winifred
Edith
b.6 Oct 1896
West Ham
d.1 Dec 67
Rochford

Thomas J.W.
b.29 Sep 1895
Tottenham

Mabel
Eveline J.
b.24 Nov 1896 Tottenham
d.1988 Waltham Forest

George & Bertram
b&d 1914
Kensington

Roy CLARK
b.21 Oct 1917 Coventry
d.30 Jan 1990 Coventry

Doris Ethel
b.27 Feb 1900
Bowers Gifford
d.23 Aug 1984
Stowmarket

Continued on next page

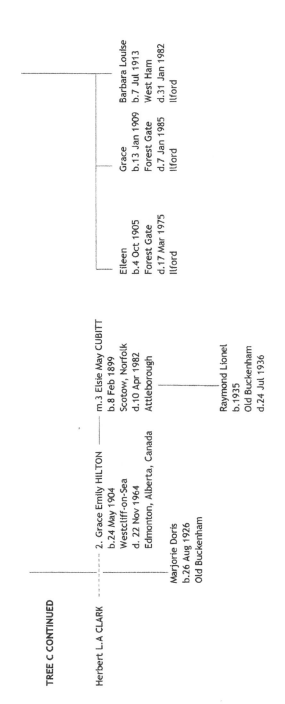

TREE C CONTINUED

Herbert L.A CLARK

2. Grace Emily HILTON
b.24 May 1904
Westcliff-on-Sea
d. 22 Nov 1964
Edmonton, Alberta, Canada

m.3 Elsie May CUBITT
b.8 Feb 1899
Scotow, Norfolk
d.10 Apr 1982
Attleborough

Marjorie Doris
b.26 Aug 1926
Old Buckenham

Raymond Lionel
b.1935
Old Buckenham
d.24 Jul 1936

Eileen
b.4 Oct 1905
Forest Gate
d.17 Mar 1975
Ilford

Grace
b.13 Jan 1909
Forest Gate
d.7 Jan 1985
Ilford

Barbara Louise
b.7 Jul 1913
West Ham
d.31 Jan 1982
Ilford

THE WESTFIELDS

Frederick Henry WESTFIELD m. 1788   Ann GORDON
b. 12 Jul 1766 Southwark   b. 1768 Dunstan, Stepney?
d. Dec 1832 Limehouse   d. Dec 1830 Limehouse

Mary Ann	Henry Frederick	Sarah	James	Ann	Kitty	Sarah	Lucy	Henry	John
b.1789	b.1791	b.24 Dec 92	b.1795	b.Dec 1797	b.Nov 1799	b.Apr 1802	b.1803	b.1806	b.1808
Rotherhithe	Rotherhithe	Rotherhithe	Portsea	Portsea	Portsea	Portsea	Portsea	Portsea	Portsea
d.?		d.?	m.Sarah	m. Robert	d.1884	m. Andrew	d.1804	d.Jun 1808	d.1808
m.		m. Edward	CLARK	MUIR 1830	Camberwell	K. RICE 1821	Portsea	Portsea	Portsea
Edward JENKINS		TURNER 1822	1816			b.1797 Ireland			
b. unknown		b. 1795	Newington						
d. 1825 Ceylon?		Southwark							

m.1 Stephen SIMS —— m. 2 Jeremiah FOWLER
of *HMS Brazen*   b. 1801
29 Nov 1819   m. 7 Jul 1856
Portsea   Bermondsey
                d. May 1861 Camberwell

Mary Ann WESTFIELD *(father unknown)*
b. Aug 1816 Portsea
d. 21 Oct 1866 Ecclesall Bierlow
m. Thomas CLARK 1839 Newington

↓
See Tree B

PART ONE

THOMAS CLARK
1819 – 1895

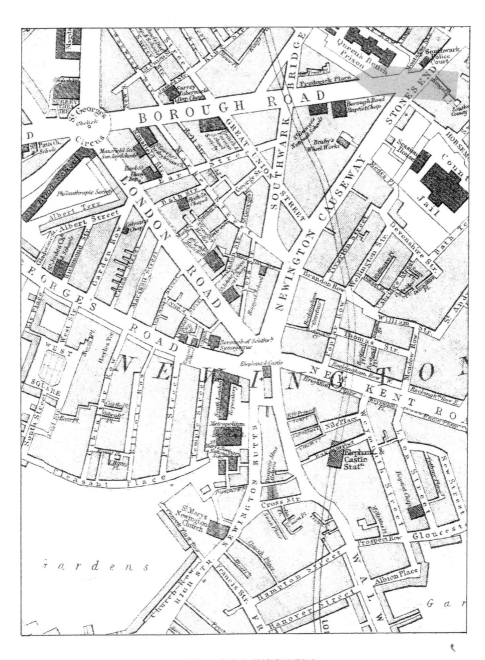

Fig 1. Map of Newington showing Frederick Place and church of St. Mary

Chapter 1

———

'GENT'

———

Newington, London

It was the best of times; it was the worst of times.
(Charles Dickens, A Tale of Two Cities 1842)

D ecember 1839 was the end of a wet year and had been a particularly wet summer in London. In the first week of December, rain had given way to fog which had enveloped the capital, very likely exacerbated by the smog created by industry and coal fires.[1]

On the morning of Monday 16 December 1839, a young couple arrived at their parish church, St. Mary's Newington, in the county of Surrey, for their wedding ceremony.[2] It was the second wedding of the morning held at the church.[3] The bride gave her address as 1 Victoria Terrace, one of the many new developments named after the new Queen who had ascended the throne just two years earlier, whilst the groom lived at 7 Frederick Place, a terrace running parallel with Borough Road, Newington.

The church was situated on Newington Butts. Newington meant 'new farmstead', denoting the rural nature of this part of the county next to the City of London south of the Thames. Butts took its name from its historic site where in former times, archery was practised.[4] The church of St. Mary in 1839 was relatively new in appearance as it had been rebuilt in 1793 following the decay of the earlier building which had caused it to collapse.[5]

The young man inside the church with a classically designed façade was Thomas Clark, a 20-year-old who confidently and proudly cited his occupation as 'gent'. Both he and his bride, Miss Mary Ann Westfield, described themselves as being of 'full age' on signing the register. This meant that both parties were, or should have been, above 21 years old.[6] Both of them signed in their own hand.[7] However, Mr. Clark was more than four months short of his 21st birthday whilst Miss Westfield was almost three years his senior. If the groom adjusted his age to disguise marriage to the older women, the bride undertook a greater act of deception in order to retain a dark family secret. It was a secret that may have never been disclosed to her husband or her children.

Family and friends joined the couple through the church's portico. The two mandatory witness signatures in the register were

supplied by Edward Turner and Ann Aldridge, the latter being Thomas Clark's elder sister, who had married Frederick Aldridge in 1836.[8] It is likely that Edward Turner was the uncle by marriage of Mary Ann Westfield as a Sarah Westfield had married Edward Turner in the same church in 1822. How

Fig 2. Mary Ann Westfield c. 1840s

(Left) Fig 3. George Aldridge (c.1854) was the brother of Frederick who married Ann Clark in 1836; (Right) Fig 4. Percy Aldridge Grainger (the composer 1882-1961) with his mother Rose (daughter of George) Grainger was the great-nephew by marriage of Ann Clark.

the couple met is not known but there were many non-conformist churches and chapels which had opened up in the Newington area over the last decades and although marriage was still expected to take place at the local Anglican parish church, it is probable that both parties were dissenters. Alternatively, introduction may have occurred through one of Thomas Clark's sisters who could have been a friend of Miss Westfield's. Possibly they could have met whilst promenading in one of the local gardens such as the Vauxhall Pleasure Gardens.

If any of the bride's family did attend on that cold and foggy morning, it is probable that they would have been aware that Miss Westfield's father was not William cited by Mary Ann on the register as her deceased parent. In reality she was illegitimate, being a daughter born to 16-year-old Catherine, baptised as 'Kitty' Westfield from Portsea, Hampshire. Kitty's daughter was baptised at Portsea on 25

August 1816, just over a year after the Battle of Waterloo ended the Napoleonic Wars. The baptism records a desolate blank space where the father's name should appear.[9]

Thomas Clark was almost certainly unaware of his chosen young lady's sad history. Illegitimacy was a social stigma and many people in this position invented a deceased father upon marriage to conceal certain disgrace. Until well into the 20th century, being illegitimate meant you lacked a family background. A child born outside the union of marriage inherited the same immorality as those who gave him or her life. Given his status as a 'gent' it would potentially be an impediment to their union. The class system played a leading role in an upwardly mobile society which saw the rise of the middle classes. Thomas Clark had aspirations and confidence for his future which meant that he wanted to be judged as a respectable middle class early Victorian gentleman.

THOMAS CLARK entered the world on the 22 April 1819 at Webb Street off Bermondsey Street in the Borough, London which was then in the county of Surrey.[10] He was most likely baptised on the 5 May 1819 at St. Olave's Church, as it is recorded in the register that Thomas Clark, the son of Thomas (a labourer) and Ann was baptised that day. Their residence is given as Marble Court, which on a map of the period, is situated adjacent to Webb Street, off Bermondsey Street.[11] His unremarkable start to life belies his perceived rise in status just two decades later.

The labourer of 1819 baptising his only son, had twenty years later risen in occupation to a warehouseman. Upon his son's marriage, he is described as a stationer – possibly an attempt by his son to make his father's job more important than it was in reality. More frequently in records he has the fuller occupation title of stationer's warehouseman or just warehouseman. The old definition of a 'warehouseman' may not merely mean someone who works in a warehouse; alternatively it was 'someone who owns a warehouse and sells goods from it or from a shopfront'.[12] Reading between the lines it is possible that he kept a warehouse for a stationer.

Thomas Clark senior's origins can be traced back to a baptism recorded at St. Nicholas' Church, Plumstead in the county of Kent in August 1785; Thomas Clark was perhaps the first child born to William and Sarah Clark.[13] It is unknown how or when Thomas Clark arrived from Plumstead to the Borough at the time of his son's birth in 1819 or indeed to confirm his marriage to his wife Ann with any degree of certainty.[14] However, life in London at this time for many was heavily influenced by, and reliant upon, the River Thames and its industries. It is reasonable to consider that he arrived in the area in connection with work opportunities in the same manner that his father had also been born in Plumstead close by the Thames. The Industrial Revolution was the catalyst for the mass production of goods for consumption; these were transported by river and canal within the United Kingdom as well as exotic goods and raw materials imported via sea journeys from its overseas colonies and around the world. A warehouseman would have an important role to play in this process.

In that momentous year of 1819, across the Thames, and a few weeks after Thomas Clark was born and baptised, the future Queen Victoria was born at Kensington Palace on 24th May. The first few days of her life were marked by a period of severe late spring frost which lasted from 27 to 30 May. The United Kingdom was in fact still in the grip of the little Ice Age which had started in the 13th century but was coming to an end at this period of time and the Thames was often frozen over; as recently as 1814 a Frost Fair had taken place.

Meanwhile, back on the opposite bank of the river, Bermondsey Street was one of the oldest streets in London and it ran diagonally south-west from Tooley Street down to Tower Bridge Road. By the time of Thomas Clark's birth in 1819, this area was well known as the centre of the tanning industry and the leather and skin market opened here in 1833. No doubt, the family would have been accustomed to the sights and foul, noxious smells emanating from the variety of buildings which were involved in the stages of processing animal skins for leather, as they passed by leading their daily lives.[15]

Thomas Clark's youngest sister Esther was born some eight years after her brother circa 1827 at Tooley Street, Bermondsey.[16] This street ran parallel to the Thames through the district of Horsleydown connecting old London Bridge with St. Saviour's Dock. The road then continued to the Surrey Commercial Docks and was a major route of transportation of goods to the City of London and the rest of Great Britain from the riverside docks. His eldest sister Ann had married a warehouseman too in 1836 when she wed Frederick Aldridge.[17]

Given the uncertainty over the exact connection Thomas Clark senior had to warehouses, consideration should be given to his son at twenty, marrying someone who in all probability was unable to provide an income to the marriage in view of her fatherless status. It was unusual for a minor to be able to marry until he had established himself and could support not only himself but his wife and any subsequent family. This gives more weight to his father being a man of considerable income; he was below the average age for a man to marry at this time.[18]

The fact that he names his occupation as 'gent' is open to interpretation. It could denote someone who has no occupation or profession. This for someone of his tender years with a father, who was supporting him probably until he reached his majority, would offer an explanation. The majority of his poorer contemporaries would have been working in hard labour occupations from a very young age to support their parents and younger siblings and had to pay their own way. The term 'gent' suggests a man of some resources at a time when most of the population lived in poverty. The new industrial and merchant classes certainly attempted to have themselves designated as 'gentleman' as a consequence of their growing wealth and influence.[19]

Chapter 2

———

THE WESTFIELDS
1788-1832

———

Rotherhithe – Portsea – Newington

*The Great silent ship, with her population of blue-jackets,
marines, officers, captain, and the admiral who was not to
return alive, passed like a phantom the meridian of the Bill.*
(Thomas Hardy, The Trumpet Major 1880)

MARY ANN WESTFIELD was the only child of Kitty Westfield and born out of wedlock. Kitty was baptised at St. Mary's, Portsea, Hampshire on 15 December 1799 at one month old. This means she had not yet attained her 17th birthday when her child, Mary Ann was born.[1]

Given that her daughter was baptised in August 1816, Mary Ann was conceived during the previous November. Britain celebrated victory at the Battle of Waterloo which took place in June 1815. Portsea being the royal dockyard of the South Coast saw great numbers of sailors and officers of the Royal Navy as well as soldiers passing through on their return home. Many of these men may have spent extra months celebrating on the continent before returning to England later that year.[2] It is easy to speculate that her father was one such individual. Given her tender years, it was probable that Kitty Westfield's relationship was brief and clandestine at best or possibly at worst, the result of rape or even prostitution. However, such assumptions are merely speculation – the truth being it can never with any certainty be ascertained. The lack of a father was very definite as no mention was made of him either in bastardy bonds of the parish of Portsea.[3]

On 29 November 1819 Kitty Westfield, now 20 years old, married Stephen Sims at St. Mary's, Portsea.[4] Stephen Sims was a sailor serving on the 28-gun Royal Navy sloop, HMS *Brazen* which had been built in 1808.[5] At the time of his marriage to Kitty Westfield, *Brazen* was berthed at Portsmouth undergoing repairs and being fitted for sea. She was recommissioned in December of 1819 under Captain William Shepheard and Sims was probably under pressure to 'tie the knot' quickly with Kitty before being summoned to sea for what could be an indeterminate time. In 1820 and 1821 the vessel served at St. Helena and Ascension Island in the South Atlantic before returning to Portsmouth on 31 October 1821.[6]

If Sims had completed previous voyages with *Brazen*, he must have been on shore leave from December 1818 or possibly earlier as the vessel had returned from a previous voyage in July of that year from Barbados taking just 31 days. It is likely that it was sometime between these dates and the wedding at the end of November 1819 that the couple first met and conducted a courtship.

Mary Ann Westfield's family likewise had a nautical background and they can be traced back in Portsea to the baptism of her uncle, James Westfield in October of 1795. Her grandparents were Henry Frederick Westfield and Ann (née Gordon) and they had travelled from London down to the South Coast port following the birth of their child before James, who was Sarah; a baptism at Rotherhithe in January 1793 confirms their residence in this parish.[7]

Henry Westfield was a rope maker by occupation and it is significant that his move from the London port of Rotherhithe to the South Coast coincided with the start of the French Wars in 1793. The French Revolution was then in full swing and King Louis XVI had been guillotined in Paris on 21st January of that year. As the revolutionaries were opponents of the monarchies of Europe, they declared war on Britain on 1 February 1793. As a result, there was a huge influx of people to Portsmouth and neighbouring Portsea at this time. It included persons in military occupations as well as people working in support of organisations like the Royal Navy. Rope makers had a vital part to play in the shipping industry and in the rigging of ships required for battle and defensive capacities.

About a third of the port's entire population worked in the dockyard. There was a great demand for labour, especially when the fleet was laid up for repairs in the winter months. While a farm worker a few miles inland was earning a shilling a week, the shipwrights' wages were six shillings and sixpence…[8]

As Frederick Eden commented when he surveyed the poor of the country in the late 1790s,

> *Watermen, at present, have constant employment; but in peace this class of men is almost starving. Tailors, shoemakers, and other tradesmen, more particularly publicans, are in full business: in short, war is a harvest for Portsmouth; and peace, which is so ardently wished for in most parts of England, is dreaded here.*[9]

The Isle of Portsea, when the Westfield's arrived sometime between 1793 and 1795, was a place where a variety of people of diverse reputations and social status lived and circulated. The area originally known as Portsmouth Common lay between the town of Portsmouth and the nearby dockyard. In 1792, the name changed from the 'Common' to Portsea and by then it had the character of this mixed dockside population, Portsea being a separate but neighbouring parish to Portsmouth, occupying much of its south-west corner.

The Westfields may have lived near the dockyard in Clock Street as it was in Clock Lane that Kitty was living when Mary Ann was baptised.

The fortifications of these two towns gave rise to crammed-in buildings creating a layout of narrow streets existing behind the more genteel façade of Portsmouth town. In these poor dwellings and filth-ridden alleyways, disease was undoubtedly rife. Almost certainly some of Kitty's siblings succumbed to infection due to the insanitary conditions.[10] The Westfield family births, marriages and some infant deaths are recorded in the parish registers of both Portsea and Portsmouth throughout 1795 to 1819 covering the entire period of the French Revolutionary Wars from 1793 and subsequently the Napoleonic.

Within the ramparts, where townsfolk took their Sunday walks, the narrow lanes of the old town ran off the High Street, with the platform at its seaward end, where people gathered to watch the boats pass. Stunned by the crowds of sailors, shopkeepers and dockyard workers, innkeepers and prostitutes, William Wilberforce, passing through in late June 1794, found it a 'shocking scene', where 'wickedness and blaspheming abound'.[11]

Of course, Wilberforce was an evangelical Anglican who campaigned for social improvement so would have found the sights particularly disturbing. Horatio Nelson was a frequent visitor to Portsmouth and it is more than likely that members of the Westfield family would have seen him on one occasion or another as he was a public face in the locality. In a letter to Lady Emma Hamilton written on 20 May 1805, Nelson described Portsmouth as 'that horrid place' clearly finding it as unpleasant as Wilberforce had experienced. Later that year just before embarking to take part in The Battle of Trafalgar, he arrived at The George Inn on Saturday 14 September 1805 and a number of people followed his Lordship and cheered him on when he boarded. It was a different story just two months later when sadly, following the victorious battle, the church bells in Portsea rang out muffled peals on 7 November 1805, the day after news of his death reached the town and one can imagine the doleful noise conveying the terrible message making a strong impact on those who heard them.[12] If the Westfield family did not manage to see the hero before the battle, they would undoubtedly have heard the bells ringing out in mourning.

Considering Kitty's youth of 16 years in 1816 and without having any independent means to raise her child, it is almost certain that Mary Ann was brought up by her grandparents Henry and Ann, or possibly by one of Kitty's older sisters. By 1820 the family had all returned to live in the London district of Newington where Mary Ann eventually married Thomas Clark in 1839. Indeed, it seems likely that Mary Ann was named after her eldest aunt, Mary Ann, who was 27 years old at the time of her birth. Her aunt had been married for over six years in August 1816 to an Edward Jenkins, the marriage having taken place back in Portsea. Could the young Mary Ann have been raised by the childless couple?

Mary Ann's uncle James Westfield married a Sarah Clark at St. Mary's, Newington on 4 April 1816, just a few months before Mary Ann's own baptism in Portsea. This may indicate either a familial relationship or friendship between the Clarks and Westfields dating back over 20 years earlier and already established by the time of the union of the 1839 couple. It certainly does provide early evidence of the return to London of the Westfield family following the end of the Napoleonic Wars.[13]

Another sister, a Sarah born in 1802 in Portsea, in 1821 and as a minor, married Andrew Rice also at St. Mary's, Newington. At this marriage, Mary Ann Jenkins (the eldest child of Henry and Ann and sister to both Kitty and Sarah) acted as a witness in the register of marriage. Finally, the first sister named Sarah born in 1792 married Edward Turner at St. Mary's, Newington (which by now can be identified as the family parish church) in April 1822.[14] Fred and Ann Westfield had baptised two of their daughters 'Sarah', a family name, due to low confidence that both would survive to adulthood.[15]

Edward Jenkins, a mariner, made his Will in March 1825 just days before setting out on perilous sea voyage to Ceylon in the full knowledge he may never return.[16] He left all of his estate to his wife, Mary Ann (née Westfield). In 1835, his Will was proved as by that time it seemed probable that he had perished either on the voyage or on the island. In 1834, Sarah Rice (nee Westfield) named one of her children Edward Jenkins Rice after her lost brother-in-law, to perpetuate the memory of her sister's husband.[17]

Chapter 3

———

THE CLERK

———

Newington – Milton – Peckham 1841-1850

O n Sunday 6 June 1841, some eighteen months after Thomas and Mary Ann's wintry wedding day, a national census took place. It was the first time that such a complete and comprehensive survey, to include every resident, had been undertaken by an English government.

This night, Thomas and Mary Ann Clark were staying at 1 Victoria Terrace, Horsemonger Lane, Newington. Their address was the same one that she gave as her residence at the time of her marriage. Almost concealed between the names of thousands of other inhabitants of this district, Thomas Clark's occupation, like over 20,000 other men at the same date, was 'clerk' or commercial clerk. This was a middle-class profession which distinguished him from the lower-classes because he used his brains and not his hands in manual labour, like the vast majority of working men.[1] Whilst Thomas Clark left home smartly dressed in his top hat and black-coat each morning, his wife however, had no visible occupation like the majority of Victorian women. On this early summer night, she was in fact living in the knowledge of an event that would take place almost exactly in six months' time; she was three months pregnant with her first child.

Possibly Thomas Clark was working as a clerk for his father, the warehouseman, or in one of many other positions that had sprung up to fulfil an increase in demand for educated young men over the last few decades. His age is faithfully recorded as 22 whilst his older wife is 24 – she will be 25 later that summer.[2]

Mary Ann Clark was pregnant at the same time as Queen Victoria, although for Victoria this was for the second time. A girl, Victoria, known as Vicky, had been born on 21 November 1840. She had become pregnant again quickly after that birth and her second child, Albert Edward, the future King Edward VII, was born on 9 November 1841 at Buckingham Palace and named after his father. The Royal couple had only married in 1840 and had produced two children in less than two years. They were undoubtedly a role model for the upcoming generation of young people who would accompany Victoria through her reign.

Across the Thames in south London, exactly a month later, on Thursday 9 December 1841, Mary Ann Clark gave birth to her first child at 1 Victoria Terrace in the parish of St. Mary's, Newington. Mary Ann did not adhere to the traditional month-long post-partem bed rest often recommended after birth. Childbirth continued to be a dangerous event for women and babies and the mortality was high for both mothers and infants. Infection was the greatest threat and poor hygiene during childbirth was responsible for the high death rates which continued throughout the 19th century. Mary Ann would have no option of pain relief either.[3]

The child, a boy, was named after his father and grandfather, Thomas, and Mary Ann went to register the birth herself just before Christmas on Tuesday, 21 December 1841 which was less than two weeks after giving birth. Mary Ann had safely delivered and must have recovered quickly enough to be up and about within a fortnight. In common with Queen Victoria, Thomas and Mary Ann Clark were to found a large dynasty.

Unlike his parents, there is no evidence that Thomas or any of his siblings were ever baptised and this may indicate that one or both parents held strong non-conformist religious views against infant baptism. Were they members of a local Baptist congregation or another non-conformist dissenter group? Alternatively, was the decision not to baptise, made unilaterally with no church affiliation involved in the decision? These are questions that cannot be answered.[4]

Did Mary Ann benefit from any support from her maternal relatives during her pregnancy or labour? Her maternal grandparents, Henry and Ann Westfield both died in the early 1830s whilst she was still a minor. She may have received help from any surviving aunts or cousins who were living in the Newington area.[5] What is known is that her mother, Kitty, was living close by at Bermondsey New Road, Southwark at the time of the 1841 census.[6] The fate of Stephen Sims, the sailor she had married in 1819 back in Portsea, is unknown but by 1841 he had either died, gone absent or missing after a period at sea or they had separated. How much contact, if any, Mary Ann had with her young mother is a matter for conjecture. Did she even know she was her mother? Kitty, also known as Catherine, is living with a 'William' Fowler and they declare to be married although there is no evidence to support the event. They are dwelling in the heart of the leather market and he works as a skinner.

A second son arrived on St. George's Day, 23 April 1843. He was named after his maternal great-grandfather as Frederick Henry Clark. As with her first child, Mary Ann trudged off to the Register Office to duly record the birth but this time, not a mere fortnight after giving birth. Instead, this had to wait until a month later, 19 May 1843.

Fred, as he was known in the family, was not born in Newington like his brother. Instead, the birth took place miles away at an address in Milton-next-Gravesend in the county of Kent. Mary Ann gave her usual address as different to the birth, 2 Rupell Street, Milton. Her husband's occupation had reverted from that of 'clerk' in the 1841 census to that of the 'gentleman' who married her less than four years before.

It is difficult to ignore the maritime location that Milton-next-Gravesend commanded. The parish was bounded on the north by the River Thames forming a union with Gravesend. As has been mentioned already, both families were reliant on shipping or trade for their livelihood.

Whatever the circumstances surrounding the family's sojourn into the rural location in north-west Kent, their time there was of short duration. Just the following year, their third child and first daughter, Mary Ann Esther, was born back in the London suburbs. She was named Mary Ann naturally after her mother and Esther after her father's sister. In spite of these names, she would always be known as 'Polly'.[7] Polly's birth was registered in the Peckham district of London which was then in Surrey. As the eldest daughter, it would be her responsibility to be a second mother to her younger siblings and help her mother to run the large family home while her elder brothers were destined to be the heirs to their father's business interests.

A third son and fourth child, James (named after Mary Ann's uncle of the same name) was born in 1846 and another girl, Emma Ann in 1848 – the middle name Ann may have been a nod towards Thomas' mother, Ann. In December 1849, Alfred arrived. It was a perilous time of year for a new born baby to survive in cold and poorly heated homes. From 3 to the 15 of January 1850 cold and frosty weather was reported and on the 15th, the observatory at Greenwich recorded a day maximum temperature of minus 2.8 degrees.[8] Ice was observed on the Thames. On February 5 and 6 a 'great gale' was recorded in London. Alfred was destined not to survive these punishing winter conditions of 1849/50 and he died of convulsions brought on by bronchitis on 18 February 1850.[9] His father registered the death of his baby son.

Chapter 4

———

COMMERCIAL BROKER'S CLERK TO COLONIAL BROKER

———

Old Kent Road, Peckham &

Great Tower Street (City) 1850-1854

*...she arrived at the drug-flavoured region of Mincing Lane, with
the sensation of having just opened a drawer in a chemist's shop.*
(Charles Dickens, Our Mutual Friend)

B y the start of the new decade of the 1850s Mary Ann Clark had
given birth to six children, all but one of whom had survived
their early years and thrived. This was good news statistically
for a time when infant mortality was extremely high.[1] However, the
following decade would be more testing as the family increased but
would also continue to experience, like others of the period, the pain
of childhood death as well as the random nature imposed by the grim
reaper's strike by way of one of the most feared and prevalent diseases
of the times – cholera.

Mary Ann Clark had little time to reflect on or mourn her loss of baby Alfred before she was once again with child. Her daughter Matilda Hephzibah was born on 26 December 1850 at Shenton Street, Old Kent Road. Matilda would be known in the family as Tilly but her biblical middle name was after her father's sister Hephzibah. Her mother Mary Ann, now weighed down by six young children to care for, as well as recovering from the loss of a child less than a year earlier, took even longer to register the new birth. In this case it was 5 March 1851. Presumably, Thomas her husband was too busy at work to provide an income for his expanding brood to bother with such trivialities so left it to his wife to complete the formality.

Later that month, on Sunday 30 March 1851, the next public census took place. Thomas Clark was by now a commercial broker's clerk, something more definite on the social status ladder from 10 years previously when he was more loosely termed a clerk. On the new occasion, his family is glimpsed at their residence, 7 Shenton Street, just three months after the birth of Matilda and he is now three weeks short of his 32nd birthday.[2] His five eldest children, even the three year old, are described as 'scholars'. The children may well have attended one of the schools in the local district or they could have been educated at home, more likely for the girls. Only the two youngest of his eventual 12 children, were sent to boarding school and this was 20 years into the future. Thomas Clark regarded an education of importance for his family, including his daughters, who were expected to become accomplished in skills which would find them good husbands of at least the same status as their father but with any stroke of good fortune it would be someone higher up the social ladder. The sons would be taught the subjects to help them succeed in business such as maths and the sciences. His family are the only ones recorded as scholars on the page of the enumerator's schedule amongst his neighbours' children. Other neighbours in Shenton Street, a small road off Old Kent Road, included an iron warehouseman, a writer for newspapers and a bullion porter.[3]

Fig 5. The Great Exhibition, The Crystal Place, Hyde Park – 1851.
The transept looking north shows visitors admiring the exhibits.

The year of 1851 was monumental in British history for it was the year the Great Exhibition was held in Hyde Park. Opening in May of that year, it ran until October and showcased Britain's achievements in manufacture and trade with the colonies and the rest of the world. The exhibition was the culmination of the Industrial Revolution which had been in progress for a century. It was a time of great national confidence and pride, Britain's trade and industry being greater than any other nation. The Exhibition was housed in the Crystal Palace, designed by Joseph Paxton it was assembled in 22 weeks. It is estimated that six million people visited the Exhibition, which was the brainchild of Prince Albert, consort of the Queen. Considering the population was 21 million in 1851, this was a significant number of people even if many visited more than once. Thomas Clark almost certainly attended and if he did, it is likely he took with him his two eldest sons, Tom and Fred then 9 and 8 respectively. They would have been in awe of the exhibits and he would have been proud to show them the greatness of the Empire and impress upon them the personal contribution to that success that he and his father had made and indeed, one day they too could influence in prominent business positions to follow in their father's footsteps. It would be an outing they would never forget.

Evidence for the wide appeal the Great Exhibition held as a family outing is supplied from Henry Michell, a brewer from Horsham, Sussex who recorded in his diary:

> *We did not go on any tour this year but made a point of devoting all the time and money we could spare on visiting the Crystal Palace and studying its contents with our children and all our servants and dependants at the Brewery, farm and brickyards and on the 24th September we went with all the school children in the parish to the number of 380.[4]*

Perhaps Thomas Clark too visited with the entire family including his parents, not just his eldest two sons like Henry Michell. Not only did the Exhibition emphasise Britain's superiority and achievements as the leaders of the Industrial Revolution but its dominance in the world, especially as it possessed more colonies in its vast and expanding Empire than any other nation and so it would have personal appeal, if not actual involvement for many.

The Illustrated London News of 26 April 1851 contained images of Bengalis carving ivory for the exhibition, demonstrating the opportunity available for British people to view commodities and artefacts from exotic and far-flung parts of the globe which was an exciting novelty.[5]

Two years after the Exhibition closed, on 17 October 1853, Thomas Clark's father, the warehouseman, died suddenly at East Lane, Walworth after an illness of eight or nine hours certified as apoplexy.[6] East Lane was not far from his son's residence in Shenton Street, however, his son-in-law Thomas Try was instead at hand when he died whilst his son was almost certainly at work in the City. Thomas Try had married Esther Clark just three years earlier. Thomas Clark senior left no Will and was buried in a fairly newly purchased family plot at All Saints' Cemetery, Linden Grove, Peckham (later to become known as Nunhead Cemetery). The first family member to be interred here was his baby grandson, named Alfred who had died in early 1850. The plot was in a prime location adjacent to the footpath along Dissenters' Road to the right, inside the main entrance gate and in unconsecrated ground, thus suitable for the unbaptised, as well as those of other denominations outside of the established Anglican Church. The Clark plot had a simple table top tomb to mark the site; on the top slab the names of those interred could be inscribed.[7] The cemetery was set within attractive landscaped gardens and was located on high ground with a fine view across London to St. Paul's Cathedral. At 52 acres, it was one of the largest of London's new necropolises.[8]

After a suitable length of mourning had taken place, an inheritance from his father as the likely only son may have paved the way for Thomas Clark to progress his working status from that he declared on the census of 1851. Before the year 1853 had ended, he had stepped forward in occupation from a clerk in a broker's office to becoming a broker himself.

On 8 December 1853, he was admitted into the Freedom of the City of London and the document which bestowed this accolade to him states his professional address as Great Tower Street. Furthermore, he had made the declaration required by law during the Mayoralty of Thomas Sidney and Sir John Key, the chamberlain. His name had been entered into the book relating to the Purchase of Freedoms (known as Redemption), rather than by honour or patrimony. This was a

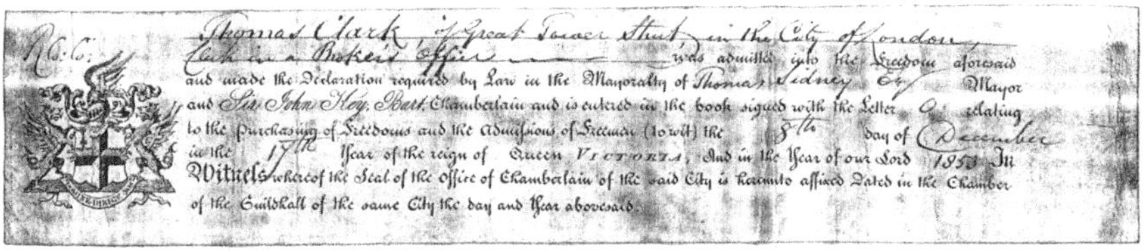
R.O.C.
Thomas Clark, of Great Tower Street, in the City of London, Clerk in a Broker's Office was admitted into the Freedom aforesaid and made the Declaration required by Law in the Mayoralty of Thomas Sidney Esq Mayor and Sir John Key, Bart Chamberlain and is entered in the book signed with the Letter Q relating to the Purchasing of Freedoms and the Admissions of Freemen (to wit) the 8th day of December in the 17th Year of the reign of Queen VICTORIA, And in the Year of our Lord 1853 In Witness whereof the Seal of the Office of Chamberlain of the said City is hereunto affixed Dated in the Chamber of the Guildhall of the same City the day and Year abovesaid.

Fig 6. Thomas Clark – certificate of Freedom to the City of London, December 1853

necessary business move for any broker operating in the City and on 17 January 1854 another document declared that on condition of a yearly payment of five pounds, he was duly admitted to be a broker within the City and was sworn for the due execution.

It is probable that Thomas Clark had previously been working as a clerk in the office of a broker named Donald Gray. Gray gained his Freedom of the City of London by Redemption in 1819 and was trading in London as early as the 1820s.[9] He appeared in the *Public Ledger* newspaper advertising his goods for auction long before 1852 but from 1854 to 1864, as the business partner of Thomas Clark who was 30 years his junior.[10] Donald Gray was born in 1789 in Dingwall, an east-coast town in the Highland region of Scotland. Gray, in the 1851 census, lived at 12 York Place, Stoke Newington, which was an upmarket district in north London. He was then 61 years old and his wife Margaret was 45 and also from Scotland. They had five sons, Donald, William, Hector, Alexander and Roderick. Their daughters were Eliza and Isabella and all had been born in Stoke Newington. Also part of their household, were his wife's unmarried sister Elizabeth Anderson and servants Rebecca and Maria Culmore, probably sisters, born in Rotherhithe. A third servant was Margaret Lord from Lancashire. 10 years later this family are at the same location. His sons William and Hector (24 and 22) were then both working themselves as clerks in his employment and would one day succeed to their father's business.[11]

In the meantime, it was the produce sold by Gray and Clark which was imported into London warehouses from the colonies and worldwide. These included raw materials for manufacture into finished products such as piano keys, jewellery, trinkets or ornaments made from slain animals from Africa, India and the Americas such as elephant ivory and buffalo horns. There were also spices to enhance the flavour of food and bring a new taste of the oriental to the appetites of the population, for those who could afford such luxuries. Other produce was harvested from the natural world to be used gainfully in the manufacture of household goods – everything from furniture

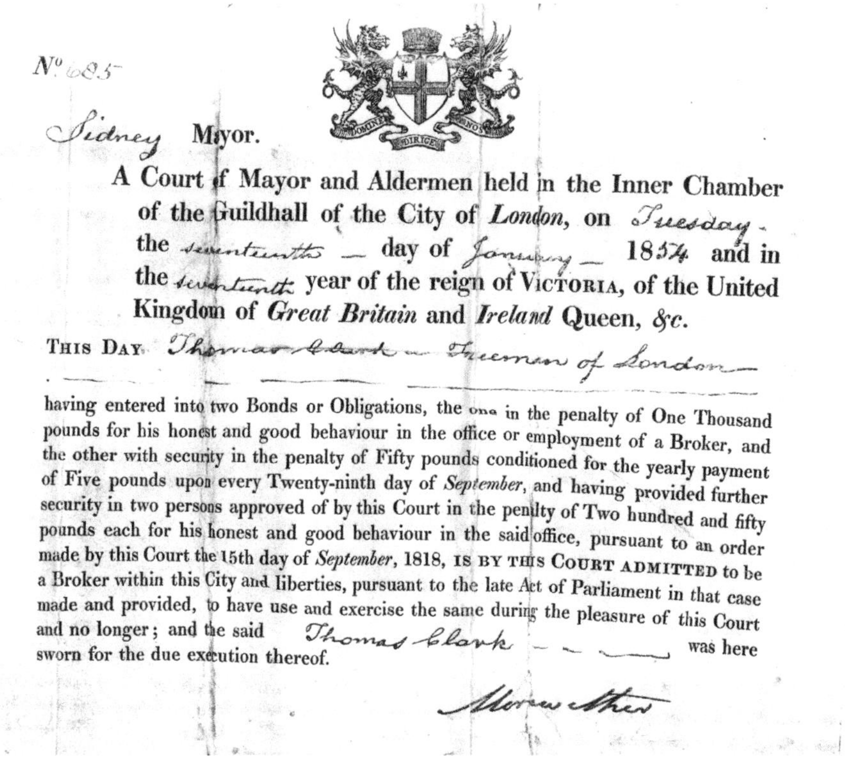

No. 625

Sidney Mayor.

A Court of Mayor and Aldermen held in the Inner Chamber of the Guildhall of the City of *London*, on *Tuesday* the *seventeenth* — day of *January* — 18*54* and in the *seventeenth* year of the reign of VICTORIA, of the United Kingdom of *Great Britain* and *Ireland* Queen, &c.

THIS DAY *Thomas Clark* a *Freeman of London* —

having entered into two Bonds or Obligations, the one in the penalty of One Thousand pounds for his honest and good behaviour in the office or employment of a Broker, and the other with security in the penalty of Fifty pounds conditioned for the yearly payment of Five pounds upon every Twenty-ninth day of *September*, and having provided further security in two persons approved of by this Court in the penalty of Two hundred and fifty pounds each for his honest and good behaviour in the said office, pursuant to an order made by this Court the 15th day of *September*, 1818, IS BY THIS COURT ADMITTED to be a Broker within this City and liberties, pursuant to the late Act of Parliament in that case made and provided, to have use and exercise the same during the pleasure of this Court and no longer; and the said *Thomas Clark* — was here sworn for the due execution thereof.

Morris Mather

Fig 7. Admittance to be a City of London broker, January 1854

to drugs. Brokers like this were driving the economy and it was a highly lucrative occupation bringing great financial rewards as well as prestige.

In the new year of 1854, Mary Ann Clark was again pregnant – this time expecting her ninth child. With his new business status as a colonial broker and Freeman of the City of London to boot, here at last was the self-made Victorian man. The River Thames was to thank for bringing him the materials of wealth and prosperity, but, ironically it was also a source of disease and death. As the goods imported by Gray and Clark were being unloaded onto the wharves lining the Thames, the river was about to deliver up disease and death in his family.

Chapter 5

THE RIVER THAMES – CARGOES AND CHOLERA

1854

On visits to London in 1859 and 1862, Hippolyte Taine, a French critic and art historian, was awestruck by the sight of the docks, he writes[1]:

The number of canals by which the docks open into the body of the river...are streets of ships...the innumerable riggings stretch a vast circle of spider-web all round the rim of the sky...[they are] one of the mighty spectacles of our planet...[the docks] are prodigious, overwhelming. There are six of them, each a great port inhabited by a population of three-masted ships...from every corner of the world. A merchant who had come to check the arrival of spices from Java and a trans-shipment of ice from Norway, told me that about 40,000 ships enter these docks every year, and that as a rule there are between five and six thousand in the docks at any given moment.[2]

It must have been a similar scene a few years earlier on Wednesday 6 September 1854 when Thomas Clark had important business to attend at the Commercial Sale Rooms in Mincing Lane.[3] Gray and Clark's latest vessel of produce had recently docked at the London wharves from Africa and 2¼ tons of elephant's teeth and 3½ tons of seahorses [ivory] had been weighed and were waiting for auction on that day.[4] From here, they would be bought by manufacturers to be crafted into luxurious items or made into human false teeth to supply demand from the middle classes who could afford dentures.

City workers on that September day may have been worried about a new wave of the deadly disease of cholera which had broken out and was killing Londoners in their droves. This was the third major outbreak in the capital since 1832. At this time, just like the earlier epidemics, it was the common belief that the disease was transmitted by a 'miasma' which floated on the air and consisted of rotting organic matter causing foul odours which was then breathed in by the unfortunate victims. The theory that cholera was in fact a water-borne disease was supplied by John Snow, a London-based physician who had come to recognise that it was contracted by drinking contaminated water. The cholera outbreak of summer and autumn 1854 affected London south of the Thames as well as the district of Soho. Snow linked the source of the Soho outbreak to a water pump at Broad Street from which the local community drew their supply of water. Once the pump had been closed down, the deaths in Soho stopped. Meanwhile in the south of the city the distribution of water direct to households was the responsibility of private regional water boards. The Clark family living at Shenton Street off the Old Kent Road, obtained their supply from the Southwark and Vauxhall Company which drew their water from the Thames at Battersea Fields.

Back in the south of the London suburbs, Thomas Clark's widowed mother, Ann, had most likely moved in with her son and family at 7 Shenton Street following her husband's death 10 months earlier. On 5 or 6 September, Ann began to suffer the disturbing symptoms of cholera including nausea, vomiting and profuse watery diarrhoea. The loss of bodily fluids rapidly led to her severe dehydration and circulatory collapse and after just 18 hours of suffering, she died.[5]

Perhaps her son Thomas was staying up in the city at this time and it is possible that he learnt retrospectively of his mother's horrific illness and demise. It was her daughter-in-law Mary Ann who was present when she died and went to register it the following day. She must have feared greatly for the rest of her family and indeed for herself, for she was heavily pregnant. It must have been a traumatic experience for a mother of eight young children and about to give birth at any time. Just 10 days after the death of her mother-in-law, Mary Ann Clark gave birth to her ninth child, a girl whom was named Eliza who would be known as Lizzie.

Thankfully, no other member of the household succumbed to cholera, they had been extremely fortunate to have avoided multiple deaths. Ann Clark's mortal remains were buried with her husband's at All Saints' Cemetery, Nunhead.

During the investigation that followed the outbreak, the microbiologist Dr. Arthur Hassall commented.

'It will be observed that the water of the companies of the Surrey side of London, viz., the Southwark, Vauxhall and Lambeth, is by far the worst of all those who take their supply from the Thames.'

In fact, all the grime of London including human effluence and animal waste products from slaughter houses ran into sewers and cesspools which were over-running or seeping into the ground before ultimately being dumped in the Thames. On examination by Dr. Hassall, the Southwark, Vauxhall and Lambeth Company's filtered water was found to contain animal hair amongst other foul both visible and invisible substances. The river was in fact an open sewer and Londoners were drinking and washing in filth.[6]

It was reported that Snow assisted by a Dr. J. Whiting visited every house in which a cholera death had occurred during August and ascertained the identity of the supply used. As a result of his survey, Snow showed that during a seven-week period, the incidence of cholera deaths in houses supplied by the Southwark and Vauxhall Company was 315 per 10,000 houses and thus more than those nearby who obtained water supplies from the Lambeth company much

A Pestilent Suburban Cottage.

Fig 8. 1854 - A house in the Old Kent Road where cholera, diphtheria and fever had all occurred. It was surrounded by a foul ditch on one side and a stagnant pool.

further upstream at Thames Ditton where the water was cleaner.[7]

Perhaps not surprisingly after the death of his beloved mother in the family home, as well as the damning evidence against the Southwark and Vauxhall Water Company as being culpable, Thomas Clark may have decided it was time to relocate his family away from that place where disease and death had struck at its heart. He now had eight living children and what would become of them in the event that Mary Ann became the next victim? If he himself were to succumb, they would lose the breadwinner, falling into destitution and who knows where that may have left his family.

Chapter 6

SHOOTERS' HILL
1855-1862

"At the opposite corner of The Lane were four houses called
Ordnance Terrace. In the garden of the first house there was
a peach tree trained up against the stable; she used to see the
flushed fruit among the long narrow leaves in the late summer,
and think how good it would be touch it with her fingers."
(Mrs W.K. Clifford, A Flash of Summer)

Prior to the birth of their tenth child, Amelia, in the second half of 1856, the family would move to the heights of Shooters' Hill in Kent, eight miles from London Bridge. Not only would they stand more chance of escaping the miasma here as the air was surely sweet and clear, but they may have needed more space due to the increase in family size; they had lived at Shenton Street, Old Kent Road for up to ten years. At 432 feet, the summit of Shooters' Hill was one of the highest points in south London. The family would have enjoyed spectacular views over the Thames as London unfolded beneath them. Perhaps Thomas Clark had been following John Snow's theory that polluted water was the cause of cholera and if so, he may have chosen this location for his family in the knowledge that the

Hill was renowned for its medicinal springs. John Evelyn the writer, gardener and diarist, came to drink them in 1699 and a mineral well was established at The Eagle Tavern.[1]

Their new abode was 2 Ordnance Terrace, situated off the Old Dover Road which was in olden times the Roman Road known as Watling Street, running straight from Blackheath to Dartford. Woolwich was a mile to the north-west of Shooters' Hill and known for its strong associations as both a royal naval dockyard and the home of the military academy. There were four houses in the terrace. Number two was a substantial family residence complete with a coach house, stabling and greenhouse.[2] A later 1889 advert for the public auction of No. 2 also stated that the house had 11 rooms, a cellar, washhouse and gardens.[3] The terrace appears to have been built during the early 1840s by Mr. Hawkins who was from Camden Town.[4] Although named a terrace, the houses seem to have been semi-detached.

A terrace though implies that this was the typical dwelling of the period with steps leading up to the front door and inside, a narrow hall would lead off to possibly two rooms on this level. The next floor may have contained the best rooms: a drawing room, for receiving guests, or study. The bedrooms would be found on the next floor up. Servants' rooms or nurseries were typically placed in the attics, or alternatively, servants could also be located in a room in the basement which received light and air, as well as a separate access, down another staircase from street level.[5]

Its location south of Plumstead where his father had been born in 1785 meant there may have been an existing family connection which made the location even more agreeable to the new inhabitant and his large family.

Thomas Clark was in the late 1850s, and perhaps for the next ten to fifteen years, at the pinnacle of his career in the City of London. His life and fortune linked with the dominance of Britain as the leader of the Industrial Revolution, its expanding Empire and world-wide trade. He was still working with his partner, Donald Gray but his eldest children were on the cusp of adulthood. This meant for his sons, an opportunity and expectation to join him as business partners so after his demise the family line would continue to flourish. Unfortunately, the 1861 census records for this area are lost so we cannot glimpse the family at home during this crucial period. However, two more girls were born at this address, Alice Mary in 1858 and Florence Ada in 1860. Mary Ann was by this time 44 years of age and at the end of her child-bearing years.

In her diary of 1872, his daughter Matilda describes the house at Shooters' Hill. At that later time, her father had offered it to her as a home of her own after she marries Alfred Bawtree and she is weighing up carefully whether to accept the house:

> *Papa has asked Alfred and me through Fanny* [Thomas Clark's second wife] *if we would like to live in Shooters Hill house, which belongs to Papa and in which we all lived for seven years and it seems likely from present appearances that that is where we shall live.*
>
> *As for my inclinations, I scarcely know what to think about it, but on the whole I rather like it. It is a better house than we can afford… the house is some distance from a station… The house is well-stocked with cupboards, we have quite as much garden as we could keep in order at first and a nice greenhouse and grape vines, which yield plentifully every year, with very little attention. There are a few fruit trees in the garden, and in the front garden the trees all bloom in their season. Red May, Lilac, Laburnum, plenty of Jasmine and Clematis too which would much improve the house if carefully trained.*[6]

The Clark's neighbour inhabiting No. 4 Ordnance Terrace was Thomas Gaspey. Gaspey at this time was an elderly man but he had enjoyed a career in newspaper journalism and magazine writing and was at one time the part-owner of *The Times* newspaper. He was also a prolific author who spent the last 20 years of his life quietly at Shooters' Hill. He is described in the 1851 census as an author and writer of history whilst in 1871, shortly before his death, as an historical writer. His

Fig 9. Mrs W.K. Clifford, 1926 – formerly known as Lucy Lane. was a neighbour of the Clarks when they lived at Ordnance Terrace.

entry in the Dictionary of National Biography describes him as a kindly man, genial, witty and an excellent mimic.[7] Gaspey's grand-daughter Sophia Lucy Lane (known as Lucy) was living with him in the 1871 census (and probably was recorded 10 years earlier too but the returns are lost) and was a 25-year-old magazine writer. Upon her marriage, she was known as Mrs. W.K. Clifford and amongst her literary output was a novel entitled *A Flash of Summer*.[8] Written in 1894, it was in part auto-biographical as she vividly recalled her own childhood memories of Ordnance Terrace and the wider Shooters' Hill area as the setting in which her heroine Katherine Kerr lived as a child. As a contemporary of the Clark children, the former Lucy Lane may have fraternised with them whilst living as a neighbour or if not, she would have certainly known them by sight. Mrs. Clifford describes Ordnance Terrace and its houses with its lush fruit trees, as mentioned by Matilda Clark in her diary, as well as placing the terrace into a wider setting bordering the Woolwich Military Academy. What follows is an intense multi-sensory recollection experienced by the young girl.

At the opposite corner of The Lane were four houses called Ordnance Terrace. In the garden of the first house there was a peach tree trained up against the stable; she [Katherine, the heroine] used to see the flushed fruit among the long narrow leaves in the late summer, and think how good it would be touch it with her fingers. Lower down was a plantation, to which the artillerymen came in the morning to exercise their horses: the clatter of hoofs, the shrill bugle, and the rushing among the trees made her wonder if it were like a battlefield. Opposite, on the other side of the main road, was a wide expanse of gorse and blackberry bushes, the great trees of Severndroog and its ruined tower showing above them on the left. On the right, beyond the Scrubs, as the tangle of bushes was called, a narrow road that led to Eltham went across the landscape, and beyond again stretched the open country, showing the Crystal Palace in the distance.[9]

She also describes the community at the heart of Shooters' Hill close to Ordnance Terrace with which the Clarks would have been familiar as they also conducted their daily lives:

Just below was the grey little church, and opposite was the post office, established for many a long year at an unobtrusive general shop; next to the post office was The Red Lion, with its wide quadrangle and tea-gardens that were almost rural. To the tea-gardens, on Sunday nights, the soldiers from Woolwich and the Government servants from the Royal Military Academy brought their sweethearts, and sat drinking beer with them at little wooden tables in trellis-made summer houses. They grew jovial as the evening went on. Katherine listened to their snatches of song and the din of voices till darkness fell, and perhaps faint in the distance the bugle-call was heard; then gradually the merriment ceased and two and two, always a he and she, the Sunday crowds went down the hill and turned to the right towards the barracks. The little road they took was known as The Lane, and led to Woolwich, at one corner of it was a stuffed bird shop, and on one side of the shop window were toys and story-books for children.[10]

If there was any friendship between any of the young Clarks and Miss Lane is unknown, but Thomas Clark's relationship with her grandfather, his prominent and genial neighbour, may not have been always very amiable. In early March 1858, Thomas Clark wrote to the Woolwich Board of Health to complain that there was an issue with water drainage into an adjacent ditch from two houses belonging to Mr. Gaspey which he believed were causing a nuisance. The Board responded that this was not an issue to concern them but a surveyor was directed to attend to the matter.[11] The following week, Mr. Gaspey wrote at length to the Board in response to the accusation from his neighbour, denying the statements made by him. Mr. Gaspey claimed the nuisances were not caused by his premises alone and he had long been anxious to do something to bring about a remedy to the problem. He named several parties who could support his statement. The Board once again reiterated their stance that it was a private matter in which they would not become involved.[12]

In early April, the Board received another letter from Thomas Clark in which he alluded to 'some alleged irregularity in his assessment' regarding the drainage of his and the adjoining houses. The Board, becoming tired of what they perceived to be a private dispute, reiterated that they had 'declined to entertain' this. Thomas Clark refused to accept this and cited that an Act of Parliament prohibited the existence of cesspools beneath houses and stagnant ditches to the rear of properties. He considered the nuisance to be 'unbearable' and urged the Board to reconsider the matter. However, they dug their heels in and it was not discussed further at this meeting.[13]

The problem with drainage and cesspools at Ordnance Terrace was in fact a longstanding issue which probably dated back to the time the houses were built in the 1840s. In 1850, Mr. Gaspey's predecessor at No. 4, Mr J. Guest, together with the resident of No. 3 Mr. J. Francis, had complained to the Woolwich Board about the offensive state of the cesspools at Nos. 1 & 2.[14] This was something of which Thomas Clark may have become all too aware.

On 22 May 1858, it was reported that both Thomas Clark and Thomas Gaspey had written to the Board. Mr. Clark requested to be informed if the Board intended to substitute an effective system of drainage rather than the existing one. He reminded them of the fatal cholera epidemic 'which was also felt in his house and those of his neighbours'. He said it had 'visited this locality' and he blamed the disease outbreak directly onto the existence of the ditch in question which drained from the houses in Ordnance Terrace. He hoped that the Board would not again say, as on the previous occasion, that the nuisance was a private matter and not of public concern.

Mr. Gaspey in his missive stated that the 'drainage of the houses was carried out in accordance with the law' and any objectionable matter which found its way into the ditch, he felt, was discharged into it from the houses at the upper part of the hill. The Board had previously advised him that the War Department had refused to allow the houses in the neighbourhood to drain any longer into the foul ditch in question. Mr. Gaspey asked the Board if they could suggest a better plan of drainage for which he would be happy to bear his share of the expense.[15]

The year 1858 was the summer of 'The Great Stink' of the Thames in London and the stench from the river was so dreadful that business in Parliament was disrupted.[16] On a more personal level, Thomas Clark must have felt keenly that he was experiencing a *déjà vu* of his life four years earlier when the foul ditches around the Old Kent Road were full of polluted water piped in by the Southwark and Vauxhall Water Company which led directly to the death of his mother. Thomas Clark had to make the local Health Board accountable for this very public health matter at Shooters' Hill.

Over a year later in July 1859 without resolution yet, matters were coming to a head. The War Department had placed a stoppage in the barrel drain thus causing the overflow of the cesspools at Ordnance Terrace. The residents all wrote to the Board bringing to their attention this calamity. It was agreed that the Board would advise the Plumstead District Board of Works that the overflowing cesspools was due to sewage from houses in Plumstead parish flowing down into the cesspools of Ordnance Terrace.[17]

On 13 August, it was reported that the Woolwich Local Board of Health had produced a sub-committee report which recommended that the board be applied to for the terms on which they were disposed to allow drainage constructed by Plumstead District at Shooters' Hill to fall into the Woolwich sewer and what facilities it would allow for the drainage at Ordnance Terrace, within the Woolwich parish. It was recommended that the sewer should be conveyed to the boundaries of the Woolwich parish at the expense of Plumstead.[18] The three residents of Ordnance Terrace, Messrs. Clark, Gaspey and Lee, wrote to the Board around the same time thanking them for the attention they had given to the defective drainage problem. However, they wanted to draw to their attention that it was 'now in a most foul condition'.[19]

The Plumstead Board had constructed a drain for relief of the neighbourhood but it did not reach further than the boundary of the parish, close to Ordnance Terrace. Plumstead authority had informed them that there was no reluctance on their part to allow the houses to drain into their sewers. It was hoped that the local board would give co-operation in order that the existing nuisance might be removed and the disease risk averted.

In early September, a letter from Plumstead Board of Works stated that the nuisance complained of by the Woolwich Board of Health arose principally from the diversion of the watercourse at Shooters' Hill by Mr. Thomas Clark of Ordnance Terrace in Woolwich parish. Evidently Thomas Clark had been taking matters into his own hands such was his frustration and had done some engineering work himself. However, they stated that they were happy to make an arrangement with Woolwich for remedying 'the evil' by draining of the locality into the Woolwich sewers and would undertake to carry a drain to the boundary of the parish. The surveyor confirmed the parish sewer was of ample dimensions for the required purpose. The storm water was provided with an outlet by another channel. A committee was appointed to consider this and make arrangements in view of the government property in the neighbourhood being affected by the proposed works.[20]

On 17 September it was reported the local Board of Health met the previous Tuesday. The Committee set up to consider the Plumstead application to connect the house property at Shooters' Hill with the sewer of the Woolwich parish terminating near the Royal Military Academy, recommended that it should be granted, provided that Plumstead parish paid a rate of 6d in the pound on the gross assessment of the property and offered facilities for the drainage of Ordnance Terrace, which was situated in a corner of Woolwich parish, with other conditions. If the Plumstead parish refused to pay the rate, a solicitor recommended that the Board should remedy the matter by severing the connection.[21]

Finally on 18 February 1860, the surveyor reported that the works of drainage carried out by the Plumstead Board were nearly completed. The Woolwich Board needed to lay down a 9 inch drain 10 feet long to cost eight pounds. This would connect the houses in Ordnance Terrace to the main sewer and thus the matter would be resolved at last.[22]

Up until this time, we have glimpsed both the family man and the business man. What of the private Thomas Clark and his interests? During the latter end of the dispute with the local Health Board concerning the drainage at Shooters' Hill, he gave a lecture at Woolwich Town Hall entitled 'Natural Magic', hiring the hall for a cost of 2l. 2s, the proceeds were given to a charity named The Soldiers' Institute.[23] Natural Magic during this period probably referred to alchemy and astrology. After the event, he found out that the board offered a discounted rate to those hirers who donated to charity. He approached the Woolwich Board to see if he could obtain the retrospective reduction and was informed that it would be necessary for him to attend the board meeting and make his application with another gentleman who had attended for a similar purpose. The board later claimed he had failed to attend this meeting but he said that he was in attendance outside, but on hearing what the difference in charge amounted to from the other gentleman, he 'thought it unnecessary to trouble the board'. He was then informed that an answer would be sent to his application and then he left. Afterwards, a discussion took place, and it was decided to refuse his application. The board seemed to be at fault however, because when the clerk put out placards advertising the use of the hall, details about the reduction offered for charity were omitted. This had subsequently been done by the placing of a white strip of paper across the coloured bills. Possibly, they had decided to refuse his application as he was well-known to them over the separate but long-standing drainage issue.

Chapter 7

———

LIFE AS A COUNTRY GENTLEMAN

———

Cudham & Crofton, Kent 1862-1867

The Clarks enjoyed an extensive home in the London suburbs for seven years but now Thomas Clark set his sights upon a country 'seat' to emulate the upper classes, so that his family could live a life in parallel to those for whom it was a birth right. It was in June 1862 that his business partner Donald Gray had died of jaundice at Brighton after seeking a cure for his poor health in the popular seaside resort.[1] The passing of Gray meant that Thomas Clark was then the sole buisness owner and he no longer had to share the profits.

Ashmore House, Leaves Green, Cudham in the county of Kent was acquired for the family in 1862 or 1863. Already a house of some maturity, it appears on an 1801 map of Kent, it was located south-west of the village of Keston and just a few miles west of Down, the home of Charles Darwin who had recently caused a great stir by publishing his controversial theory *On the Origin of Species* in 1859. Back in its 1820s heyday, Ashmore House had been inhabited by Luke Pocock, who had seen service in the East India Company Army in 1779.[2] His daughter, Belinda, married the artist Thomas Landseer in 1825 at Cudham.[3] The census returns from 1841 to 1861 shows that the area was vastly rural and agricultural. It is possible that the Clarks took up residence under a short-term lease in continuity with the way the house appears to have been run since the vacation of the Pocock family in the late 1830s.[4]

The Clarks must have just settled into their new residence when Amelia (Amy) their six-year-old daughter who had already been ailing with typhoid for six weeks in June 1863, died on the 21st. The onset of typhoid was rather subtle and could be mistaken for influenza or a common cold as the symptoms were similar and, like cholera, it was caused by water-borne bacteria. Typhoid was not always fatal but in Amy's case she then contracted scarlet fever, a highly contagious childhood disease which was endemic in the mid-19th century. Amy sadly succumbed to the combined diseases and her 20-year-old brother Fred was present at her death and duly registered it.[5] She became the fourth family member to be laid to rest at the family plot at Nunhead cemetery back in Peckham. Whatever the circumstances, whether it was the threat of disease the property posed, the unhappy association of a childhood death, or the expiry of a short term lease, the family were once again on the move.

Crofton Hall in the hamlet of Crofton close to Orpington, Kent, had been built circa 1780 on land owned by Admiral Sir Francis Geary. It then passed on to the Reverend Alexander Platt, who leased it to the three Miss Percevals, Margaret, Mary and Isabella, the half-nieces of the Prime Minster Spencer Perceval who was assassinated in the House of Commons during 1812.[6] Upon the death of the last sister, Isabella, in early 1860 the Hall was then sold to Sir Richard Madox Bromley. Bromley was a direct descendant of Elizabeth I's Lord High Chancellor Sir Thomas Bromley (1530-1587). He was in residence at the time of the 1861 census with his wife Clara and children Juliana, Walter and Edward complete with a large retinue of household staff as befitting the needs of a substantial residence of the upper class.[7] The servants who waited on this family inside the Hall were a butler and footman, a housekeeper and cook, an upper housemaid and an under

*Fig 10. Crofton Hall, rear view c. 1864, with unknown lady
wandering in the gardens, possibly Mary Ann Esther Clark.*

housemaid specifically for kitchen work and an under gardener. Other
staff occupied two cottages on the estate; in the Gardener's Cottage, a
coachman and his wife who worked as a laundress, together with the
gardener himself. In Ivy Cottage, an agricultural worker, his wife and
son were in occupation.[8]

The area of Crofton was very rural indeed. In ancient times it was
the location of a Roman villa, the centre then of a large farming estate,
but in more recent centuries, the oldest house was Crofton Court,
followed by Crofton Lodge, then Crofton Pound Farm, belonging to
St Thomas' Hospital, then Crofton Hall itself. Not only was Crofton
Hall to be the new home for 13 Clark family members, but it was part
of a working country estate complete with a farm of 91 acres. The
attached farm was mixed arable and livestock with dairy cows, sheep,
a breeding sow and pigs and chickens. In addition, there was stabling

for horses and ponies, both to ride and drive as well as for use on the land. The farm contained several varieties of transport both for agricultural and leisure use on the estate including a park phaeton, pony chaise, dog carts and two waggonettes.[9] Thomas Clark purchased the lease for the property but was not himself the landowner.[10]

It is unlikely that the Clarks on moving in sometime between July and early September of 1863 would have retained such an extensive compliment of domestic servants as the Bromleys, but there would certainly have been a few retainers. The 10 children, ages ranging from 21 down to 2, would have enjoyed the freedom and space to roam all the outbuildings, park and pasturelands attached to the house and gardens built with its fashionable glasshouses. Matilda Clark later

Fig 11. Crofton Hall, front view c. 1864. Behind the gate in the shadows
stands Thomas Clark junior (born 1841) with perhaps, his sister,
Mary Ann Esther, (Polly) seated on the ground.

recalled an incident when she had sustained an injury on the gate railings in an attempt to imitate the feats of the French tightrope walker, Charles Blondin who was performing in London around this time to vast crowds of spectators.[11]

The older children probably became proficient at driving some of the carriages with horses both on the estate, as well as trips into Orpington or the surrounding area. They would probably have driven Papa to the nearest railway station in order to catch a train into London, 12 miles away, thus mimicking the lifestyle of the country gent. Typically, a working father of the family would be driven into London in the morning and his carriage would return for his wife to use, if she so desired, he would then make the return journey by cab. If the family employed a coachman, this arrangement would mean that the coachman would have quite a lot of spare time on his hands for the rest of his day.[12]

On May 2, 1864, Thomas Clark liquidated his business partnership with Donald Gray which was a necessity as Mr. Gray had died two years earlier in Brighton and his sons Hector and William now took over his business.[13] Thomas' sons Thomas (22) and Frederick (21) had now reached their majority and it was time for them to become his business partners in a City office at Great Tower Street. No doubt, they had already been groomed and educated for this moment. On 3 May, a sale was advertised for the first time by T. Clark & Sons, brokers, of 92 Great Tower Street.[14]

In the City Press of Saturday, 22 July 1865, it was reported under the City Courts column that Thomas Clark and Frederick Henry Clark were sworn as brokers during a meeting of the Court of Aldermen held the previous Tuesday at The Guildhall and in the presence of the Mayor.[15] Furthermore, on Wednesday, 15 November of the same year:

At the First Court of the Mayor and Aldermen, held at Mansion House of the Lord Mayor of the City of London, on Tuesday, the 14th November, 1865, and in the 29th year of the reign of Victoria, of the United Kingdom of Great Britain and Ireland, Queen, &c.

Thomas Clark and Frederick Henry Clark both of 6 Great Tower Street were admitted to act as brokers within the City of London and its liberties.[16]

Just as the family had reached stability by creating their own family firm, in the New Year of 1866, tragedy was once again just around the corner. In October, Mary Ann Clark (Thomas' wife) was staying in Sheffield. It is not known if she was accompanied by her husband on this visit, but it appeared that the family were regular visitors to Sheffield. Daughter Matilda noted in her diary entry at the end of 1873 that her sister Polly had been staying at Sheffield for two months and Papa and Fanny spent Christmas there that year.[17] The purpose of the visit to Sheffield in October 1866 was surely at the invitation of a business acquaintance named John Chester, a horn dealer and local manufacturer, whose home was at Sunny Bank, 24 Newbould Lane, Broomhill, Ecclesall Bierlow.

Sheffield was a Yorkshire town well-known for the manufacturing of steel which was greatly enhanced in 1856 by the invention of Henry Bessemer's convector. The locality became successful for its cutlery manufacturing in support of the demand for high quality tableware to furnish the dining tables of middle and upper class households.

John Chester and his family were local entrepreneurs who found themselves in the right place at the right time to benefit and joined the ranks of the *nouveau riche*. An advert in the local press in 1889 for Chester Brothers promoted their manufactured wares of table cutlery, scissors, fine pen, pocket and sportsmen's knives produced at their premises at West End Cutlery Works.[18] Other than the steel blades, these finely finished items would have exquisitely carved handles made with luxurious materials such as ivory or buffalo horn. No doubt Chester was one of the Clark's biggest clients at the London auctions. Not only did they have common business interests, but it seems likely that they shared a non-conformist Christian faith which would have bonded them together in friendship. John Chester was a leading member of Mount Zion Congregational Chapel in Sheffield, his connection lasting over 50 years. In addition, he was well-known in the area for his philanthropic financial support to local charitable organisations and causes. He possessed shrewdness in business dealings and a quiet humour.[19]

On 21st October, Mary Ann Clark died whilst staying at Sunny Bank. The cause of death was stated as organic disease of the stomach and John Chester was present.[20] She was only 50 years old and her youngest child was not quite six. The loss of the matriarch must have been devastating to the entire family. She was taken back to London, presumably by train, and interred at Nunhead a few days later on 27 October. Only the two eldest sons, Thomas and Fred, had left the family home both having married in 1865 and early 1866 respectively. The remainder of the family were all girls, except for 20-year-old James. Their father was a successful businessman whose job took him away from home most of the time and family life had been turned upside down.

The news of his wife's death appeared in some London papers but it was in Sheffield the loss was reported in the greatest detail in the Sheffield Daily Telegraph of Wednesday 24 October:

> *On the 21st inst. At Sheffield, at the residence of an esteemed friend, Mary Ann, the dearly beloved wife of Thomas Clark, Esq., of Crofton Hall, Orpington, Kent, and 6, Great Tower Street, city, deeply regretted by her family and friends.*[21]

The Clarks' marriage had lasted almost 27 years and Thomas was just twenty years old when it began; he was still only 47. His wife ran the home for him and was there to provide a comfortable place for him to return to from life in the City. She was also by his side to meet his business acquaintances with whom deep friendships were forged such as that with the Chesters. Furthermore, she was the mother of his 10 living children.

With the tragic death of his wife, Thomas Clark faced a challenging situation. His eldest daughter Mary Ann (Polly), now 21 and of age, would have been called upon to step-in and look after her younger siblings, a task with which she was probably already familiar. There is no doubt that she continued to act as a substitute mother to her family, largely due to the fact that out of the seven sisters, she would be the only one to remain a spinster. Polly must have been a source of great strength to the family in the dark months of mourning and the years to follow.

Chapter 8

―――

PENGE – ANERLEY – SYDENHAM

―――

1867-1872

The Crystal Palace was the wonder of the age, and for the years that it existed, it brought trade and wealth to Penge and Sydenham and the people living there were at the centre of one of the most popular places in England. …it could be seen for miles around, glistening in the sunshine.
(Doris E. Pullen, Penge)

It was obvious that the family could not remain in the remote location of Crofton Hall, so distant from the City of London. The family needed to move back to the suburbs and Papa to his working place. On Tuesday 5 February 1867, an auction of live and dead farming stock and effects was to take place at Crofton Hall. The agent had disposed of the lease and taken instructions from Thomas Clark who was moving in haste to Sydenham, South London.[1] In an act of conspicuous consumption, the advertisement was designed not only to inform the public of the goods he had acquired and of

Fig 12. Anerley Road and Crystal Palace photographed circa 1900.

his status, but that his wealth was going with him to the prime new location. Around the same time, another advert sought the 'valuable long leasehold' of the property he owned at 2 Ordnance Terrace, Shooters' Hill.[2] Sydenham was a fashionable new suburb due to the relocation of the Crystal Palace in 1854 following the 1851 exhibition. Prosperous Victorians were building spacious mansions here to be near the Palace and its numerous attractions. It was a world away from the rural backwater of Crofton.

His eldest son Thomas was then living at 5 Palace Road, Norwood and a reunion was also to take place so father and son had mutual support privately and in business.[3] Meanwhile the younger Clark children would have access to so many educational and cultural pursuits to keep them occupied. In the years following the relocation of the Crystal Palace to Sydenham, it became the cultural hub of south London life. There were exquisite gardens and fountains laid out by Joseph Paxton. Inside the great structure, which had been enlarged, could be found the ten Architectural Courts reconstructing in plaster the ancient buildings and figures of the world's greatest civilisations. These included the Lions Court situated within the Alhambra Court, and the Assyrian Palace which was guarded by winged bearded figures. The Byzantine Court offered a copy of an 8th century cloister from a museum in Cologne. Some of the other Courts were inspired by the classical worlds of Greece and Rome. There was also a court which celebrated contemporary success; the manufacturing prowess and prominence of the Great British cities of Birmingham and Sheffield. Produce hailing from these centres was marketed to the masses, who, if not living locally, arrived by train. Two million people were transported for the first 30 years after the Palace was opened at Sydenham. Thomas Clark would have appreciated the opportunity to patronise the classical music concerts held every Saturday. The Palace had its own resident orchestra too. Music of all genres could be heard daily; as well as classical, brass and military bands also gave regular performances.[4]

In the 1871 census, the family is living at Anerley Road, Penge so it is reasonable to suggest that this location was the approximate vicinity of their next home after Crofton Hall.[5] Like the former residence at Ordnance Terrace, Shooters' Hill, it was an area next to one of the highest points of London at Sydenham Hill. Matilda wrote her diary in 1872 from 4 Norfolk Villas, a location that today cannot be found. The motivation for the move was in part, to remarry as soon as a respectable period of mourning had been observed. Victorian middle-class etiquette demanded this should take place in bereaved families and this was encouraged by Queen Victoria who famously grieved for Prince Albert for decades following his early death in 1861. For widowers, mourning was brief and low-key in comparison to that for widows. Male mourning attire consisted of a black mourning coat, black hat-band, cravat and gloves and so would not have looked very different from everyday dress. There was no set time period for this display, but *Cassells Household Guide*, a Victorian manual for the middle-classes, advised that widowers should observe deep mourning for a year. For widows, a full period of mourning was two years followed by a further period of six months at half-mourning. During this time, they had to observe a strict dress code of specific black mourning garments accompanied by appropriate restrained social behaviour.[6]

Just over a year after his wife had died, Thomas Clark re-married. A new wife could take care of the domestic sphere whilst enabling him to concentrate on his life as the breadwinner. It was of utmost importance that a wife was present to oversee the appointment of servants, run the household and act as an intermediary between him and his children as well as providing moral and practical support and guidance.

His new wife was Miss Frances Colebatch (known as Fanny). Miss Colebatch was eminently suitable for the role. Her father Joseph Colebatch was, according to the 1861 census, a warehouseman and Fanny was then 35 and the eldest child in his household. There were several unmarried younger siblings in the family home at Islington at this time.[7] Fanny would have been educated and raised with the expectation that she would make a good marriage. Had she lacked the social opportunity to meet someone earlier in life? However, she was probably not expecting to be a step-mother to such a large brood of children into the bargain but she had experience of looking after younger siblings. Joseph Colebatch was probably someone Thomas knew in the city or had been introduced to by an acquaintance or friend. The marriage took place on 23 November 1867 at Stoke Newington Parish Church, the local church of the 42-year-old bride.[8] Her father would have been delighted to have her taken off his hands at an age considered to be well and truly beyond hope of marriage and know she would be amply provided for when he and his wife had died.

No members of the Clark family acted as witnesses and one wonders what their thoughts were about their father's speedy courtship, which must have taken place well before the year's period of mourning had ended, and supplanting a new mother figure in the household. The evidence supplied by Matilda in her diary of a few years later does not paint a very receptive welcome to the newest family member. However, the bride had her younger sister Mary for support at the wedding and another relative, J. Colebatch (either Joseph himself or her sister Jane) signed the register.

In the 1871 census at Anerley Road, Penge the family are young adults. Fanny, Thomas' wife of over three years is not at home this census night. Instead, she is staying with her sister Eliza and her husband Isaac Simon and their family at Paradise Row, Stoke Newington.[9]Daughters Mary Ann, Emma, Matilda, Melina and Eliza are all at home with Papa. 12-year-old Alice is staying with her brother Tom at his home in Sutton, Surrey and enjoying the companionship of his growing family, as many of the girls also did at this time.[10] James is now the only son at home at 25 years old. 10-year-old Florence is not recorded and her whereabouts on this census night are unknown.

For the first time in a census, Thomas Clark has two servants employed within his household. A 21-year-old housemaid, Esther Holden and Ann Fox, 26, who is working as a cook. Both young ladies are recorded as being born in the county of Sussex. One of the important markers denoting a middle-class household was the ability to employ a servant or two. In 1871, Thomas Clark's wife had help at hand to run her large household. The appointment of a cook and housemaid meant that she was released of the more mundane aspects and could focus on overseeing and directing the servants' work. It is likely that Thomas Clark enjoyed uncomplicated meals and favoured plain cooking.[11] The neighbourhood they were living in during the time of this census created a glimpse into the expanding suburb with the newly built grand houses, some unoccupied or established. Some were being run as boarding houses by single or widowed women to provide them with an income. The immediate neighbours include Ellen Jones, a 69-year-old widow who has a coachman, cook and housemaid living with her. Then there is Sarah Brind, a single lady of 45 who is a lodging housekeeper from Essex with a cook, housemaid and page staying at her accommodation.

Chapter 9

'THE ROCKLANDS'

Upper Norwood 1872-1873

'Nil Desparandum' (Never despair)
Clark family motto

The wedding stationery for Thomas Clark's daughter Matilda in 1873 bore the family motto which perhaps was chosen as a reflection on how the family had overcome the obstacles they had endured over the previous two decades. The deaths of two strong matriarchs who ran the family homes and lives had sent shockwaves of despair but had seen the family emerging resilient and stronger than ever. Wealth and success now defined the Clark family.

The years between 1872 to 1874 are recorded in the diary of Matilda Clark who, as a young woman aged between 21 and 23, chronicled her inner most thoughts as well as opening up a window into family life and events leading up to her marriage to Alfred Bawtree on 10th May 1873 and just beyond.[1] She describes her interactions with her father, step-mother and siblings, life at home, various needlework and craft projects, the servants, and her courtship with her soon to be husband as well as national events such as the death and funeral of the

Fig 13. Matilda Clark kept a diary between 1872 and 1874 which threw open the window onto the Clark family dynamics.

exiled French king, Louis-Philippe (Napoleon III) which occurred at Chislehurst, Kent in 1873.

Matilda's step-mother Fanny Clark was undoubtedly relieved to escape the household of the man she had married, on the census night of 1871. Matilda confides to her diary just the following year on Wednesday 8th May 1872:

> *Papa and Fanny are very unhappy together just now, I am so sorry for it and it makes home so unhappy too.*

Fanny's father had died in 1869 and her mother, also named Frances (née Hoppe) passed away on 17 March 1872 and so Matilda's comment can be read with a recent bereavement in mind.[2] The will was proved on 12 April. In her diary, dated Saturday 29 April 1872, Matilda states:

> *Fanny and her family have behaved rather strangely since Mrs. Colebatche's death. Fanny has made a will without Papa's knowledge and he does not even now know anything about it.*

Mrs. Colebatch had directed that the residue of her estate following the payment of her debts and funeral expenses should be divided equally amongst her five daughters. Also Fanny was to inherit equally with her sisters 'plate, books, clothes and jewellery' from her mother. Perhaps Fanny wanted to keep the inheritance herself or pass on to a member of her own family rather than have it fall into the hands of her step-children.[3] If what Matilda had recorded was true and her step-mother had indeed made a will, this would be a very rare occurrence indeed in 1872 for a married woman. Before the Married Women's Property Act of 1882, married women and their possessions were treated as property of the husband and they could only make a will with the consent of their spouses.[4] Matilda states that her father is unaware of this development.

In April 1872, Matilda's diary reveals that her father is having a new home built for the family.

The house is getting on so slowly.

On Wednesday 24 April, the entry reads:

The house progresses slowly. Alfy and I are very anxious about it, as so much depends upon when it is completed.

For Matilda, the completion of the house is imperative because once it is finished she hopes her father can turn his attention to arranging her wedding to Alfred Bawtree. She concedes it will not take place during the present year.

On 9 June 1872, she records that her two youngest sisters, Alice (13) and Florrie (11) had been sent to Miss Wheeler's boarding school that May. Matilda asserts that she is 'very glad for they need school discipline sadly'. Perhaps this is a reflection of the poor relationship between the girls and their step-mother, particularly the youngest two, who may have felt their Mama's loss the most heavily. Matilda herself took them to the school and her entry for Wednesday 8 May shows that this took place the previous Thursday. She remarks that she hopes that 'school life will do them good'.

Very unsettled weather predominated throughout 1872 and Matilda often refers to rainy days, thunder storms, lightning and humid conditions.[5] In her diary entry of 1 June, written retrospectively as she had been away staying with her brother Tom in Sutton, she recounts a meteorological event which took place at the family home on Thursday 9 May, two days after her departure:

> *Our house caught on fire while I was away, there were hundreds of people collected round the door. The chimney caught fire and the chimney pot split to pieces but nothing was destroyed. The people all waited to come in and they wanted to let them in, but luckily Papa was at home and made them keep the door shut.*

Matilda did not elaborate on the cause of the 'fire'. However, a lightning strike was reported in the Norwood News and Crystal Palace Chronicle newspaper on Saturday 11 May. The date of the incident being 9 May seems to fit her diarised account.

> **A HOUSE STRUCK BY LIGHTNING** – *During the thunder storm on Thursday, the inhabitants of No. 9, Hawthorn Close, were considerably alarmed in consequence of a stack of chimneys being struck by lightning. Fortunately beyond loosening the brickwork and displacing a few slates, no damage was sustained.[6]*

Yet, there was more high family drama just around the corner. Matilda records on Saturday 9 June that her youngest sisters Alice and Florrie had run away from boarding school the previous Sunday and returned home.

> *We did not know what to do with them, but Miss Wheeler sent a telegram to say she knew where they were. She then went on to Papa's office to see him about it, so that when he came home he was quite*

prepared to see them. I am glad to say he gave them a good scolding although he gave Polly and me one too. It was a miserable day and a more miserable evening. I cried very much and my darling Alfred was so kind and comforted me a great deal. On Tuesday morning Lizzie and I took them back and spoke very seriously to them. Miss Wheeler was very kind to them and to us. She got us some lunch and forgave the children very readily. Oh! It is very hard to do what you think is for the best and to be thought hardly of for it. They all turned round upon Polly and me because we had been the cause of the children going to school.

Matilda does not explain or expand as to the reason why both she and her sister Polly (Mary Ann) were 'given a scolding' because the children had run away. Nor do we know why she and Polly 'had been the cause of the children going to school' in the first place but can only surmise that it had been a proposal that they made which was authorised by Papa. In the light of the subsequent truancy it seemed to have failed to bestow any improvement in their wayward behaviour.

I am not sorry for my part in sending them and this only makes me feel more how much they need some restraint. Florrie told me that Alice tried to choke and starve herself – poor Alice she has a proud hard disposition. They have all taken a great fancy to Florrie, but they seem to think and I fear they are right, that Alice tries to make herself unamiable. My opinion is that the child made up her mind from the first not to stay, and that she has left no stone unturned to accomplish her purpose. She understands Papa's weakness and has written him the most pitiful letters. The last one she sent was on the Monday they came home, and we decided to withhold it from Papa, because one would think to read it that she was in a dying condition. She says she is growing weaker and weaker and is in great pain. I have no doubt that she will suffer just now, but I am sure that even from this cause alone she is better at school, than at home for she has far more consideration shown her. Even she, has never said a word about any unkindness on their part. Miss Wheeler makes her lie down every afternoon and gives her an interesting book to read. When they go for a walk, Miss Mann consults her as to the distance she should walk and they give her an egg every morning.

In the entry for 9 June, she writes that around this time, her Papa decided a break to the coast might be a good idea to heal family divisions and tensions that summer and provide a welcome diversion whilst the house was being finished. Matilda records:

Papa talks very decidedly about taking us to Brighton but I shall scarcely believe it until we are on our way there. Although it seems so far settled that I have gone as far as to buy a bathing dress, at least the material which I shall make up into one. We have had a great deal of wet this June – it is very much like last year for that.

Fig 14. Eugenio Arbib, (c. 1910) feather merchant, was a business acquaintance and a guest at Matilda's wedding in 1873.

On Wednesday 19 June she reflects on the last few days and the difficult relationship with her remote and authoritarian Papa:

Papa has given me my guinea, thanks to Lizzie for asking Fanny who asked Papa. It is quite unexpected and I am very glad to have it. I have given Lizzie eighteen pence for asking. Mr Arbib too has sent me my Ostrich feather at last although my pleasure in receiving it was somewhat damped through Papa scolding me for having written to remind him of it.[7] I don't see much harm in having done so, myself, (except it was) the same evening in which I received it and (then) the scolding was a most unfortunate one.

Then with an air of excitement:

We are all going to Brighton on Saturday and my darling is coming down the following Friday for a fortnight's holiday. Oh! It will be a happy time for us. I have made a bathing dress and hope to be able to bathe everyday.

Some weeks later, Tuesday 9 July 1872:

We came to Brighton on 22nd June. We have nice lodgings facing the sea. No. 35 Marine Parade.[8] We have the drawing room floor at present and a very nice drawing room it is too – it has panelling of looking glass at two windows and has a nice balcony.

Brighton was at this time a new and fashionable seaside resort. The arrival of the railway to the town earlier in the century brought day trippers and holiday makers from London in their droves hoping, like Matilda, that the sea air and bathing 'will do me a great deal of good – for my nerves seem so upset that they need a little strengthening'. Bathers would have used horse-drawn bathing machines to change into appropriate dress and take the waters.

Matilda records that she and Alfred had 'been several times on the new pier in the evening…it was such fun.' The West Pier had opened a few years earlier in 1866. She also spent 'one afternoon on the old pier'. This was the Chain Pier opened back in 1823 after Brighton was first developed as a Regency bathing town akin to earlier Georgian spa towns like Cheltenham and Buxton.

They also enjoyed a day trip to Hastings leaving on the 7.55am train.

…and did such a lot of walking, but I hope to go there again one-day. We went over the castle and saw the different names of the Bawtree's cut on a rock… I cut out A.B. and Alfred cut Tilly and Alfred and put them in a small square. We went to the lover's seat there too and to Fairlight Glen.

The Victorians were enjoying increasing amounts of leisure time and this was encouraged by the Bank Holiday Act of 1871 passed by Sir John Lubbock in which year a bank holiday in August was created.

In total, Matilda stayed at Brighton from 22 June until approximately 24 July as her diary states she was in Brighton for a month and two days. Reflecting on the holiday after her return, she ponders over a family outing:

Another day Papa took us all to Bramber Castle and Alfred [Bawtree] went with us. We came upon the prettiest little village I have ever seen there. We enjoyed ourselves very much, and in Bramber Village and Churchyard there was nothing but people of the name of Woolgar. The woman who attends the chapel told us that thirteen years ago when she went there, there were only two families not bearing that name.

At the end of the summer reflecting on the holiday and subsequent stays with Alfred's family also her brother Tom and his family, Matilda looks forward once again to the new family home being built at Norwood:

Friday 30th August 1872 – *'My darling boy and I shall be so thankful to get married and settled in our own comfortable little house, and however grand the Rocklands may be, I don't expect there will be much comfort there under present circumstances'.*

Her diary entry for Wednesday 25 September reads:

> *Home at last, really in our house... [I] am glad for many things to be*
> *at home again. We are not all here although Alice and Florrie are at*
> *Tom's and Lizzie at Fred's. I shall be glad when we can all be together*
> *again. The house is still filled with workmen but they are getting on*
> *nicely. Ours is considered the best house in Norwood and it certainly*
> *is finished off beautifully. There are from twenty to thirty rooms in it,*
> *but I long to leave it for my own home.*

The new house was situated in a prominent position next to Crystal
Palace High Level Station, Upper Norwood, and was a fine property

Fig 15. The Rocklands, College Road. The 20 to 30 room home built for the Clarks in
1872 was considered the best house in Norwood, according to Matilda.

built in the fashionable High Victorian Gothic style, an architectural design made popular between 1850 and 1880 by the architect Sir George Gilbert-Scott. The house has a substantial size porch flanked by neo-classical columns at the entrance over which the Clark family coat-of-arms is proudly emblazoned. At the windows, smart venetian blinds lend a very modern fresh look. It appears so stunningly new and stylish that it's possible to think that even today you could grace the entrance, knock upon the door and be admitted as a family member.

Inside the commodious home, you would expect to see the material possessions of conspicuous consumption acquired by a successful Victorian gentleman which would define his middle class status. In his Will written in 1880 he inventories the effects to be found amongst the usual household furniture: plate, plated articles, china, glass, books, linen, prints, pictures and musical instruments.[9] However hard Thomas Clark had worked to rise to the top and give his children a privileged lifestyle, it would seem that as always, money and property could not secure personal happiness. Tensions and friction continued to exist within the pristine walls of the family mansion. Matilda sadly noted, even as the paint was drying, that 'she longed to leave it for her own home'.

On Wednesday 30 October 1872, she confides to her '*old friend*' – her diary:

> *I do pity the girls at home so, and I seldom have more than one evening a week at home. I always dread it when it comes, for Papa is so very touchy and tyrannical that it is almost unbearable. At least I cannot be as patient under it now as the other girls are and as once I used to be. My darling has spoilt me for that, though unless I am mistaken, Papa is much worse than he used to be.*

Matilda had thought that the attitude of Papa towards her and Alfred concerning the possibility of living at his house and the former family home, 2 Ordnance Terrace, Shooters' Hill was 'shabby'. As part of the proposed deal, they could live there rent free and he would pay the ground rent but Alfred would have to pay for all repairs (about sixty pounds) and rates (about twenty pounds).[10] In her diary, she states:

We declined the offer with thanks and I thought it very shabby of Papa proposing such a thing for his daughter which he would most gladly get a stranger to undertake on the same terms. I hope this is not the sign of future liberality in kind, or else 'twill be a poor look out for my Trousseau etc.

Thomas Clark had by 1872, achieved the aspirations of the middle-classes in the Victorian era. He had given his family the suburban house with a semi-circular drive, very likely that drive could take their own carriage, and they had more than one servant and were taking a lengthy seaside holiday.[11]

However, perhaps Papa was worried that he had over-reached himself with the new house. The completion coincided at a time of financial insecurity in Great Britain due to the start of The Great Depression in 1873 which was to last until 1896. Britain no longer was the powerful manufacturing world leader it had been as other countries, namely Germany and the USA, were catching up and the competition creating economic uncertainty. On Friday 6th December 1872, Matilda is aware of her Papa's decline in outlook which may in part, have been influenced by this development:

Papa is in such a miserable state just now – it is a most unhappy sight to see him so, not only miserable himself, but making everybody else miserable too. He is one continual groan about the times and yet nobody else seems to find them so bad. Of course I know that he has had to spend a great deal of money on the house, but it is all twaddle to say that it is all done for us. We should be much happier in a smaller house with fewer decorations, than to be here, afraid to move for fear of getting scolded for some mark or another on the paint. I hope I may not be doing dear Papa an injustice but I shrewdly suspect that in spite of all this expensive outlay being for us, the house will make my trousseau and wedding suffer.

The acquisition of the grand new house seemed to have done nothing to improve Papa's quick temper; Thomas Clark was recalled for having a very bad one. Matilda recalled an incident which demonstrates this all too well:

Papa nearly hammered the door in the other night because the bell was not answered quickly enough for him, and he came home quite unexpectedly too. It is so silly and childish of him.

On another occasion, one of Matilda's great-granddaughters recalled an anecdote, perhaps retold by Matilda herself that he once threw a joint (of meat) on the floor declaring it to be done to rags![12]

In an earlier diary entry on Saturday 23 November 1872 Matilda mentioned a commotion going on outside the new house which actually did not involve Papa:

There is a Spring-Heal-Jack [Victorian folklore figure] *about just now frightening everybody out of their wits, wicked fellow. I wish he were caught. We were awoken the other night by hearing a man calling loudly for the police but no one came to his aid. I think it is a disgrace to think that the police are never near when they are most wanted. We heard afterwards that it was a drunken man calling out. I am sure I hope it was no worse.*

On 28th December, reflecting on Christmas 1872, Matilda declared it to be, 'the most miserable we have ever spent, even including the one shortly after Mamma's death'.

Not only was Papa bad-tempered, but it seemed that his son Fred had inherited this trait too and Matilda was annoyed that her father had invited Fred and his wife Annie to stay at The Rocklands whilst they were house-hunting.

> *We all stood out against that although Fred and Papa think it very unkind of us. I know too well what it would be with two fiery tempers in the house instead of one. Papa has been very miserable for the last six weeks and very cross too. I have not even dared to ask if I might have a few friends to keep my birthday.*

On what should have been a happy family gathering, the first Christmas Day spent at The Rocklands was certainly not filled with peace and

Fig 16. The Rocklands, c.1873. The young ladies on the left and right in the porch are two of the Clark daughters, flanking their step-mother, Fanny. Their downcast eyes reveal the strained relationship with their step-mother.

goodwill and conviviality was in short supply. Instead, it seemed to resemble Ebenezer Scrooge's home before he had been visited by the ghost which changed his outlook on life. To us, it seems far removed from the image of a Victorian Christmas encapsulated by Mr. Charles Dickens. Matilda told with sorrow what happened that day:

Papa came downstairs in a bad humour to begin with and everything seemed to go wrong from the first. I was in the kitchen the greater part of the morning making Cocoa nut cakes… It is true that he had good cause for complaint but he need not have stormed and raved the house down as he did. We had lunch at one and then the storm was at its height. "The place is in a filthy condition" and he made them turn cupboards out and clean places that ought to have been done long before.

Matilda then lays the blame squarely on the shoulders of her step-mother Fanny for failing in her duty to ensure that the house was cleaned for Christmas:

We have told Fanny over and over again to have things cleaned up for Christmas day and that is all we could do, and it ought to have been done. [Her sister] Emma has done a great deal more than I would do in cleaning the place, when there are three servants to do it.

The arguments continued into the afternoon.

Fanny would not come down to lunch and this made things worse, but he [Papa] began to storm and rave at us poor girls so that at last I could not stand it any longer and spoke out. He said we ought to do our duty and I said we did do it and could do no more. I said it was too bad to think of us poor girls suffering for the negligence of his wife and I told him how Emma slaved. Then he turned upon me and said that I should soon be out of it. I said in an undertone, "a good thing too", and he told me not to be insulting and told me to go out of the room.

Of course I went, and as I went upstairs I felt so ill and worried, that I went off into the most violent fit of hysterics I have ever had. Alfred says I threw my arms about a good deal and called out, 'my home, my home'. I remember saying once too 'God have mercy on my home'. The fit lasted for some time and I felt weak when it was over.

Alfred was so gentle with me, and they all surrounded me in alarm. Fred [her brother] was very kind and sympathising, he kissed me and tried to calm me and I threw my arms round him and said 'Oh, Fred'.

As I look back upon it, it seems all a miserable dream...we had dinner at six and that was the only cheerful part of the day. The evening was miserable and we went to bed miserable. Some of it I am obliged to laugh at when I think of it for it was quite comic sometimes. Alfred laughs so when he thinks of Papa standing at the top of the stairs with the bread and fat he had found in the fowls' house. He said it was a waste, and so it was, but not so much so, as though they had thrown it away. If it is not given to them, it will be wasted in some other way with such management as there is here.

Thursday 26 December was Boxing Day and Matilda's 22nd birthday. This day, like the August bank holiday, having only been introduced as a public holiday the previous year. Matilda wrote there was a little improvement from the previous day but not a great deal:

The morning passed very happily indeed though the rest of the day was uncomfortable. I forgot to say that yesterday after lunch I kissed Papa and made it all up. I was disappointed the rest of the day because I had expected a nice family party and neither of my brothers turned up.

Her birthday was saved by her fiancé Alfred who

came round about eleven o'clock and handed me a small packet. I felt a little disappointed at first, for I thought it would be a work table, but

I don't think I showed it. I unrolled the paper and at last found a large steel key. Then I was silly enough to think it meant he had chosen our house and that was the key, a romantic idea. At last the truth flashed upon me, and I knew that my present was already in the house and I went up and found the key fitted the workroom's door, and on opening it I found my beautiful worktable. I have never seen such a beauty – walnut wood, inlaid with tulip wood, it seemed such a long time before I could open it, while Alfred was taking the tray off. But oh! I was delighted when it did open – it was full of everything I could possibly want. It would take too long to describe them, but the scissors and thimbles, and needles and cottons and silks, etc, etc, and all the little ornamental fancy things besides. I was so pleased, and it will always be a pleasure to look at it and think of it and use it.

In the Clark household, gifts seem to have been exchanged by the family on this day when employers traditionally gave a Christmas 'box' to their workers and servants. The majority of Victorian children, whose fathers could not afford luxurious commodities as presents, often could look forward to an orange or a bag of nuts as a gift. The middle class Clark family could use their well-lined pockets as well as their imaginations, to purchase what many would consider expensive items which the recipients would have been delighted to receive. The age of materialism was still in its infancy and gift giving was a novelty which was appreciated more than it is today.

In view of her forthcoming wedding, Matilda considered herself lucky to receive gifts at all on the day which was her birthday as well as exchanging seasonal gifts:

Fred has given me three shillings for a Christmas box. Papa has given me a nice black Vulcanite brooch for a Christmas box and he is to give me a nice-sized bag too, just large enough to take a few necessary things when I go out to stay. The others have all had similar presents. Little Florrie has given me a handkerchief with my name worked in the corner. At present these are all I have had.

To add to the Christmas holiday woes, the new house was flooded on Boxing Day morning when 'the pipes burst…I baled [sic] out the water and it came in as fast as we could bale it out but at last was stopped'.

That afternoon, Matilda and Alfred Bawtree joined the household of her future brother-in-law Josiah Bawtree and his wife Jane who lived in Croydon. Matilda noted that they walked there, a likely distance of over three miles from Sydenham. The couple found them engaged in a merry game of blind man's bluff. 'I could not help contrasting the two homes', she wryly commented.

December 1872 was like the rest of the year had been – very wet. It had been the wettest year on record in England and Wales. 21 December to 18 January 1873 was very mild with limited frost and snow with constant southerly winds.[13]

January 1873 started off on a sombre note as the exiled French Emperor Napoleon III died at Chislehurst on Thursday 9th following a risky operation to remove gallstones. On that day, a housewarming party took place at The Rocklands. This was an opportunity for Thomas Clark to show off his brand new stylish residence to all his family, friends and acquaintances. Matilda reported six days later on the 15th that 'there were fifty-five people present and eighty-five were asked. It all went off happily with the exception that Papa was very fretful and cross the first part of the evening.'

I wore my Maroon silk dress and a beautiful white Camelia, which my darling gave me, and a few small pearls in my hair. Directly I went into the room Miss Beckham poured a lot of hot milk down my dress, and when I had attended to that I came in again and Mr. Willis poured a cup of coffee down me. During the evening Mr. H. Raw tore the skirt right off my back so I had a chapter of accidents.[14] Alfred introduced Mr. Ross to us and I like him very much – he seems so gentlemanly.

Perhaps Papa's mood had improved and he was able to relax with his guests by this time as she reports that 'Papa made a very nice speech'.

Henry Raw was so mischievous he danced with me a great deal and kissed me under the Mistletoe and the next morning he was as bad. He Johnny and I drew chalk figures all over the drawing room floor. Alfred and Mr. Willis and Mr. Ross went away before breakfast. Mr. Ross had one of his boots taken away by mistake, so he and somebody else went off with odd boots. This is my last party at home as a Miss Clark but nothing was said about it, by Papa or anybody.

Perhaps the party and the clearing up were all too much for one of the servants. Matilda says scornfully that 'the housemaid left us the next day all in a muddle, ungrateful creature'. Perhaps this was Esther Holden, the housemaid at the time of the 1871 census, or more possibly could have been a later employee given a likely high turnover.

Matilda makes comment about the ways in which the death of the French emperor affected the family. Her step-mother Fanny travelled the short distance to Chislehurst, Kent on Tuesday 14 January to his lying-in-state and she reported back that many people were present as there was 'a great crush' and that it was 'quite a sight, all the people in mourning'. Matilda has some strong feelings about this too. She adds that she feels that 'at present the English have shown the family more sympathy and respect than the French, much to their disgrace I think'. Not surprising perhaps, considering the popularity of the British monarchy was on the rise again after years of decline since Victoria had withdrawn from public life following Albert's untimely death. The Prince of Wales, who contracted and survived typhoid, an illness that reputedly was responsible for killing his father, reinvigorated support within the last couple of years and was perhaps evident in Matilda's strong statement of support.[15]

Chapter 10

THREE DAUGHTERS AND
FOUR MARRIAGES

1873-1878

In her diary, Matilda does not say how she met Alfred Bawtree. However, it would seem possible that their paths crossed at the congregational church at Anerley in which Matilda was deeply involved as a church member who took a children's Sunday school class and played the piano.

Alfred was the youngest child in his own large family and was born in 1846 in the affluent northern district of Stoke Newington; he was four years older than Matilda Clark. At the time of the 1871 census he is 24 years old and lodging within the household of his brother Josiah, his wife Jane and their children in Croydon. He is on the threshold of his career in the insurance industry as one of the masses of commercial clerks. His future success and earning ability however is an unknown quantity.

The theme running through Matilda's diary in 1872 leading up to their marriage in May 1873 is that she doubts her Papa thinks Alfred financially viable enough to maintain his daughter in the manner to which she is accustomed. Matilda, for her part, does not appear to be swayed by the necessity of material comforts as much as her Papa. However, she is deeply unhappy living at home with her parents. Also, she does not get along very well with some of her siblings, notably Lizzie (who is flighty and a 'material girl') and her bad-tempered brother Fred of whom she seems to have mixed feelings.

A month after her wedding Matilda reflects on an incident with Fred, which occurred a few nights before her marriage, together with the absence of her mother who had died over six years earlier:

Thursday 22nd June 1873 Fred and I had a sad quarrel a few nights before I was married and he cursed and swore most horribly, and [I] prayed that God might strike him dead if he came to the wedding. Of course I forgave him, but having once said that, I dared not ask him to be present at my marriage. However he came at the last – not one of our family was absent. I am glad he was there. I wonder, was my dear dead mother there to behold my happiness? Who knows.

The only way to escape her unhappy home life at this time was by marriage which was the usual route for daughters in their early twenties. If marriage was not an option, another path for middle-class young ladies was often to become a governess. Matilda writes on 24 April 1872 that an acquaintance named Lucy Lord was 'having a very good situation as governess, beginning with thirty pounds and several advantages such as having the same music master as the grand lady without charge'. However, if this seemed tempting Matilda seems genuinely in love with Alfred whom she refers unceasingly in endearing terms as 'my darling' 'the darling' or 'darling boy' and describes him as 'a dear noble good-natured boy'. She was exceedingly fortunate to have found a young man who was able to placate her temperament – which was actually not unlike other family members in its ferocity on occasions. Alfred Bawtree in turn became a well-liked and respected addition to the Clark family using his undeniable strengths of patience and perseverance.

Still considering the offer by Papa of 2 Ordnance Terrace, Shooters' Hill as their first marital home, Matilda states in January 1873 that

…the offer is a slight improvement upon the last, as he is having it repaired. If we go we are to live rent free, but I think Alfred will refuse the offer on my account, as I should be so far away from everybody and shall be so lonely, and I am in such a nasty nervous state just now.

Papa had given Matilda a 'generous' present for her trousseau of twenty pounds but had deducted her quarterly allowance in lieu of the gift, she pointedly states: 'But of course I have taken no notice of this and have pretended not to understand him in this'.

The family has informed him that it is not considered enough so she is confident that there will be an increase. 'I will not buy a wedding dress unless I have fifty pounds. I think according to our position I ought to have a hundred'. Matilda will be making much of the garments required to complete her trousseau herself so 'it will be worth a great deal more owing to my care in sewing and working so hard and getting good things'.

A few weeks later on Wednesday 5 February, she confirms that Papa had increased the offer of her trousseau money to forty pounds which she thinks is still insufficient although acknowledges it as an improvement. Members of the family are all helping with the needlework. Annie (Fred's wife) has made a strip of embroidery for a pair of drawers and has made a pair of drawers too. Fanny is making embroidery for a nightdress and Polly (her elder sister) is assisting with the nightdresses although Matilda acknowledges there is still plenty to do.

We are getting through the hardest work – first I have made five already, there are only five more. The price of coals is very high – I hope they will soon go down. It is a good thing my darling and I will be looking forward to summer weather when we are married.

She hopes that upon her marriage, Papa will be generous with contributions towards setting up of things for their new home 'little things which he has in the house and would cost him nothing, but I don't like to suggest it to him, and am afraid no one else would'.

Matilda has probably overlooked or forgotten that she is the first of seven daughters he has to marry off and with each of them likely to marry over the next decade or so, he is in for a very expensive time ahead in providing money for trousseaus and all the other associated expenses that marriage entailed.

Monday 14 April and Papa has increased the trousseau money to fifty pounds and she hopes for another ten. The wedding day has been fixed for Saturday 10 May. She feels this date is inconvenient to her but 'convenient to Pa and that is considered everything here. We are to be married at Sydenham Hill church. This is not our wish

Fig 17. *The wedding between Matilda and Alfred was arranged by Papa and the guests responded to this invitation.*

but Papa was disposed to be nasty to Alfred though he had better please Alfred for my sake, for we are very anxious for everything to go off smoothly'. They have after all considerations 'taken a house at Sutton' where they shall be neighbours of Lydia (Alfred's sister). 'I am so pleased, for I did not want to live at Norwood. We have a small garden nine rooms and a scullery, no gas and we have pump water.'

Her next diary entry of Wednesday 21 May is written after the wedding and reflects on the day and the wedding dress entirely made by Miss Beckham and her sisters Polly and Emma 'who made it so well I am sure as any West End dressmaker could do it'. Papa had coughed up the sixty pounds so that she was able to complete her trousseau.

We had a beautiful day for the wedding and I noticed a great many people whom I knew there. I think I must have been a cheeky little bride but my only thought was that I was very very happy. I did not seem to trouble about leaving home at all. I was quite calm and self-possessed – the only time I really cried was when I wished them all good-bye and then I tried not to. I felt a little faltering when I heard my own voice in the church, but Alfred says no one would have noticed it. I took a little church service with me and that helped me a good bit. Part of the service was conducted at the steps leading up into the altar, and it was concluded at the rails of the altar.

We had Mr. Meen to play the wedding march etc at the church. We had a beautiful cake. Polly packed us up a piece to bring away with us. It looked so pretty to see them all in the grand porch with all their bright dresses and their rice and old shoes.

The wedding ceremony took place at 11am at St. Stephen's Church, South Dulwich and the wedding guests reconvened to The Rocklands for the traditional wedding breakfast (usually held at the home of the bride) and a lavish display of food was enjoyed. The celebrations

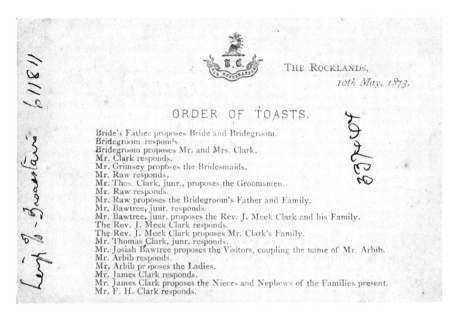

*Fig 18. The Order of Toasts at the Wedding Breakfast
reveals several family members participated.*

continued with speeches and toasts made by the family including Papa and Matilda's brothers, Tom, Fred and James. Matilda noted in her diary that although she and her new husband had departed by that time, a musical evening was held at The Rocklands to end the wedding day and that she had received several letters from friends informing her that it all went off very well.

I think it must have been a very pretty wedding, indeed everyone says it was. The bridesmaids, nine in number, including my little niece Annie were dressed in Brussels net dress silk net veils and beautiful blue sashes, blush roses, the new forget-me-nots, an expensive flower but very pretty, and Lilies of the Valley. The visitors were all beautifully dressed and it made altogether a very bright and pleasant scene. It was a very happy breakfast.

Matilda does not describe how her Papa behaved at the wedding ceremony but he arranged the date, location and the entire ceremony itself only informing Matilda and Alfred of the details within the last three months beforehand. He did shed tears on the big day whilst Matilda said she 'was determined not to, and didn't'. Her thoughts were very much with her sister Polly, who was her senior by six years and had not yet married. 'I do hope that she too may soon find a kind and loving husband, for certainly our house is not the happiest there might be'.

Perhaps Polly realised, not just that she was a spinster at the age of 29 but that she was losing a much loved sister who had always supported her, a very much needed quality in the inharmonious household. Matilda acknowledges the 'evident struggle to keep back the tears'.

Thursday 11 September 1873, now married for four months, Matilda recalls an outing with Papa that had just taken place at Westminster 'with all the girls [her sisters] and Jenny Smith at the office in a private omnibus and had great fun although it was a very showery day'.

Christmas 1873 was very different to the previous year and it probably was best for all that Papa and Fanny spent it in Sheffield as guests of their friend and business associate, John Chester and family, as Matilda records in her first entry for the New Year of 1874 on 8th January. Meanwhile, his daughters (except for Lizzie who went with Fred and Annie to the Potters' – Annie's parents) went to spend the day with eldest brother Tom and his wife Fanny at Sutton. Matilda and Alfred were also present and in contrast to the last year, thankfully, 'they had on the whole a very happy evening, although we did not feel fit for much after late dinner'.

Papa was back from Sheffield after Christmas, as Matilda recorded that

> On New Year's night Papa had a family party at The Rocklands. All were present (but not Polly) nephews, nieces and all but it was by no means a happy gathering as Pa was in a dreadful rage in the evening.

A return to the family home did not do Matilda any good as she had 'felt miserably unwell all day and would end up with a good cry'.

23 February 1874 – Matilda mentions that 'Old Mrs. Hall has lately died and left Papa a legacy, to which Papa has added more and bought a handsome piano for the girls at home'.[1]

The window which had been thrown open revealing the secrets of family life by Matilda's diary would be firmly shut forever. In this last journal entry dated 23 February, she reveals she is pregnant with her first child and no doubt the forthcoming arrival of the baby created a permanent change as her time and responsibilities would become channelled into raising a family of six children over the next 20 years.

With hindsight it seems strange that Thomas Clark decided to build such a large family home during 1871/2 considering that it coincided with the start of the decade when several of his daughters, being of marriageable age, would leave to start married life.

After Matilda's marriage of 1873, the next daughter, perhaps unsurprisingly, to walk to the altar would be Lizzie (Eliza) on 18 September 1875 to Frederick Albert Field.[2] Lizzie had finally settled on a marriageable man and stayed the course. Fred Field was also a colonial broker like Papa and his family perhaps rival merchants in the City. Papa probably would not have approved of the union and there were no family witnesses to sign the marriage register. Within a year, Lizzie and Fred did what many others were doing at the time; they sought a new and exciting life in Australia and would never return.[3] Following the birth of her two daughters in the late 1870s, Lizzie and Fred separated and Matilda probably would have wisely told her diary that she saw it all coming.

Matilda and Lizzie (four years her junior) were as different as chalk and cheese. Lizzie freely attached herself to any wealthy suitable paramour. Matilda's diary reveals that she despaired of her sister's lack of seriousness concerning seeking a suitable marriage partner, as engagements were made only to be broken off.

In January 1874 Matilda notes that an engagement was broken due to Lizzie expecting a second proposal from an Arthur Wyvene whom she doubts will actually propose at all, because it is merely a flirtation on his part. Papa apparently 'made such a deal of him (her fiancé) when he went there and encouraged him so openly'. He was annoyed to think of the broken engagement because the suitor 'had a little money'. Matilda is upset because Papa did not make enough of Alfred, a son-in-law of whom he may now be proud. Lizzie was considered the most physically attractive of the daughters but she was vain and had a mercurial nature when it came to her choice of men.

> *I think she is right in giving him up and her mistake was in engaging herself to him. As far as I could see it would be the worse thing that could possibly happen to Lizzie at present with her extravagant ideas to marry any one very well off it would be best for her to learn a few lessons of economy first.*

Not only was this disconcerting to her sister, Matilda, but Lizzie undoubtedly damaged both her reputation and social status by her broken engagements. Another aspect of Lizzie's personality Matilda found difficult was her predilection for borrowing items of her clothing, only to return them after Matilda wanted to wear them again, invariably soiled or damaged. She also forgot to pay back monetary debts.

> *Oh! I do wish she would alter, I believe she will and I do hope so. She is so bad tempered that she makes herself quite disagreeable to them all at home, and excepting that she is a good looking girl I really don't know what to say in her favour, and yet I know there is a true vein running underneath it all.* Matilda recognises that she has faults too *which are the same as hers, so what God has done for me he can certainly do for her.*

No sooner had Lizzie departed England's shores when on 24 November 1876, daughter Melina (Milly) married Edmund Howe Lilley at Camberwell Register Office by licence. After all the recent turmoil caused by Lizzie's courtships, marriage and departure to the other side of the world, Melina must have felt that she could not approach her father to seek his approval to her plans. Time and time again, we see that his children do not conform to his expectations. What of Edmund Lilley? He is deceitful on the certificate, stating that his father, Thomas, is a deceased ship owner when in fact he had over another decade to live![4] The young couple, both in their mid-20s, must equally have felt a mixture of both power and despair at their situation.

Less than eighteen months later, on 2 March 1878, the pair married again at St. Saviour's Church, Pimlico, again by licence, with Papa acting as a witness together with Edmund's mother, Eliza.[5] Edmund Lilley stated he lived in Lewisham whilst his bride apparently spent the night before the wedding at 14 Lupus Street, Westminster. They married in a London district far away from familiar people and places. Perhaps Melina's Papa knew someone prepared to give his daughter the required residentiary address. This raises all kinds of questions. More than likely Papa would have been belligerently hostile to the union, so that Melina and Edmund married without the knowledge of their parents in 1876. If so, how long did the secret endure? Perhaps

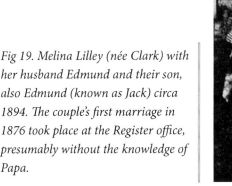

Fig 19. Melina Lilley (née Clark) with her husband Edmund and their son, also Edmund (known as Jack) circa 1894. The couple's first marriage in 1876 took place at the Register office, presumably without the knowledge of Papa.

until enough time had elapsed that they were more confident to bring the suit to Papa and in receiving a positive response.

In spite of these bizarre circumstances, the nautical theme was constant, as Edmund Lilley was a chief officer (First Mate) in the Mercantile Marine service, a job that would take him away from home for long periods at sea. Melina perhaps returned to The Rocklands during his prolonged periods of absence to spend in the company of her family. Indeed, she is present with the family at the time of the 1881 census when her husband is on a vessel named *Marlborough* moored off Shoeburyness in Essex at that time.[6]

Chapter 11

———

BRIXTON – GIPSY HILL

———

1879-1894

As the 1870s retreated, Emma Ann was the next daughter to walk down the aisle; on 15 November 1879 she wed Arthur William Hill.[1] Older than her other sisters who had so far married, at 31, her husband is two years her junior. Although she was positively an old maid by the standards of the day to marry, the couple would go on to have seven sons – the highest number of children born to the children of Thomas and Mary Ann Clark. The marriage took place at St. John's church, Brixton and Papa must have approved of this match as he is one of the witnesses in the register, the other being her unmarried elder sister, Mary Ann (Polly). The address she marries from is 12 Wiltshire Road, Brixton which reveals that sometime between November 1876 and November 1879, Papa and his family had left The Rocklands having lived there from between just five and seven years. We don't know why this was – it could have been a combination of a number of factors. Four daughters had departed the family home leaving only three still unmarried by the end of the 1870s. Also of course, Papa had paid a total of four trousseaus and weddings since 1873 which must have bankrupted him! The financial uncertainty caused by The Great Depression also would have taken

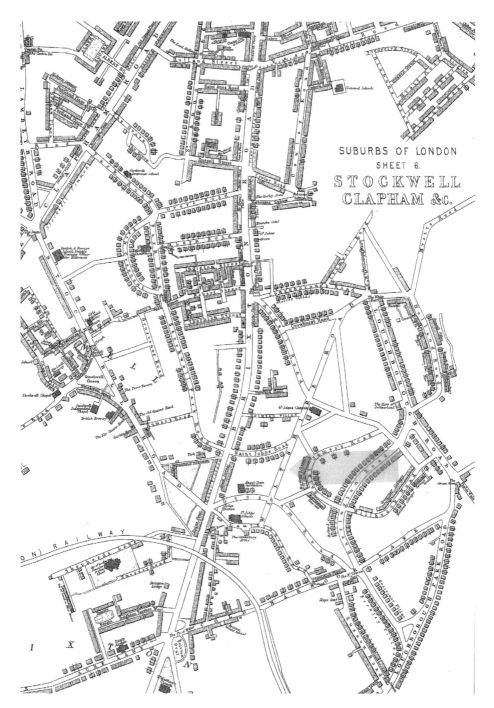

Fig 20. Map of Stockwell and Clapham showing Wiltshire Road where the Clark family lived during the late 1870s and 1880s.

its toll on business.[2] By this time, Thomas Clark was 60-years-old and perhaps the house at 12 Brixton Road was more accessible to the City as well as more manageable although still of generous proportions.[3] With his age in mind, turning 61 in April 1880, Thomas Clark made his extensive Will on 12 May that year.

At the time of the 1881 census, the household is much reduced. In residence at No. 12 with Thomas Clark is his wife Frances, daughters Mary Ann (36) Alice (22) and Florrie (20). As already mentioned, Melina is staying there whilst her husband is at sea. The household now just have one servant, 28-year-old Isabella Pearson. The neighbours are at No. 10, John Hart a 54-year-old accountant born in Shoreditch, his wife Elizabeth from Rotherhithe and two adult children, his widowed mother and a servant. At No. 14, Arthur Trevener, a 46-year-old solicitor born in Cornwall and his 49 year-old wife, Mary Ann, from Halifax, Yorkshire and their three servants.[4]

Brixton was at this time, a popular new district in the suburbs for middle-class city working men, it being convenient for omnibus and tram routes. Wiltshire Road was a long straight avenue, which ran parallel north to south with the Brixton Road. St. John's Church, where Emma had married, was along Wiltshire Road at the junction with Angell Road. In the 1891 census, Thomas Clark's son Frederick is living nearby at Loughborough Road.

The area formed what was known as 'The Angell Estate' and was extensively developed in the mid-19th century which shows that 12 Wiltshire Road was a relatively new dwelling circa 1880. St. John's Church was only completed and consecrated in 1853. The layout of Angell Town was influenced by Humphrey Repton's theories of parkland landscaping, which in residential construction converted to wide curving streets rather than being set to a geometrical plan, the traditional format for town planning. The idea here was being always to give a pleasant vista to a focal point and in this case, towards the tower of St. John's.[5]

Some of the houses in Wiltshire Road were erected by James Barker of Bath Road, Peckham. Like The Rocklands, the houses were

Fig 21. Wiltshire Road, Brixton, looking towards St. John's Church c. 1900.

constructed in the Gothic style and were described as having bay windows, segmentally-headed, and crudely gabled porches. Twin-arched windows to the upper-storeys rose from coarsely designed foliage capitals.[6]

On 23 July 1884, the wayward daughter Alice married Edward Alexander Troup at the Parish Church of Hove, Sussex. She is the first child to marry outside of the London environs and her husband, born in 1864, was six years her junior.[7] Possibly she had made her choices in defiance of Papa once again and left home to escape her unpopular step-mother. It is interesting to see that she married in Hove adjoining the family favourite seaside resort of Brighton; perhaps she met him there and enjoyed a secret holiday romance. In the 1891 census, her age is incorrectly recorded as 27. She was in fact a more mature 33 during that year.

The date that Thomas Clark and the remains of his family still at home moved from Wiltshire Road is not available. However, by 1891 he had relocated to what would be his final address: 17 Alexandra Road, Gipsy Hill, Norwood. The house was called Oakleigh and the district marked a return to the area near Sydenham where The Rocklands had once been his dream home, completed at the pinnacle of his success. Gipsy Hill was a remote rural area until the railway arrived there in 1856 and it took its name from the presence of gypsies. In the 1891 census, the household at Gipsy Hill was formed by Thomas and Frances Clark, Alice (now Mrs. Troup) and her son, Edward who had been born in 1886 both perhaps temporary visitors, Florrie Clark and a young servant named Emily King (16) born in Bromley, Kent.[8] The youth of the servant perhaps is indicative of not such successful times as before. Emily did not stay beyond the end of the year of 1891 for an advert was placed in the Norwood News and Crystal Palace Chronicle on 21 November appealing for a replacement.

WANTED, General Servant, about 18, plain cooking: small family: an early-riser. – Apply personally, between 11 and 1, or after 7, at Oakleigh, 17 Alexandra Road, Gipsy Hill, S.E.[9]

Polly was not at home on census night but was enjoying the company of her sister Emma, her husband and large family in Wandsworth.[10]

The Clarks' neighbours in Alexandra Road included at No. 19, William Graham, a 30-year-old police constable born in Cockermouth, Cumbria, with his wife Mary and their young family. At No. 15, Mary Cooper, a 70-year-old widow from Maldon, Essex lived with her single daughter, Emma (33) who was born in Leicestershire and they employed a cook and housemaid at their home.

At the beginning of 1893, tragedy was to strike on 28 January although perhaps not unexpectedly. Thomas Clark's second son, Frederick, died at the early age of 49 at his home, 183 Loughborough Road, Brixton. His faithful unmarried sister Mary Ann (Polly) was present at his death which must have been following a long period of suffering, as his death certificate states that his demise was caused by tumours of the brain and neck. He was the first adult child known to die in the family.[11] The news of his son's illness and passing must have been a terrible blow to his father who probably did not expect to outlive his second son.

The youngest daughter, Florrie, had to wait another decade after her sister Alice to exit her father's household. On 15 November 1893, having just turned 33, she married Thomas Alfred Page at Wandsworth Register Office.[12] Like Alice, she was the older woman being born almost nine years before him. Perhaps this register office wedding was clandestine, just like Melina's, because the following year, there was a further church wedding at Christchurch, Norwood, held on 24 May 1894.[13] Florrie knocks off a few years to reduce the gap between her age and that of Tom Page stating she is 30 instead of 33 in the register. Perhaps her new husband had been a neighbour of her brother Fred – his address is the same road, Loughborough Road, Brixton. Once again, there is a seafaring connection like her sister Milly; Florrie marries a master mariner in the mercantile service whose father was also a ship owner. Thomas Clark had built a trade emporium and three of his daughters married men who were linked with the industry.

Chapter 12

———

GIPSY HILL

———

1895

Fear no more the heat o' the sun, nor the furious winter's rages;
Thou thy worldly task hast done, home art gone, and ta'en thy wages:
Golden lads and girls all must, as chimney-sweepers, come to dust.
(William Shakespeare, Cymbeline Act IV Scene II)

In March 1895, Thomas Clark was a month away from his 76th birthday and his health was failing but being the stubborn and authoritarian man that he appears to have been, he refused to seek medical attention and probably ignored the pleas of his family too. It had by this time been two years (possibly following the death of Fred) that Doctor William Gandy of Gipsy Hill had last seen him.[1]

Thomas Clark was found dead in bed on the morning of Wednesday 20 March 1895 at his home, 17 Alexandra Road, Gipsy Hill. The young Scottish doctor John Josiah Douglas was summoned by the family, he examined him and declared him deceased but refused to issue a certificate.[2] Instead, the coroner was informed. The death certificate was issued two days later having been registered by his wife, Frances, and the causes of death were listed as bronchitis, asthma and syncope but with the absence of the usual doctor's certification.[3] His death was reported in the *Norwood News and Crystal Palace Chronicle* on Saturday 23 March as occurring suddenly and the family desired no flowers by special request.[4] His body would most likely have been kept at home until the funeral and burial which took place on Monday 25 March when he was interred in the family plot at Nunhead cemetery.[5]

There was always an element of mystery regarding his affairs, as a tin box supposed to contain some of his papers went missing after his death, and was never found!? My mother remembers her father (Alfred Edwin Bawtree) telling her that tale with all its unanswered questions as to 'what happened to the tin box?[6]

His will was proved on 27 July 1895 and probate was granted to the two people he trusted most; his dependable single eldest daughter, Mary Ann (Polly) and his son-in-law, Alfred Bawtree who was sensible and with a proven track record in business and in possession of a level-head. His Estate was valued at £8286 4s 2d.[7] To have some idea of his wealth in terms of the modern age, using the Bank of England inflation calculator the present day equivalent would be £1,097.702.[8] Nowadays millionaires are common, but few people possessed money to this level towards the end of the 19th century (See Appendix 1).

So what became of Mrs. Frances Clark following her husband's death? It is not known whether Frances lived in accordance with the will of her husband or if she rejected any agreement and made her own arrangements with perhaps the support of her blood family. However, she remained a widow and lived on for another 21 years afterwards.

In the 1901 census, she is living as a boarder on her own means in the household of Alice Bun, who presumably ran her premises of 35 South Street, Greenwich as a boarding house. Frances' sisters Mary and Martha Colebatch, also boarded at the same address. Frances' age is incorrect at 67; she was then 75 years of age.[9] It is to be hoped that she had found some solace at this time in her life in the company of her beloved sisters.

Ten years later in 1911 there is a totally different picture. Frances is a visitor at 93 Park Lane, Stoke Newington. This is the district she lived in before her marriage whilst she was with her parents and younger siblings. She is visiting her sister Jane Whyte (a widow) who is staying there as a boarder in the household of Albert and Victoria Hancox, both 42.[10] Mrs. Hancox is running her home as a boarding house to bring in extra income. We do not know Frances' circumstances at this time or where she lived permanently.

Then in 1916, there are documents which confirm that Frances was admitted to the workhouse at Islington where she passed away on 2 July of that year.[11] The cause of death on her burial record is given as senectus (old age) heart failure. She had lived a long, but probably not always happy, life of 90 years. She was buried at Islington cemetery the following day by friends.[12] At the end of her life, she seems to have been without financial support or family. She was certainly forgotten and abandoned by her step-children although this may not have been entirely their intention and she had outlived all but one of her siblings.

PART TWO

THOMAS CLARK
1841-1927

Chapter 1

————

SCIENTIA POTENTIA EST

————

Crofton Hall – 1862-1863

On 9 December 1862, a young man came of age. He was the eldest child of Thomas Clark, colonial broker. Thomas, or Tom, as his sister Matilda refers to him affectionately in her diary, was just 22 years younger than his successful father. They were both born in the first half of the nineteenth century in the neighbouring south London districts of Bermondsey and Newington. His father had worked his way up the ladder starting out as a 'clerk' or 'commercial clerk' in the 1840s and early 1850s. By 1854, he was a broker and in partnership with an established trader who may at one time have been his employer.

Tom did not have the same slippery ladder to climb; his father in the early 1860s, was a wealthy successful man whose assets could cascade downwards to his children. Like his business partner, Donald Gray, Thomas Clark's sons would become his own partners in the same manner that Gray's sons followed in his footsteps. Whether Tom liked it or not, this was the way his career was going to pan out. In just a few years he would be sworn in at the City of London as a broker and join the ranks of the other traders of Mincing Lane and Great Tower Street and it would be unlikely that he would try and break the mould.

Fig 22. Thomas Clark circa 1862

But for now, Tom's early footsteps on the path of life had been different to his father's back in the 1820s and 30s. His father would have ensured that throughout the 1840s and 50s his son would have received a fine education befitting the eldest son of a gentleman in business. Although there is no evidence that Thomas went to university, he was clearly a highly educated individual with great knowledge and interest in the subjects deemed to be essential for young well-to-do men in this exciting era to be alive. The disciplines that held value for Tom were science, religion, geography, geology and biology including botany. He would have also studied mathematics, English, history, literature and perhaps the classical languages of Latin and Greek. As the saying goes, 'Knowledge is Power' and Tom would have gone out of his way to absorb as much information as he could and relate it to the world around him.

For his 19th birthday his Mama had given him an illustrated copy of *Milton's Poetical Works* that must have later inspired the poet within him. In the inside cover she dedicated it to Thomas Clarke [sic] as 'a gift from his affectionate mother'.

To mark the occasion of his 21st birthday, a photograph was taken

Fig 23. This photograph was placed inside his book 'Westfield's Essays on Universal Science'.

in a London studio; it was a full-length portrait and depicts a slender, smartly-attired man looking older than his years due to his full beard. He exudes confidence as his gaze is set on distant sights off the camera. His hair is swept back neatly and he wears a dark velvet jacket with trim on the sleeves and the front edgings. His lighter waistcoat is complete with a chain concealing a pocket watch, his light coloured trousers have a hint of a check pattern and his left hand is casually placed in his trouser pocket whilst in his right hand he grasps an ink pen. His right knee rests on a richly upholstered chair whilst the gleam of the back of his shoe reflects in the camera lens. The portrait is framed by a draped curtain complete with a tassel hanging down parallel with his head. To his left stands a small gothic-style table laden with papers and books. The studio backdrop consists of a bookcase – perhaps especially selected by the young man to demonstrate his devotion to learning and writing. Perhaps he had in mind a career as a writer, for six months earlier newspapers had carried adverts of his first book *The Japanese*.[1]

Although he almost certainly never visited Japan, travellers to the country would have been in his orbit. He would have also had access to books, newspapers and magazines such as *The Illustrated London News* and *The Leisure Hour*; these two publications are amongst those he acknowledges as sources for some of his detail garnered about Japanese culture and life.

His commonplace name Thomas Clark, would not set him apart from the many other men bearing the same name so to become distinctive, he added the maiden name of his mother 'Westfield' thus becoming Thomas Clark Westfield for the first of his literary and artistic works. *The Japanese: their Manners and Customs* was originally written and delivered as a lecture at the Marylebone Literary and Scientific Institute at 17 Edward Street, Portman Square[2] (Plate i). In the preface to the book, he states that it was written in the realisation of 'The manifest interest with which Japan has been regarded of late...'[3]

1862 had been a successful year for the 20-year-old Tom. At the end of February, he had applied for membership to the prestigious Royal Society of Arts and he had been accepted in mid-March paving the way for giving his forthcoming publication more credence. This organisation, founded in 1754 for 'The Encouragement of the Arts, manufactures, and commerce of the country' was the ideal vehicle for a young businessman to join if he wanted to get ahead in life.[4]

It was the year when the lure of the orient was an enticement to over six million visitors to the International Exhibition held between 1 May and 1 November at South Kensington, London. This world fair was held to showcase the advances made since the Industrial Revolution and especially since the Great Exhibition of 1851 at Hyde Park. An enormous structure of cast-iron with two massive domes was built on the site to house the exhibition which was even larger than the Crystal Palace. Japan had just sent its first embassy to Europe and it was the first official contact between Japan and the west. The Japan Court in the exhibition displayed the unofficial collection of Rutherford Alcock (British Consul-General of Japan) and contained

Fig 24. The 1862 International Exhibition was held at South Kensington.

parasols, ceramics and other exceptional Japanese commodities. The Japanese embassy visited the exhibition and Japan, in the spring and early summer of 1862, was a major news story for not only its exoticism, but for trade reasons. The London Protocol was signed on 6 June, just two weeks after images of the official embassy appeared in *The Illustrated London News* ensuring the future of trading relations between the two nations.[5]

The slim volume published by Thomas Clark Westfield was illustrated with six stereoview photographs and it had the distinction of being one of the earliest books to contain actual photographs of Japan. These images were the work of Swiss photographer Pierre Rossier.[6] Rossier was commissioned by the London photographic firm of Negretti and Zambra to document the progress of the Anglo-French troops during the Second Opium War in China of 1858-1860. Although he did not, after all, complete this mission he was active in China, Philippines, Japan and Siam (later known as Thailand). His 1859 images taken in Japan were also exhibited in May 1862 at the International Exhibition by Negretti and Zambra.[7] Perhaps this was the very occasion where Tom acquired copies for his book after visiting the great show whilst he was completing his work for imminent publication, if not before. Tom must have been spellbound by the wonders of the exhibition as well as interested in what the forthcoming trade deal would mean for business.

Up to this time, Japan was a country still largely closed to the rest of the world although they had allowed some limited trade with the Chinese and Dutch. The Dutch had occasional ambassadorial contact with Japan and Thomas Clark states that it is due to 'journals of the Literati accompanying their embassies that we are chiefly indebted for the little information we possess...'[8]

His lecture was delivered and book published in the context of the dramatic events of 1861 in which the newly installed British Legation was stormed by a xenophobic group known as the Ronin on 5 July, an attack which was deflected by Rutherford Alcock and his staff. Laurence Oliphant at the time was First Secretary of the British Legation working under Alcock and he was seriously wounded in the assault.[9] Japan was therefore a hot topic on multiple levels and seemingly at a junction of looking forward as well as back.

Tom mentions (no doubt with pride) the types of produce being imported to London from Japan of which he has personal knowledge:

> *A short time since we were much interested on being shown over a warehouse, the property of a gentleman who imports largely from Japan. The first thing which struck our attention was an entire set of Japanese armour; it was made of iron, beautifully wrought, japanned black, and lined with leather. The helmet was especially heavy, and of a somewhat singular form; with this they wear a mask of iron, made as ugly as possible, with thick red lips, and white bristly moustachios: this, I suppose, is intended to work upon the enemies' fears.[10]*

Then whilst discussing foodstuffs and drink in Japan he once again implies personal experience:

Within the last few months we have had several imports of tea, and should it be liked by the public, no doubt it will be shipped very largely.[11]

He was both advantaged and encouraged by his father's position and world trade connections to enhance his knowledge of the exotic corners of the globe such as the Far East and Africa. Furthermore, artists and writers at this time were bringing the cult of far eastern countries to the masses in Europe as travel, ever increasing, was broadening horizons and trade was opening up barriers between east and west. The artist James Abbott McNeil Whistler (1834-1903) was producing paintings during the 1860s and 70s of ladies dressed with an air of *Japonisme* about them as they held parasols aloft in dresses resembling kimonos.[12] The use of Japanese motifs and techniques were employed in art, in much the same way as the *Chinoiserie* had dominated art and architecture from the 18th century onwards and seen in such structures as The Royal Pavilion at Brighton and The Pagoda at The Royal Botanic Gardens at Kew. The fascination with the exoticism of Japan remained strong into the 1880s with Gilbert and Sullivan producing their famous comic opera *The Mikado* to great public acclaim.

The years 1862 to 1863 were some of the most meaningful for the young Thomas Clark. As well as a career as a writer and the excitement of the major London trade fair, it was during this period too that his parents and siblings moved from Ordnance Terrace, Shooters' Hill to the Kent countryside, firstly to Cudham near Bromley and later to Crofton Hall, Orpington. Sometime during these years, although he was not yet working as a partner in his father's business, he would have been involved in life in the City and a frequent visitor to his offices and warehouses around Great Tower Street. It is also likely that he networked and mixed with his father's associates in these places as well as the coffee houses in the area which dated back to the 17th century in origin but were still operating into the early 1860s. Perhaps it was in this setting that he was introduced to a certain William

Bailey. Mr. Bailey, according to the 1861 census, was a shipping clerk at the insurance brokers' company, Lloyds of London.[13] He lived with his family at 2 Clarendon Place, Coburg Road, Camberwell and was 43-years-old. William Bailey's wife was Jane (née Muir) and they had married in December 1839 the same month and year as Tom's own parents.[14] William Bailey had been born in Hackney and was the son of an apothecary and surgeon, and he and Jane initially lived in north-east London before moving to Camberwell after 1842. Tom may have heard William and Jane Bailey had four young and unmarried daughters Jane, Ann, Mary and Frances and had evidently been informally introduced.

Miss Frances Charlotte Bailey was born on 9 June 1846 at Albany Road, Camberwell and so she was just 17-years-old in 1863.[15] There is no way of knowing how or where Thomas Clark actually met Miss Bailey, but it is possible that the contact came through their fathers, due to her extreme youth she would not have gone out unchaperoned. According to the 1851 census, the Bailey sisters were educated at home. This task was most likely carried out by their mother, Jane.[16] As a clerk, William Bailey was placed firmly in the lower middle class and therefore of a lower social status than the Clarks who were mercantile class. The Baileys would not have been able to afford a governess although in the 1861 census they had progressed to having a 17-year-old general servant. In 1861, Frances' sister Jane was staying in Bristol in the pursuit of a musical career – appreciation of music, another link between these families.[17]

Photographs taken in the period 1863-5 show that Frances (or Fanny as she was known) was a strikingly attractive girl with dark hair and she dressed fashionably in the crinoline dress styles of the early to mid-1860s. Thomas Clark fell hopelessly in love with the young woman who may have only been 16 when they were first introduced. He himself was only 21 or 22 at the time but he was older than his father when his father married at just 20. Tom gave a copy of his book *The Japanese* to her dedicating it 'to Miss F.C. Bailey with kind regards'. Miss Bailey needed parental consent to marry as she was

Fig 25. The young Miss Frances Charlotte Bailey.

under 21 years old. This was not the only impediment as her father's lower social status would have been a serious barrier. A third problem would have been that Thomas Clark junior had no official occupation at this time. He would not become a broker for another year or so, therefore he was reliant on Papa's money for his own livelihood.

During summer 1863, Tom's sister Amelia died of typhoid and scarlet fever at home in Leaves Green, Cudham. We don't know if Tom was at home with the family at the time of her illness and death but the loss of a sibling must have had a profound impact on the entire family. No doubt his mother was distraught and not for the first time was this family forced to meditate upon the brevity of life and the random way that death claims its victims. Before the onset of winter 1863, the family had moved to Crofton Hall and it was from here that Thomas Clark Westfield wrote the Preface to his next book *Westfield's Essays on Universal Science*.[18] Like *The Japanese*, the book was first delivered as a lecture to the Marylebone Literary and Scientific Institute and it must have been completed earlier in 1863.

Tom recorded in his completed manuscript that he wrote the Preface to his *Essays* on Wednesday 9 September. On the very same day, he and his young love Miss Bailey eloped to Kew, Surrey. The date was also that of her baptism, 17 years earlier, and they were wed in secret that morning in the church of St. Anne situated on The Green, outside of Kew Gardens[19] (Plate ii). The location must have been chosen because it was sufficiently distant from areas where either of them was known but also accessible by some form of transport. A third reason must have been for its romantic setting. Thomas stated that he was residing at Kew at the time whilst his bride was from Camberwell. They falsely declared, just as Papa had done when he married, that they were both of full age. Perhaps the romantic young couple had viewed the elopement and ceremony along the lines of a betrothal ceremony and knew that another public wedding with their families would have to take place.

Six months earlier, the Queen's eldest son Albert Edward had married Princess Alexandra of Denmark at St. George's Chapel, Windsor. Born just a month earlier than Tom, the Prince's wedding must have been a topic of conversation and surely another reason for justifying his own marriage at the same age. Alexandra was a mere 18 years old at the time.

The young curate, Percy Wemyss Nott, only three years older than Tom, conducted the ceremony.[20] There can have been no family at the wedding and the witnesses were two strangers, perhaps parishioners, William Granger and Jane Bass.[21] Thomas Clark, just as his father had done, declared his occupation as a 'gentleman'.

Following the marriage, they may have paused at the historic church where the bodies of the great and famous were entombed in the churchyard, amongst them the artists Thomas Gainsborough and Johann Zoffany. Once outside, they may have enjoyed a stroll around the picturesque Kew village and a visit to the gardens must have been made since it was over 100 years old and a great tourist attraction. One thing we can be fairly certain of is that the young couple would not have spent their wedding night together and they would have returned to their respective families taking with them their secret.

Fig 26. Percy Wemyss Nott was curate at St. Anne's Church, Kew in 1863 and unknowingly married the eloping young couple.

The Reverend Percy Nott.

Tom, as the man, must take the larger responsibility for what happened that day. Here was a young man in thrall to his wealthy and class-conscious Papa who was, no doubt, also a model of Victorian discipline towards his offspring. Tom was conscious however, that Papa had married young too at 20. Look how successful his marriage had been producing 11 living children (although one had just died) and the company of a devoted wife. Perhaps it was the feeling too that he had to seize the moment and marry his heart's desire, life was still short for most and with his young sister's recent death in mind, it is easy to see how the impetuous youth took this step. *Carpe diem.* With his new book about to be published, it is possible that he thought that literary success would soon be knocking on the door.

He too must have doubted that Papa would have ever consented to the match. He was desperate to assert himself as his own man. He was now over 21, so why not? Was the marriage ever consummated at this stage? That is a question we cannot answer, although I think it unlikely. Certainly, there was no child born nine months or so later!

For an impression of how much Thomas Clark adored his young wife, we look forward in time to a poem that he wrote following her early death in 1904:

…The ring I placed upon thy finger that glad day when I espoused
thee, and first called thee mine;
The ring, thou dids't so cherish and esteem,
As mad'st thy boast never to have removed.
The deep devotion each to each did bear,
That every separation was a pain,
Almost beyond endurance and did prove
Our married life to be, through all its days
One long continued joyous honeymoon.[22]

Chapter 2

———

WESTFIELD'S ESSAYS ON
UNIVERSAL SCIENCE

———

1863-64

*The immensity of the heavenly bodies, as well as the vastness of
the celestial spaces, are as such to overwhelm the mind of man,
to humble his pride from its grandeur and magnificence, and
bid him recognise the handiwork of an eternal creator.*
(Essay VI, Westfield's Essays)

That autumn Tom's second book was published. Once more,
the book was previously delivered as a lecture or a series of
seven lectures (it was considerably longer than *The Japanese*),
to the Marylebone Literary and Scientific Institute.

Magazines and newspapers carried reviews from October into the
new year of 1864. One from *The Sun* published on 28 October 1863
was overwhelmingly supportive but the majority were critical – some
scathing and these must have been a disappointment to the young
man, if, as he probably did, read all the reviews:

Westfield's Essays on Universal Science… are here presented to us by Mr. Westfield, who very emphatically and truthfully observes that "God's works cannot contradict his words." Therefore, as he most logically proves, every apparent discrepancy between the sacred writing and the world around us, is due to some misconception on the part of the expositor or the translator. "We have repeatedly found," says Mr. Westfield, "that when men employ their scientific knowledge to the detriment and injury of the scriptures, the knowledge possessed has neither been very deep nor very profound.[1]

Another review of 12 December in *The Examiner* found the selection of his full-length portrait in poor taste and stated that the aim of his book was to 'overturn the doctrines of Bishop John Colenso and all other infidels.'[2] Colenso was a contemporary cleric of the Church of England who was a polygenist, a supporter of co-Adamism, a belief that some of the races of the world were created separately from Adam, as science had proved them to be different. Clearly the reviewer had not bothered to read the book in detail otherwise he would not have found any direct reference to the doctrines of Colenso. The review glosses over the meticulous content describing it as 'for the most part geological'.

An equally succinct review in *The Globe and Traveller* of 31 December, stated:

Mr. Westfield is not adverse to all theories, for he maintains the existence of a Pre-Adamite race, and that the race consisted of the angels. He considers that such a belief will explain many scriptural difficulties. Possibly it will suggest more.[3]

These reviewers had evidently skimmed over the content of the book with one suggesting that Mr. Westfield wrote in opposition of Colenso's beliefs whilst the latter review found evidence that it was the existence of a pre-Adamic race which he favoured.

The write-up in *The Spectator* of 19 December had an overall contemptuous tone whilst acknowledging that Mr. Westfield's speculations, particularly his hypothesis for the pre-Adamite existence of angels, are often 'ingenious'.

> *An air of ridicule is thrown over this work by its pretentious title, and by the author's having been so ill advised as to prefix it to his portrait and autograph, a step which is not justified by the fact that he appears thereby to be a well-looking, smartly dressed gentleman of about thirty-five. Mr. Westfield is a firm believer in the scientific exactness of the Mosaic cosmogony,* [the account of the origin of the world given in Genesis i and ii] *and his object is to set forth his reasons for the faith that is in him. That he succeeds in proving his thesis we cannot truly say, nor does he appear to us to have by any means that acquaintance with physical science which would justify any one in undertaking so difficult a task. However, his speculations are often ingenious, as when he contends that there is no discrepancy between the accounts of the creation of man in the first and second chapters of Genesis, because the first relates to the creation of angels, or Preadamito men glorified under that title. We fear this sort of support of the theory of verbal inspiration will not be acceptable to the Record, and we are sure that it introduces ten difficulties for every one it removes.*[4]

So what is the true story and message conveyed in the Essays?

Just a few miles away from Crofton Hall, where Tom lived with his parents, a prominent scientist named Charles Darwin was writing from his own home at Down House and conducting scientific experiments to advance his views on the theory of evolution. Whilst Tom shared his passion for the discoveries of the scientific age, unlike Darwin he was a committed Christian. It was a counter-blast from the perspective of a Christian to demonstrate that both science and faith could co-exist and that science did not invalidate the Bible but instead served to enhance it.

In the Preface, Tom states emphatically:

> *We believe, most assuredly, that there is not one fact stated in the whole Bible that is not scientifically correct, or may be accounted for,*

either by some slight error in translation, or our imperfect knowledge of the subject. God's works cannot contradict His words.[5]

He acknowledges that: 'The study of geology, although comparatively a new science, has thrown much light, and introduced many new truths… and in many instances have entirely reversed long and established opinions.'[6]

Perhaps a direct and pointed remark directed at his famous but controversial neighbour, Mr. Charles Darwin, or indeed others, he goes on to elucidate: 'The reason many writers have been endeavouring to disprove the truth of the scriptures arises from the development of a certain class of infidelity and antichristian spirit.'[7]

In the following paragraphs, extracts are selected from some of the seven essays in which Tom writes with conviction and sensitivity concerning his views on scripture and science.

Essay II – On the Six Days of Creation

In 1854 the Crystal Palace Gardens had opened at Sydenham. Amongst the attractions were full-scale statues of extinct animals created from the study of fossilised remains. Still to be seen in the 21st century are the iguanodon and pterodactyls mentioned in Tom's essay. These were sculptured by Benjamin Waterhouse Hawkins, a natural history illustrator, and the sculptures were set in a landscape designed by Joseph Paxton. As a child and young man, Tom must have spent many a leisure hour strolling at Crystal Palace and observing them with keen interest. Tom discusses the extinct creatures that 'are well represented at the Crystal Palace Gardens, at Sydenham, and such were the occupants of the earth on the fifth day'.[8]

He found no conflict between the biblical account of creation and the recent discoveries of the 'abundance of reptilian fossils in lias [rock strata of western Europe], the lowest formation of the middle secondary strata, would seem to point out this, the colitic system, as analoguous to the fifth day's creation.'[9] He argued that on the fifth day of the Genesis account of creation, where it states 'bring forth abundantly' suggested that such large and fantastic creatures did exist before day five but this day 'was set apart for the progressive development of these creatures.'[10]

Essay III –On the Probability of the Existence of Man before Adam

The Book of Genesis appears to contain two different accounts of creation in chapters 1 and 2 and Tom concluded that these point to 'two distinct and separate creations, the creation of man on the sixth day bore no reference whatever to our first parent Adam.'[11]

He came to the conclusion that the angelic host must have been the pre-Adamite race. In a footnote at the end of Essay III, Tom recommends a book entitled *Pre-Adamite Man* published by J. Nisbet & Co. 'a work we feel proud in recommending, and one which we must admit has given great tone to our opinions on this subject.'[12]

What Tom probably did not know was that the author of the book he closely shadowed in writing his own tome was a woman. Her name was Isabelle Wright Duncan (1812-1878) and the book's sub-title: *The Story of our Old Planet and its Inhabitants told by Scripture and Science* was an 1860 reply to Darwin's *On Origin of Species*.[13] It is considered to be the first full-length treatment of pre-Adamism by an evangelical Christian. In this, Isabella Duncan was keen to demonstrate that scientific theories were not incompatible with Biblical accounts.

Essay VI – On the Immensity of the Universe

The writer happened to be travelling at dusk in late autumn 2020 at the end of a sunny afternoon. The blue sky was a sight to behold with the rising and almost full moon like a giant lamp illuminating the tranquil scene. A solitary large column of white cloud stood out opposite the moon but just as stunning in its composition. This celestial beauty observed in all its glory was evident this day just as it may have been almost 160 years earlier at a time when Tom Clark was a young man for whom both the heavenly bodies and the wonderful temperate climate of England brought forth abundantly the splendour of nature in which he believed he observed the hand of God.

Tom wrote despairingly of his contemporaries:

The lightness with which people regard things that are going on around them... it is indeed remarkable; but there are many, we think, who would scarcely know the existence of an atmosphere in which we live and move, were it not for a good stiff breeze now and then to refresh their memories. Much less, however, do they take notice of the stars, oh! dear no, they have nothing to do with them, that is the work of astronomers.[14]

Tom describes what observing the heavens means to him:

...to the lover of nature they are ever a source of gratification and enjoyment. He loves to trace the planet in its course, to watch the setting sun.[15]

Tom believes that the study of astronomy is:

the one which points pre-eminently to the existence of an infinite and Omnipotent Being. The immensity of the heavenly bodies, as well as the vastness of the celestial spaces, are as such to overwhelm the mind of man, to humble his pride from its grandeur and magnificence, and bid him recognise the handiwork of an eternal creator.

He then takes the reader on a journey describing the attributes of the sun and the planets each in turn, followed by comets, meteors and shooting stars, the stars and the Milky Way.

Essay VII – On the Multiplicity of Worlds

This essay centres on a discussion on whether the heavenly bodies are inhabited including the sun, moon and planets and whether any of them were inhabitable and speculation as to where mankind may live in the future.

Over 100 years before man would land on the moon, Tom wrote:

It has been supposed that the moon is void of atmosphere. Could this supposition be established, it would at once put an end to the idea of its being inhabited – but this stupid theory is fortunately dying out.[16]

We cannot well see how matter can exist without an atmosphere; but to suppose there is no atmosphere in the moon is simply absurd, when we see such abundant traces of its existence in the lunar mountains: the craters testify to the great volcanic action. And this, as everybody knows, is caused by the expansion and explosion of gases; besides this, there is combustion. This must be supported by the most important constituent in our atmosphere – i.e. oxygen. Therefore we are bound to admit that the moon, in common with this world, has an atmosphere, and therefore capable of supporting inhabitants.

He concludes the chapter giving full rein to his creative mind:

This brings us to the inquiry, as to where man, in his future state of existence, is likely to reside? He will then have, as now, a spiritual nature and a corporeal frame, and therefore must live in a material world. Now, at the present time there are existing on the earth upwards of a thousand millions of inhabitants; and if to these you add those who have gone before, and those who may follow after, it will be clearly evident that the earth will not be able to accommodate them all. Where then, we ask, after the resurrection, are they to go, if not to some planet whose inhabitants have ceased to exist, or to planets, either in our own or other systems, which have been in a state of preparation for the reception of the intellectual life?[17]

Chapter 3

PENGE – CAMBERWELL – SUTTON

1865-1876

Never mind the why and wherefore love can level ranks, and therefore though your nautical relation in my set could scarcely pass though you occupy a station in the lower middle class.
(Gilbert and Sullivan, HMS Pinafore, 1878)

O n Tuesday 18 July 1865, Tom and his brother Fred were sworn in as brokers at the London Guildhall.[1] They were now joint partners with their father as City of London merchants.

Just two months later, and two years exactly to the date since they eloped to marry clandestinely at Kew, Tom and Fanny were once again in church for their second and this time legal marriage. On the morning of 9 September, their respective families joined them at Fanny's parish church, St. Giles, Camberwell. St. Giles, a 21-year-old architectural gem in 1865, had been erected as a replacement for the medieval church which burnt down in 1841. The new church was consecrated just three years later having been the first major gothic edifice designed by the architect George Gilbert Scott whose most famous buildings were St. Pancras Station and the Albert Memorial. Behind the altar, if the couple had eyes for anything in the building, they would have gazed on the east window which was designed by John Ruskin, who was at that time a resident of Camberwell too.

Fanny was now 19 years of age and although still a minor, she would have received the consent of her parents. Now that Tom had an occupation and an income of his own, Papa had perhaps become amenable to the match. Signatures as witness to the ceremony are Fanny's father, William Bailey, her eldest sister Jane Bailey, Tom's eldest sister Mary Ann Clark and Fanny's first cousin Robert Vizer, who was the son of William's sister Charlotte.[2]

The happy and devoted young couple went to a studio to have the customary photograph of their marriage as a record to leave their family in years to come. Tom is dressed in a dark formal jacket and holds a top hat with a trim. His bride is wearing a plain crinoline dress. She wears a high bonnet adorned with flowers and tied under her chin with wide pastel or white coloured ribbons or ties. Another image taken around the same date, shows Fanny alone and standing

Fig 27. The wedding portrait probably shows the happy couple at the time of their 1865 marriage in Camberwell.

without a hat displaying her dark hair styled into ringlets. This may have served the purpose of an earlier betrothal or engagement portrait.

After the ceremony there would have been the usual wedding breakfast which may have been held at the home of the bride and then the honeymoon, perhaps to a seaside resort on the South Coast or West Country given the family's known attraction to these areas which were now accessible by rail.

Unsurprisingly, given the passion and devotion of the pair, as well as the two year wait to consummate their first marriage, when they had solemnly promised themselves to each other, their first child was born nine months later. Fanny had just turned 20 when their son whom they named Thomas William Francis, entered the world on 25 June 1866.[3] The names selected can be explained thus, Thomas naturally after his father, William after Fanny's Papa and Francis, the masculine form of her own name.

The baby was born at home, 5 Palace Road, Penge near to the relocated Crystal Palace and the birth was registered on 11 August by Tom. This would set the trend for all six of the future births as unlike Papa, Tom would be the person to attend the register office after his own children were born. Perhaps he may not have spent as much time in the City as Papa; after all, his father held all the business reins in all probability. However, may be it was possible that the tide was turning and it was one responsibility he did not want his beloved to become over-burdened with. Here was a sign of a dutiful and caring husband.

Papa likely owned the lease for their address of 5 Palace Road. It was a middle-class district and in a few years hence, a property in this same road would be occupied by the French artist, Camille Pissarro. He came to live in London to escape the danger of the Franco-Prussian War raging in Paris from 1870 to 1871. However, by this date, Tom and Fanny had moved from the area and their stay appears to have been of a short duration. Pissarro's famous painting *Lordship Lane Station* of 1871 was painted from his residence at Chatham Terrace, Palace Road and he painted many other scenes depicting bucolic life on the edge of London during his short stay in the Sydenham and Penge area.[4] The houses in Palace Road were built in the steep hill surrounding the Crystal Palace and they had four floors with fireplaces in each room.[5]

In 1866 with one child on the way or already born, Tom had a burst of written creativity; a pamphlet entitled *England's Past, Present and Future in Connexion with Rome* was published. Its title is, as it suggests, a Protestant's diatribe against the papacy through the ages. At this time, Britain was a largely Protestant country, stanchly loyal to the act of the 16th century English Reformation which severed ties with Rome; one which felt under threat firstly by the Catholic Emancipation Act of 1829 and then Tractarianism which later became The Oxford Movement. The Oxford Movement was led by John Henry Newman, a high Anglican who converted to Catholicism in 1845. In the Introduction, Tom does not withhold his vehemence:

> *It is our peculiar boast – at this time – of the extension of civil and religious liberty to all, forgetting that in doing so, we are extending it to those who are its deadliest enemies, and who, in the name of civil and religious liberty are conspiring towards its overthrow, and the substitution of priestly intolerance, despotism, and persecution. Now, I would ask, Are you content to let this be so? Will you stand quietly by and see your dearest, holiest rights, filched away from you by a set of snivelling priests? Nay! God forbid that Englishmen should come to such a pass as this!*

Both Tom's and Fanny's parents were now first-time grandparents and it is hoped that Mary Ann, Tom's mother, had some interaction with her grandson before her untimely death on 21 October 1866. A photograph of Fanny with a baby, probably taken in 1866/7, shows her wearing a black dress and jewellery; in all probability the family were still in mourning for the death of Tom's mother Mary Ann Clark in the autumn of 1866. Young Tommy is seen in photographs as a baby and young child with very fair hair. He is dressed in fashionable child's clothes at this time still much like miniature adult apparel. Boys

Fig 28. Fanny dressed in black, with her first-born son, possibly in mourning for her mother-in-law 1866/7.

and girls were dressed alike as babies and young Tom's hair is worn long and in one photograph in particular he appears very feminine due to his long hair and tunic dress.

The next child arrived on 5 March 1868, less than two years later. Ernest Percival Frederick was born at Clarendon House, Coburg Road, Camberwell.[6] His first two names may have been conferred on him because they were popular at the time. His third name was after his uncle Fred and was a family name. However, in this case, his parents decided for him, that there was no importance in being Ernest after all, and he would always be known by his second name 'Percy'. The birth took place at an address previously associated with the Bailey family. It was here in the 1861 census where Fanny lived with her uncle by marriage Charles Vizer, his brother Robert and her sister Ann, whilst her parents lived next door at 2 Clarendon Place with her sister Mary. It is possible that Tom and Fanny lived here as a temporary arrangement whilst they were waiting for Tom's Papa to make another property available to them. We do not know if the Bailey family were also living here in 1868 or whether they had moved on.

Fig 29. Fanny with her second born son, Ernest Percival Frederick, circa 1868.

In 1869, Tom's brother Fred decided to leave the family business and records reveal that he left his Papa and Tom's partnership and started out on his own as a broker.[7] It is possible that a disagreement lead to this as Matilda hints in her diary in 1872 that Fred had not 'been the best of sons'.

Sometime in the late 1860s or early 1870s, Tom, Fanny and their two young boys moved to Sutton, Surrey to a house in Brighton Road named Claremont.[8] They settled probably very happily here for up to a decade. Sutton was distant from both central London and his father's home in Anerley. However, Sutton had grown from a village to a town in just a few decades since the railway came in 1847 providing faster access into London. Brighton Road was not developed until the 1860s when it became a fashionable place for wealthy Victorians to set up their new homes. Much earlier in the century, an increase in horse-drawn traffic from London to Brighton resulted in a strip of land being purchased on the west side of the eventual Brighton Road and the bank was cut away to allow for widening. The houses on the opposite east side had retained the

*Fig 30. Brighton Road, Sutton, circa 1900. The home of
Tom and Fanny was situated here in the 1870s.*

bank and the houses on that side were above road level and on the west, below it.

In 1865, the Epsom Downs railway line was opened. It ran behind the western side of Brighton Road down to Belmont Station at the southern end of Brighton Road whilst Sutton Station was at the northern end's junction with the High Street.

Surviving photographs, show front and rear views of an immaculate detached house with landscaped lawns at the rear. At the front of the house, a foot-scraper leads the eye from the bottom steps to the entrance porch flanked by classical Corinthian columns. On both sides of the door, a vast number of potted plants are placed in large curved window-boxes rising to the front of the windows showing Tom's love of botany and horticulture. A boy seated on the steps leading to the rear terrace could possibly be young Percy and if so, would date the photographs to the late 1870s.

His sisters all loved to stay with him and his growing family, and 12-year-old Alice was staying there on census night 1871. Other

Fig 31. Front view of Claremont House, Brighton Road, Sutton, 1870s.

Fig 32. Rear view of Claremont House, Brighton Road, Sutton, 1870s.

than the five family members at home that night, were Susannah Wimhurst, a 19-year-old general servant and Charlotte Potter, a 16-year-old nursery maid employed to help to look after the two young boys, Tommy and Percy.[9] The neighbours at Brighton Road included Edward Goldsmith, born in Hailsham, Sussex and his wife Mercy with their four children. There was also Josiah Seal, a farm servant from Leicestershire and his wife, Sarah, a sweet shop keeper.

Tom's sister Matilda was a regular visitor to the family as recounted in the journal which she kept for the years 1872 to 1874 and she relives several stories of domestic life at Sutton during this period. In addition, she refers to stays that her sisters Emma, Lizzie, Alice and Florrie made during this period. Probably they all found a welcome haven from the unpleasant atmosphere at The Rocklands where they lived with Papa and their step-mother, Fanny.

Not only was Tom's home a refuge, a haven of calm and pleasantness, but Tom was a more agreeable brother than Fred. Tilly compares them:

> *Dear Fred, he has done very wrong, more wrong too, I daresay, than I*
> *know of. He has not been the best of sons, nor the best of husbands, but*
> *I hope he will improve as he gets older. Tom is such a contrast to him*
> *surrounded by every comfort, with a happy wife and home and Fred's*
> *house always with an air of discomfort about it but his own fault and*
> *not wholly Annie's [Fred's wife] – 22ⁿᵈ June 1873.*[10]

On 4 December 1871, Tom and Fanny's third child, another son, was born at Claremont House, Sutton. He was named Herbert Lionel Alexander.[11] His third name was in tribute to Fanny's maternal grandfather, Alexander Muir who was still living in 1871 but some distance from his grand-daughter and her growing family, across south-east London in Lewisham.

The family featured from Spring to Autumn 1872 in the diary of Tilly who regularly stayed for lengthy periods.

Wednesday 24th April

Fanny wants me to go to Sutton very much, so I am going to stay the week after next.

It seems Fanny and Tilly enjoyed a warm relationship as sisters-in-law and probably Fanny served as a role model to the slightly younger woman who was on the threshold of her own married life and family to come. Fanny probably enjoyed some female company too.

Wednesday 8th May

I am staying for a few days at Sutton, and came here yesterday, and of course got into a great muddle in coming. Had to have a boy to help 'Anne' with my box to the station, and when there the box came undone at Norwood Junction and had to pay for a porter for cording it. Left a band box in the train and had to pay a porter for finding it, then Alfred [Alfred Bawtree, her fiancé] paid a porter for seeing after me altogether and then another porter for bringing my box from the station to Tom's. It was a wild stormy kind of day and I felt very sorry to part with my darling although he will be here again on Thursday. Today we have had some awful flashes of lightning although the thunder was not very loud. One flash that I saw was awfully grand and beautiful, a flash of forked lightning came zig-zag down and sent a ball of fire upwards – it was very beautiful, but I have felt far from well through it all day long. I have trembled twice violently, and my head ached badly. I commenced cutting out my Trousseau today and have got on pretty well though of course I stopped when the storm came.

Little Tommy [eldest son age 5] and Percy [4] have amused me very much today, they say such strange things, dear little things. Tommy said he saw the thunder, and it was so beautiful and the dear little thing could not understand that I did not want to see it. He jumped with glee when a flash came, while I trembled, and longed for his happy feelings. He called it lighting afterwards, and asked me "who made it?" I said God and he said "why did God make it?" I said I did not know, and he said "does he do it for fun?" Of course I told him no.

Fig 33. 'Little Tommy and Percy' amused their aunt with their comments during a thunderstorm at Sutton.

Tilly's fiancé Alfred Bawtree was a frequent visitor to Claremont during her stay in Sutton. On 10 May, she describes the weather as dull and mentions that 'her darling boy came last night' following thunder and lightning in the afternoon. On Monday 14 May, they both walked for fourteen miles during which time she picked wild flowers and went up a fairylike lane called Howe-Lane and then onto Howe Green.

Wednesday 15th May 1872

Tom has given me rather a valuable book of Chinese paintings in a papier-mache case. I like them so much.

Saturday 1st June 1872

Home again and not sorry to be here, although they were all so kind to me in Sutton. I went there for a week and stayed three. While I was there we had a nice fright. Little Percy fell down on the steps and cut his head very badly and he lost a great deal of blood. The doctor when he came sewed it up. He was a brave little fellow and never cried even when the needle went through or when the stitch was taken out. Two days afterwards, we were all in a great way about him and two or three days after, he fell upon the same place in the nursery and made his head bleed.

I was at Sutton on the Derby day and saw a great deal of it, but was surprised to find a few respectable people going. They were mostly bad women and publicans and company, and we saw some disgusting sights.

That Derby day in 1872 was immortalised by the French painter Gustave Doré in his work *Tattenham Corner*. Just a few years before, when the Epsom line opened, it carried 70,000 passengers.[12] Matilda held a condescending view of horse racing and almost certainly would not have approved of gambling or drinking, both of which were associated with the activity then as they are today. After 150 years since Derby day 1872, it seems that her account of the clientele drawn to the races has not changed in the extremes of its diversity and would still be valid in the modern world.

Fig 34. Matilda Clark was staying at Sutton on 1ˢᵗ June 1872 and said the family 'saw some disgusting sights' amongst the race goers passing through to Epsom.

Following her extended family holiday in Brighton from late June, Tilly records that she went from there straight to Josiah Bawtree's in Norwood. She stayed two to three days before again staying in Sutton with Tom for another week. Then she returned once more to Norwood for another week but she felt that somehow she was unwelcome at Norwood.

> *I went from there to Sutton again for a fortnight to Keep Jenny Baily* (sic) [Fanny's sister] *company while Tom and Fanny and Mr and Mrs Baily* [William and Jane, Fanny's parents] *and Emma* [her own sister] *went out of town partly to Torquay and part at Hastings.*

William and Jane Bailey must have joined Tom and Fanny to live at Claremont sometime in the first half of the 1870s for William Bailey wrote his will in 1874 and stated that he lived at this address.[13] It is evident that Tom enjoyed a good extended family life with the company of not only his sisters, but his wife's family too.

Hastings like Brighton had grown into a popular seaside resort and it seems probable that Tom and Fanny's family holiday had coincided with the grand opening of the newly built Hastings Pier on the first ever August bank holiday on the 5th of the month. Unfortunately, the weather let the occasion down as a fierce wind blew and there was torrential rain all day.

Wednesday 25th September 1872
Alice and Florrie are at Tom's [the two youngest sisters].

This is around the time that Papa's house The Rocklands, is being finished for the family to move into. It was to The Rocklands that Tom and Fanny almost certainly went on 9 January 1873 for the grand house-warming party attended by 55 guests.

Tilly mentioned her disappointment that her brothers had not visited on Boxing Day 1872 (her birthday). 'I had expected a nice family party and neither of my brothers turned up,' she moaned.

Perhaps Tilly was being too optimistic to expect that her eldest brother would leave his wife and three children and rush to Anerley Road some distance away from Sutton, or to contemplate the difficult task of bringing out the family on a mid-winter's day. However, all winters turn to spring… and on 10 May 1873, Tilly married Alfred Bawtree at Sydenham. Tilly wrote extensively in her diary about that happy day and there is no doubt that this was an occasion when her brother Tom would not fail her.

Little Tommy, just a month shy of his seventh birthday, assisted his cousin Annie (Fred's five-year-old daughter) as a 'groomsman baby' and was dressed exactly like the bridesmaids, bouquet and all. The visitors were all beautifully dressed… it was a very happy breakfast. Baby looked a dear little thing'.

Tom's brother-in-law by marriage, Josiah Fountain Meen, who was the husband of Ann Bailey, was also present. Tilly mentions that 'We had Mr. Meen to play the wedding march etc. at the church'.

At the wedding breakfast, the printed 'Order of Toasts' reveals the parts that her family played to make it such a happy event and brother Tom had a prominent role to play. He proposed the groomsmen and also responded to the Rev. J. Meek Clark when he proposed Mr. Clark's family. James Clark (youngest brother of Tom) proposed the nieces and nephews of the families present – a generation many of whom will live through the two wars of the 20th century and into the nineteen-fifties.

Several months after the wedding, life had settled back to normal routine and in Sutton Fanny was preparing to give birth to her fourth child. Tilly records this birth in her diary, no doubt wondering as a new wife, when she herself will welcome her first-born.

Thursday 18 September 1873
Fanny had another little boy the day before yesterday. I had almost hoped it would be a girl as this is the fourth boy.

Undoubtedly, his mother Fanny must have shared the same sentiments. The new baby was named Sydney James Douglas, James after his paternal uncle and Douglas perhaps in recognition of Fanny's Scottish ancestry.

The longed for girl was to elude the couple throughout the 1870s. Two more boys arrived after Sydney. Firstly, Bertram Allan Leslie (two more Scottish names) was born on 29 June 1875, he would always be known as 'Bertie'.[14]

Tragedy was to strike in between the birth of the last two boys, just as it had with the two infant deaths amongst Tom's siblings and it was part of life in the Victorian era. Sydney died after just two and half years of life on 24 March 1876 at Hill Side, Sutton. The cause of death was given as laryngitis but this was merely a symptom of a much more serious condition.[15] The most likely cause of death was diphtheria, a childhood illness that was not eradicated in Europe until well into the 20th century by mass vaccination. His father Tom, no doubt grieving heavily alongside Fanny, duly registered his demise on 31st March, the same day as the small boy was buried.

Like his Papa had done more than 30 years previously, Tom acquired a family plot at Nunhead Cemetery along the path of Dissenters' Road, opposite and a little further along from Papa's own plot already filling with family members[16] (Plate iii). Both Papa and Tom had not had any of their children baptised so they were buried in unconsecrated ground.

Sometime between Bertie's birth in June 1875 and Sydney's death on 24 March the following year, the family had moved to a different house in Sutton – Hill Side. It was here that the last son was born, Walter Vivian Harold, on 15 August 1876.[17]

On Friday 13 October 1876, Tom attended the Lord Mayor's Banquet held at the Mansion House in the City, the Mayor's official residence.[18] No doubt he was joined by Thomas, his Papa, for the occasion. The Right Hon. William James Richmond Cotton MP was the mayor from 1875-6; he was elected MP for the City of London in 1874 and was also a merchant. The Banquet was held for the men who kept the commercial heart of London beating: the Committee of Lloyds, The Stock Exchange, The Commercial Sale Rooms and The

Baltic and New City Club. A song recital took place and the artistes included Miss L'estrange, Miss Florence Winn, Ms. Coates and Mr. Winn and the audience was regaled with a rendition of the English folk song, *Drink to me Only with Thine Eyes* after the assembly had joined in the singing of The National Anthem.

Chapter 4

TOTTENHAM – LEYTON

1879-1891

A nother move across to the other side of London would occur before the birth of the seventh and final child on 29 April 1879. At last, it was the longed for daughter who was named Beatrice Frances Mary, Frances after her mother and Mary after Fanny's sister Mary and also Tom's sister and his beloved mother who were both Mary Ann. Beatrice, always known affectionately as Bea, was born at 2 Lansdowne Road, Tottenham.[1] In the 1881 census, the family are still in residence and as part of the household of Fanny's parents, William and Jane Bailey, with whom they had previously lived at Sutton. Neighbours in the 1881 census at No. 1 Lansdowne Road were Peter McIntyre, a 60 year-old retired master mariner born in Scotland, his wife and two unmarried daughters, a young grandson and domestic servant. At No. 3, Isaac le Marc, 46 years-old, a shoe mercer born in Hackney, his wife Susan born in Liskeard, Cornwall and their young family with extended family too.[2]

Tottenham was several miles from the city and in 1880 it lay within the county of Middlesex becoming part of the county of London following the Local Government Act of 1888. Due to the advent of the railway expansion, Tottenham was transformed from its previous low-lying fields and market gardens into housing which provided easier and cheaper access to the city. It was the end of an era; Tom and his family would never again return to south London. By the early 1880s, Tom's eldest sons, Tommy and Percy, had been sent away to boarding school. The 1881 census reveals that both of them were boarders at Chipping Ongar Academy in Essex.[3] As the two eldest, they were being educated and groomed towards becoming successors in their grand papa's business and of course, as the sons of a gentleman.

By this time too, Tom's Papa had seen a decline in fortunes having moved from the large home specially built for him in 1872 known as The Rocklands. As Papa held the business, Tom's fortunes were inexorably linked to those of his powerful father.

Tom, with more time available was able to indulge in some of his own passions and interests and immerse himself in London life. In Islington, north London, his sister-in-law Annie lived with her husband, Josiah Fountain Meen. Known as Fountain Meen, his brother-in-law was born in 1846 and then educated at The City of London School. Furthermore, he was a self-taught pianist and organist becoming associated with Union Chapel, Compton Terrace, Islington, as the organist from 1880 for the rest of his life. The Meen family lived conveniently next door to the Chapel. Fountain Meen was indeed a prominent musician of the day and he accompanied many famous singers such as Adelina Patti, Antoinette Sterling, Charles Santley, Sims Reeves and Dame Clara Butt. He was also acquainted with several composers, in particular, Camille Saint-Saens and Sir Arthur Sullivan.[4]

Coming from a very musical family himself and in an era when many middle-class families learnt to play piano as it was considered an accomplished and genteel pastime, he would have enjoyed a warm relationship with Mr. Meen, at least when music was the topic of conversation. No doubt, the families would have met for musical evenings or concerts in Union Chapel, Islington, perhaps Exeter Hall or recitals elsewhere in the city or North London.[5]

Tom was a committed Christian from a non-conformist

Fig 35. Josiah Fountain Meen with Fanny's sister Mary in 1904. Mr. Meen was Tom's brother-in-law by marriage, and a prominent organist and pianist.

background which was probably instilled by one or both of his parents from a young age. His education too would have given him a wide knowledge of the Bible which he would use as a base for life and he continued to study and interpret biblical content throughout his life. He was fascinated with new and sometimes controversial theories that were becoming prominent in the mid-Victorian era. These new ways of reading the Bible often used the prophecies which littered the Old Testament to try and predict the future or interpret the past. His Bible would be a lifelong companion and the margins of the Old Testament pages were annotated in his fine calligraphic handwriting with pertinent revelations to support of one of his main interests through the late 1870s and 1880s – British Israelism. As early as 1866, Tom had written of his belief that the Saxons were the descendants of the Tribe of Ephraim in his pamphlet *England's Past, Present and Future in Connexion with Rome.*

British Israelism was a movement with roots in the 16th-century but it reached its zenith by way of several 19th-century English writings such as John Wilson's 1840 book *Our Israelitish Origin*. John Wilson's book may even have been the catalyst which ignited Tom's interest. Many years later, in 1922, the author's son gave Tom an early 1865 copy of the volume.[6] Various organisations in support were set up throughout the British Empire from the 1870s onwards and the movement had great attraction and appeal to men such as Tom whose own empirical involvement was through his trading connection. It was an imperialistically orientated movement and its proponents believed that the British race was so advanced and ahead of other nations that they were the descendants and inheritors of the ancient Israelites. Each generation views biblical content through the parameters of their own times. Genetically, racially and linguistically, these Victorians believed the Anglo-Saxons were the descendants of Ephraim, one of the Ten Lost Tribes of Israel, and that there was firm evidence for their belief in the Old Testament. With the British Empire at its height, circumstances were particularly propitious for the emergence of this distinct organisation.

Edward Hine, Edward Wheeler-Bird and Herbert Aldersmith were the men responsible for developing the British-Israelite movement and in 1878 the Anglo-Ephraim Association of London was absorbed into the Metropolitan Anglo-Israel Association espousing the Anglo-exclusive view which Edward Hine promoted. It seems that Tom became very involved in the Metropolitan Anglo-Israel Association and had a prominent position often orating at meetings in London.

Anglo-Israelites saw themselves as privileged inheritors of the promises made to the Israelites in the Old Testament. However, although it was a movement for the British peoples, it was also supported by several Jewish members and was backed by rabbis throughout the 19th century. In a way, this was surprising because Jews viewed the Torah's purpose as instructive whilst Christians viewed the Old Testament as prophetic. Perhaps it is easy to speculate that some of these Jewish supporters were men who were also profiting from business in Britain, men perhaps like Mr. Eugenio Arbib, the Jewish

Copyright, London: Robert Banks

Fig 36. Isaac Levinsohn came to England in the early 1870s and later became a Baptist minister.

merchant who was a family friend. One such known Jewish friend of the British-Israelite movement was a naturalised British citizen – a Russian Jew named Isaac Levinsohn.

Levinsohn was born in 1855 in the town of Kovno which was then in Russia. At the age of 16, he had a conversion experience to Christianity which caused him to leave his parents and homeland behind on a quest to find his own spiritual home. Following a perilous and lengthy journey across Europe, he arrived at the port of Hull and from there he sailed to London where he later met a missionary, the Rev. Henry Aaron Stern, who helped him find the path towards that of becoming a baptised Christian. Stern had himself been born into a Jewish family in Germany. Levinsohn became a Baptist minister and in 1878 he published his autobiography, *The Russo-Polish Jew: The Narrative of Isaac Levinsohn Conversion from Darkness of Judaism to light and liberty of the Gospel of Christ*[7]. Tom had a copy of this book which he kept all his life. It may or may not have been a personal gift to him by Levinsohn as they must have been acquaintances if not actual friends.

The fourth meeting of The Metropolitan Anglo-Israel Association took place on 19 May 1882 at Exeter Lower Hall in the Strand. It was recorded that Thomas Clark Westfield read the report of the Council in which he stated that there was an ever growing interest among British subjects in the identity of the Anglo-Saxon race with the Ten Lost Tribes and to support this, fortnightly lectures had taken place throughout the preceding winter. Isaac Levinsohn also addressed the meeting but it was not recorded what points he may have made. The Chairman remarked that it had been said that the association favoured the Conservative cause but he wished it to be known that they did not identify with any political party. Resolutions protesting against the persecution of the Jews and against infidelity (disbelief) in the land were also passed.[8]

Through his connection to the Metropolitan Anglo-Israel Association, Tom was almost certainly introduced to the study of Pyramidology, a concept which dated back to the time of Isaac Newton which became prominent in the mid-19th century. It was characterised by its religious or pseudoscientific speculations regarding pyramids but most prominently, the Great Pyramid of Giza. Pyramidology was then fused to British Israelism by the books of Charles Piazzi Smyth, Astronomer Royal of Scotland who was a committed adherent, and made copious numerological calculations on the pyramids and published them in his book *Our Inheritance in the Great Pyramid* in 1864, a copy of which was most likely analysed by Tom.[9]

On 17 May, 1879, Tom had a letter published which was submitted by someone with the initials 'M.M.J', who stated that 'it may prove interesting' (presumably because it seems to calculate an imminent date) in the *Hastings and St. Leonard's Observer* newspaper amidst a flurry of correspondence on British Israelism.

A CRUCIAL TEST OF GREAT PYRAMID CHRONOLOGY
From The Rainbow, April, 1879.

A date of some extraordinary importance appears to be registered on either side of the grand gallery's wall by a longitudinal groove of 4178.4 units in length. If that measure is absolutely to be relied upon – and we may reasonably conclude that it is – the date indicated by it is close upon us, and will terminate before the close of the ensuing May. It must not, however, be forgotten that a difference of one only in the decimal figure would represent considerably over a month of time – one-tenth of a year, in fact. With this proviso, and assuming that the Christian year begins approximately at the date of our Lord's birth, I think we have before us an opportunity for practically testing the value of the Great Pyramid's indication of prophetic chronology. As to the nature or the significance of the event, it is not easy to offer an opinion. It may have a double significance from the fact of its appearing on both walls. It should certainly be an event which should signally affect all Christendom, as the groove extends throughout the entire length of the grand gallery at that point. To any further assertion respecting it, I should hesitate to commit myself. But, at the same time, I think it is of the very highest importance that the fact should be noted some time previous to the date indicated.*

THOMAS CLARK WESTFIELD Tottenham.
The third edition, Piazzi Smyth's work, "Our Inheritance in the Great Pyramid".[10]

If these subjects seemed convoluted and impenetrable to the masses, there was always the certainties of life to bring the family down to earth with a bump. In 1885, Fanny's father William Bailey passed away. His 13-year-old grandson, Herbert, later recalled a rumour in the family that Grandpa Bailey was a considerably wealthy man and he reputedly told his young relative that this was just not so, 'No, I am not my boy!' he exclaimed.[11] Grandpa Bailey did leave a will which was proved on

21st April that year, his personal estate of £685 12s 1d was all left to his widow, Jane.[12] He was laid to rest at Highgate Cemetery, one of the so-called 'famous seven' new cemeteries encircling London.

Some changes to wealth must however have occurred around the mid-1880s for Percy's grandson later recalled:

> *The family had some trading company which crashed causing my grandfather to curtail his education and having to work for the Midland Bank.*[13]

It must have been after the loss of his father-in-law that Tom, Fanny and the children who were not away at boarding school moved to a new north London district accompanied by Fanny's widowed mother, Jane. In the 1891 census, Tom is 49 and described this time as a colonial broker's clerk (undoubtedly working with his 72-year-

Fig 37 and 37a. Portraits of Thomas and Frances which date from the 1870s or early 1880s.

old Papa). Does this change in job title mean that he had taken a step down from the operational side of the business? Their new abode is a house named Devonia, on Queen's Road in Leyton which was situated just off Leyton High Road. All six children are living at home; the eldest son Tom is employed as a mercantile clerk and so is Herbert, whilst Percy is working as a bank clerk. Bertie, Walter and Beatrice are all at school. An obvious decline in wealth is apparent as the large family of nine have no help of live-in domestic servants as they had previously and in contrast to Papa's household when he was a similar age to Tom.[14]

Leyton, like Tottenham, lies five miles north and to the east of central London. Its name derives from the River Lea, and 'the tun'. The parish was traditionally known as Low Leyton, because part of it lay low by the Lea. The civil parish was known by that name until 1921. It was two miles long from north to south and three miles along its northern boundary with Walthamstow. As in many other London districts, Leyton's mid-19th century growth was attributable to the railways after which time it became a lower/middle-class dormitory suburb, 'its growth in the 1880s was the fastest of any comparably sized town in England'.[15]

Neighbours in Queen's Road include on one side, at Meta House, Isabella Fife, a 21-year-old daughter of parents not at home on census night. She has charge of four younger siblings with the help of a 28-year-old domestic servant. On the other side, Clifton Villa is occupied by Maria Harris, a 67-year-old widow from Nottinghamshire and her four unmarried children in their 30s and 40s.[16] Her family were all born locally at Stratford. Whilst the adult children in the Harris' household were still at home with mother, over the next decade the Clark family would gradually marry or fly the nest.

Chapter 5

LEYTON – UPPER CLAPTON – BOWERS GIFFORD

1891-1901

Sometime between spring 1891 and the first half of 1893, a new servant was employed, probably at Devonia. Her name was Miss Edith Frances Mary Reader. Miss Reader was born in 1876 in Leytonstone, a local girl she was the daughter of Dennis and Sarah Reader. Her father in the 1881 census was a general labourer with roots in the Essex town of Saffron Walden.[1] At the time of the 1891 census, Miss Reader was just 14 years of age (just shy of her 15th birthday) and working as a domestic servant for a schoolmaster, Ernest Stollery and his wife Catherine with their two year old twin daughters at 8 Winifred Terrace, Napier Road, Wanstead.[2] However, this position was not to last for an extended period of time as Miss Reader arrived in the Clark household where she naturally met and knew their young sons. Herbert had always been a cheeky looking boy with a twinkle in his eye and in 1893 he surprised and shocked his family by declaring himself in love with the family servant – Miss Reader. Herbert was then 21 and Edith just 16 or 17 years old. Tom was furious with his son but unlike his parents, Herbert did not elope to another parish to marry his heart's desire although it may have been done furtively as far as his Papa was concerned. The couple were wed nearby at West Ham register office, no doubt very quietly, on Monday 4 September.[3] Ironically, the couple were exactly the same ages as Tom and Fanny had been when they ran off to marry at Kew! Edith declared herself to be 18 when she was in fact a year younger.

The marriage certificate confirms the marriage between the son of a colonial broker and the daughter of a builder's labourer. It was all the more shocking because you might have expected that Edith was pregnant and Herbert was merely doing his duty. There is no known evidence for this and their first known child was not born until 1895. Herbert's marriage to a servant broke all class boundaries. Although it would have been perfectly acceptable to have had a dalliance with her, marriage was a step too far. Goodness knows what Herbert's grandpapa must have thought of his grandson marrying a working class girl when he had set all hopes upon the future of the family being upwardly mobile!

Fig 38. An informal photograph, circa 1891, of Bertie, Beatrice and Percy.

A surviving photograph of Bertie, Beatrice and Percy dating to the early 1890s is an informal, relaxed pose showing the youngsters seated on a rug over a grassed area with shrubs and a winding pathway in the background. Herbert was most likely behind the camera. Beatrice, always a cat lover, which was probably inherited from her mother, has the family tabby on her lap with a small mouse toy. It is easy to speculate this was taken at Devonia, the family home where they all lived. It was a distant scene from the discordant atmosphere caused by Herbert's decision and there was more to come.

Following in Herbert's footsteps, the next son to leave the family was Tom, the eldest. On Saturday 31 August 1895 he married Rose Eveline Clara Carter at a north London register office.[4] In this case, it probably was her pregnancy that was a deciding factor – Rose gave birth just a month later on 29 September. Like her sister-in-law, Rose came from a solidly working class stock. In the 1891 census, her father was a jewel case maker whilst Rose made stays[5]. This was likely to be another disastrous union from Tom's point of view.

Whilst dealing with his recalcitrant sons marrying beneath their class, Tom's own life was also set to change dramatically in 1895. On 20th March that year, his father and to a large degree, benefactor passed away. His working life had in all probability been controlled and shaped by his Papa who was, unlike him, a driven and successful businessman. In his will proved on 27 July, Tom, like the rest of his siblings was a beneficiary to the residue of any estate as well as the interest dividends payable from the investments that Papa had instructed be set up following his death.

All such sums of money as have already been advanced, given by me or for the benefit of any of my sons and which at my death appear in my current account book to be entered against such son shall be taken in or towards satisfaction of the share herby provided for such son or (as a son dying in my lifetime) for his children taking in the place of such son and shall be brought into hotchpot and accounted for accordingly.[6]

If any sum in the account should exceed the amount of the share of his residuary estate, including his share of that part of his estate, the income of which was payable to his wife Fanny, it was directed that the executors (Mary Ann Esther Clark and Alfred Bawtree) could release the son (Tom) from so much of the sums so advanced as should be in excess of such share. The sums would have to be offset against the provision made for Tom (his son) and be included in the computation of the amount of his residuary estate, the income of one third which was to be paid to his widow.

Following his father's death the business partnership was dissolved. Tom did not possess the same business head or prowess as his father and his eldest son, Tom, who would normally have been expected to have been considered an inheritor, was rather an uncomplicated and unsophisticated kind of young man who now had other responsibilities and cares.

We cannot be certain what happened but in 1897, Tom was seemingly declared bankrupt[7]. Family lore has it that he made some unwise investment decisions, took chances that did not pay off; the details are lost in the mists of time. In any case, by the end of the 19th century, the golden age of colonial trade was waning. Britain no longer 'ruled the waves' in the global market dominated by other world powers. It was not a favourable time for any one working in this field, let alone for those not naturally inclined.

Around this time, Tom moved to another new address in Upper Clapton, which may have happened following Papa's demise. Like Leyton, Upper Clapton borders the River Lea to the east with Lower Clapton to the south. Springfield, the road name where they lived, adjoined a vast green area which was officially opened as a public park in 1905 and it contained only a few houses before mid-Victorian housing was erected in the area. It was close to Clapton railway station GER and tram routes so ideal for travel into London as well as other places east of the city.

Increasingly, Tom now turned more towards his artistic endeavours for enjoyment and relied again on his pen name Thomas

Clark Westfield which he had first used when writing his books 35 years earlier. Instead of pen and ink, this time he took up his easel and paint box and began to complete landscapes in oils. The surviving work that he completed around the turn of the century shows that he enjoyed creating moonlit scenes and rural compositions. Like his siblings, he may have used his artistic talents at times of financial insecurity as a means to supplement his income, as it was mentioned in family circles that he also sold his paintings.

As well as painting, photography was a popular hobby or occupation with Tom's sons, as well as their first cousins such as the Bawtrees – his sister Matilda's family. Photography was still a great novelty. Tom's son Walter also adopted the surname 'Westfield' around this time and seems to have had a photographic business or studio at 27 Springfield, Hackney, the later 1890s address of Tom, Fanny and their family[8].

The third son to marry was Percy who wed Gertrude Susie Clarke, known as Susie, she was no relation. This marriage, unlike the previous two, was perhaps one of which Tom approved. Miss Clarke was certainly of a different class to the two other ladies and the nuptials were celebrated at St. Botolph's, Bishopsgate in the City on 14 August 1900. Tom added his stamp of approval by signing as a witness.[9]

On 15 December 1900, Fanny's mother Jane Bailey died at the age of 85, an advanced age for the time and she was buried with her husband William at Highgate Cemetery. Just a few weeks later on 22 January 1901, the end of the Victorian era came to pass with the death of the Queen, both ladies having been born in the 1810s and living on into the dawn of the new century.

In the spring of 1901, Tom and Fanny are at home at 27 Springfield on census night. He claims he is still occupied as a colonial broker but that probably is more of a throwback to his past. The only children at home are 25-year-old Bertie, working as a commercial clerk and Beatrice (21).[10] Their brother Walter, the only other unmarried son at this time, is staying with his brother Herbert now living a life in the Essex countryside at Bowers Gifford with his wife and young family.[11]

In addition to the two children at home, the Clarks are entertaining some guests on census night. Matilda Andre, a 32-year-old visitor with two children, Bertha and Nora (15 and 14 respectively). Matilda is of French nationality but born in China whilst her children were both born in Trinidad, West Indies. It is possible that they were guests as the family of an unknown yet absent man who was a business associate of Tom, who may have been attempting to revive a flagging business. Ever interested in different cultures and countries, one imagines some lively discussions took place between hosts and visitors. Herbert's grand-daughter Eunice recalled it said that the family were using exotic spices such as ginger in cooking at a time when generally these were unknown in the kitchen to the masses.

The neighbour at 26 Springfield was Bernard William MacDermott, a 50-year-old newspaper sub-editor born in Stoke Newington with his wife Georgina and three adult children and his sister-in-law, Annie White. The other side, 28 Springfield, is unoccupied in 1901.

Herbert and Edith had moved out to the country around the turn of the century to Bowers Gifford, a village in south Essex. He had bought a plot of land in this newly expanding area, known as Clifton Road New Estate. Tom too had tired of London life. He was now in his 60th year and with retirement and a new century having dawned, he also bought a plot of land next to Herbert his son. The remaining family, who had not yet married, Bertie, Walter and Beatrice, must have spent some time with him at this location once the house was finished. It is hard to imagine now, but Bowers Gifford was a small remote place – not part of the town of Basildon as it is today. The house where Tom lived was ironically named Edith Cottage most likely for Herbert's wife who'd come a long way since being employed by Tom as a domestic servant; the property in which he now lived was ironically named after her!

Just a few months after the census of 1901 Tom was making plans to move out of Springfield and join his son Herbert in a newly built house in the countryside of South Essex. An advertisement in the *Hackney and Kingsland Gazette* of 20th September, advertises some items of furniture that he wishes to dispose of before starting his new ascetic life.

Beautifully designed walnut over-mantel, 17 bevelled plates; 8ft. extending dining table, superior dining room suite, saddlebags and other effects.[12]

The family were reducing in number and now downsizing in preparation to lead a simpler uncluttered country life. A photograph of this time shows Tom seated in a sumptuously decorated room dwarfed and surrounded by the accoutrements of wealth and success. Perhaps it was taken to promote what appears to have been the final sale by auction of his luxurious furniture before departing for a new beginning. It is reminiscent of the advert placed by his Papa in 1867 when the family left country life at Crofton Hall for a new life in suburban Sydenham.

Fig 39. Tom seated in a sumptuous interior, probably at Springfield, Upper Clapton, circa 1900.

The whole of the nearly new well-made furniture and effects of the residence, comprising massive all brass Italian and French bedsteads, clean wool and hair mattresses and bedding, blankets, quilts, and sheeting, a noble 6ft bedroom suite, a 5ft ditto, and others in various designs and woods, with pedestal Duchesne tables, chests of drawers, a fine carved walnut wood dining room suite. In Morocco, walnut overmantels, bookcases. dining tables, occasional ditto, a massive 6ft sideboard, with lofty plate-glass back, drawing room suite upholstered In the best style, a fine tone 7 oct. upright grand pianoforte, by Erard, China cabinets, Brussels, Wilton pile and Axminster carpets, rugs, brass fenders and implements, coal cabinets, china dinner, dessert and tea services, oil paintings, water color drawings, artists proof engravings, hall furniture, stair carpets, refrigerator, plated articles, and a gents free-wheel bicycle and youth's ditto. MESSRS. DRYSDALE, NURSE and Co. will sell by auction on the premises as above, Thursday, NOVEMBER 7th, 1901, at one o'clock prompt. On view, day prior and morning of sale. Catalogues on the premises, and the Auction offices, 14. Manor-road. Stoke Newington. Telephone No. 56 Dalston.[13]

Chapter 6

―――――

BOWERS GIFFORD

―――――

1901-1920

*Clifton Road, Bowers Gifford – it is an unmade road
and there are not many houses. I don't think the road is
very different from when your family lived in it. It is like
a little oasis of "depth of the country".*
(Bowers Gifford Rector's wife – February 1990).

By May 1902, Tom, Fanny and perhaps one or two of their children had moved to Bowers Gifford their newly built house with just five rooms having been finished. An advertisement for a position wanted appeared in the *Southend Standard and Essex Weekly Advertiser* on the 1st and 8th of that month:

*CLERK used to ledger, invoicing, town travelling and collecting; good
reference – Apply Clark, care of Westfield, Clifton Rd., Bowers Gifford.[1]*

As Walter was working as a travelling photographer in the 1901 census, it seems likely he is now seeking employment and advertising his services from his father's new abode.

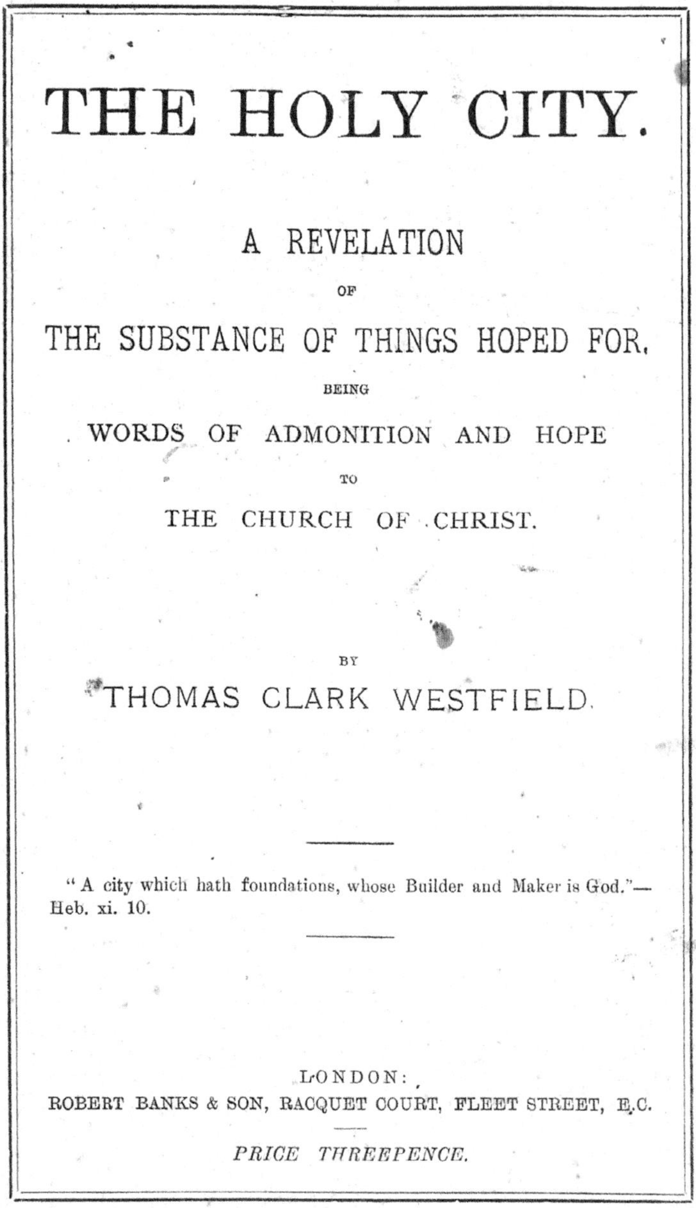

THE HOLY CITY.

A REVELATION

OF

THE SUBSTANCE OF THINGS HOPED FOR,

BEING

WORDS OF ADMONITION AND HOPE

TO

THE CHURCH OF CHRIST.

BY

THOMAS CLARK WESTFIELD.

" A city which hath foundations, whose Builder and Maker is God."—
Heb. xi. 10.

LONDON:
ROBERT BANKS & SON, RACQUET COURT, FLEET STREET, E.C.

PRICE THREEPENCE.

Fig 40. Front page of a religious pamphlet written by Thomas Clark in 1903.

Bertie was spending time at an address in Notting Hill, north London – perhaps staying here whilst working in the City. For this is the address he was living at when he got married to 23-year-old Miss Ethel Lamerton at All Saints' Church, North Benfleet, her home parish in 1902, and neighbouring to Bowers Gifford. His sister Beatrice was one of the witnesses to the marriage.[2]

Since the move to the country and retirement, Tom had more time available to devote to his love of the Bible and writing. In 1903, he wrote a small treatise entitled *The Holy City: A Revelation or The Substance of Things Hoped for*.[3] In the introduction dated 9 December that year, Tom sets out his purpose as being to draw the reader's attention towards not the temporal Eternal City known as Rome, but 'it will be well for all who are of the Household of Faith to remember that here we have no continuing city, but we seek one to come. It is of this city I fain would speak…' As an evangelical Christian, he has become disillusioned with the Established Church stating that the church has 'degenerated into a belief of vague, shadowy, and etherial [sic] nonentities'. Tom's writing closely studies the Book of Revelation and he quotes heavily from it in support of his belief that the last book of the Bible contains important truths about the life and world which is to come to all those who believe.

In Revelation, the writer John describes the holy city, the New Jerusalem, coming down from God out of heaven; using an analogy, he says she is prepared as a bride. Just over six months later a physical bride in the shape of Tom and Fanny's daughter Beatrice stepped down the aisle of St. Margaret of Antioch, Bowers Gifford on 22 June 1904. It must have been the perfect family wedding when the only daughter married at the country church. Her mother signed as a witness accompanied by many more family members eager to stamp their seal of approval on the match.[4]

A photograph of the happy party survives and shows Tom and Fanny surrounded by their children, grandchildren and Fanny's sister Mary with her husband, Fountain Meen. They must have all been delighted that their son-in-law, Edmund Palmer (known as

*Fig 41. The wedding party assembled at Bowers Gifford in June 1904
for the marriage of Beatrice to Edmund Palmer.*

Ted) came from a musical family. His father ran a piano showroom
and in the 1901 census, Ted was a music and instrument dealer who
was working on his own account.[5] It was a fine occupation for the
new husband of a girl with a musical family herself. There must have
been much rejoicing on that midsummer's day. However, within the
assembled group, Fanny appears to be much older than her 58 years.
Gone is the vivacious and attractive young girl with the dark hair and
bright features to be replaced by an elderly looking lady with white
hair who appears to be very tired but contented.

In late October of the same year, during a family meal, Fanny began
to act strangely picking up food with her fingers she exclaimed 'aren't I
funny!'[6] It perhaps was a transient ischemic attack, the forerunner of a
much more serious stroke and Fanny died on 31 October 1904 leaving
behind her devastated husband Tom.[7] They had been together since
she was just 17-years-old, 41 years earlier. Their six children must have
also keenly felt the loss of their dear Mama. Fanny, like most women

of her era, had led a quiet life overshadowed by her husband in many ways. She had been a dutiful wife and mother, successfully raising five boys and a girl to adulthood and did not leave a mark for posterity in any other sphere. Fanny was interred at the family plot at Nunhead Cemetery to join her son Sydney who had died at the age of 3 in 1876 and whom they had both mourned.[8]

Tom would never recover from the loss of his beloved wife. Unlike his own Papa, he did not remarry. A year later, on the first anniversary of Fanny's death, he wrote a poem to her memory in which he poured out his profound sense of loss and despair. Their married life had been one long honeymoon and her loss turned his life into a living death. His one hope was that they would be reunited, kindred spirits that they were, beyond the grave. Fanny's untimely death would make Tom more introspective and perhaps eccentric as he faced the decades that followed alone.

The contrast between how father and son dealt with the loss of their wives after long marriages could not be greater. The senior had

Fig 42. Fanny in later life with a pet cat.

risen out of grief to act practically even unemotionally, marrying just a year later in order to give his large young family a new mother figure: perhaps hoping that this would give them greater emotional stability whilst he was away working. The paterfamilias, his emotion was muted by the need to keep his young family together. His son Tom, whose children had all reached adulthood, became immersed in grief and sorrow with no outlook or optimism for the future and his response as the first anniversary of his wife's death passed was not to look for a replacement, but to reminisce about what he had lost. Tom would continue to look for comfort in his artistic and spiritual world.

In 1908, Walter became the final child to marry when he wed Gertrude Dennis and they made a home at West Ham. Tom was fortunate that he lived next door to his son Herbert and no doubt other family members visited regularly out in the country.

In 1909, Tom's brother-in-law, the eminent musician J. Fountain Meen died at the age of 63 following a short illness at his home in Islington.[9] Tom would have been one of the mourners at the funeral to offer condolences to his sister-in-law Mary, the long-time companion of Fountain Meen after the death of his first wife, Ann, who was Mary's sister. They would now share in the grief of lost spouses as Mary's other sister (his wife Fanny) had died just five years before and his emotions were no doubt still raw.

The 1911 census revealed that Tom was no longer living a solitary life in his new house at Bowers Gifford. His eldest son Tom had returned to his father following the collapse of his marriage to Rose Carter and may have already lived there for some years.[10] The marriage which took place with eight month pregnant Rose, had ended when she left him sometime following the birth of their third child in 1898. Times were changing and in an earlier generation it would have been unthinkable that a woman should take her children away from the marital home should she flee. It was unlikely that Tom junior would have been too upset by his wife leaving with the children and it is something he would not have contested. Tom is still working as an artist at the age of 69 whilst his son is employed as a fruit salesman.

In the early 1910s, life at Bowers Gifford perhaps entered a more settled phase. Tom's sister Alice eventually took up residence at Hebe Cottage, Clifton Road and her presence a few doors away must have been a comfort. As a young girl with an unhappy home life with her step-mother, then sent to boarding school, she had escaped periodically to the happy home life of her brother Tom who was 17 years her senior and a much less austere figure than her Papa. Like Tom, Alice was now supplementing her income by working as an artist and the two perhaps used to take up their easels and paint *en plein air* in the rural idyll of south Essex.

Unfortunately, this tranquil phase would not last and storm clouds were gathering across the nation and in September 1914 outbreak of war with Germany was declared which would change many lives. For Tom, his sons were too old to volunteer for active service that year and they also escaped call-ups when conscription was introduced for men up to 51 years old in 1916. However, some of his nephews born in the 1880s and 1890s were not so fortunate and in the war years that followed, two of them would be killed in action, one in France and another in Greece and two of Tom's sisters would mourn their lost sons greatly.[11]

South Essex was exposed to the hostilities across the Channel due to its proximity to the Somme and the Ypres Salient, the two most notable theatres of war for the British Army. The horror of modern warfare was apocalyptic to the intellect of Tom and he marked the end of 1914 and the outbreak of war by producing a religious tract in which he prophesied that this World War was no less than the biblical armageddon as written about in the Book of Revelation to include the resurrection of the dead resulting in a religious revival proclaiming the Kingdom of Christ was at hand, the anti-Christ appearing with the outbreak of war, the reestablishment of the Jews to the land of Judaea and the Battle of Armageddon resulting in the establishment of the Lord's Kingdom on earth.

The nation had been whipped up into frenzy against the enemy 'the Hun' and the eastern region of England often bore the brunt of air raids from German Zeppelins from 1915 onwards. In Essex,

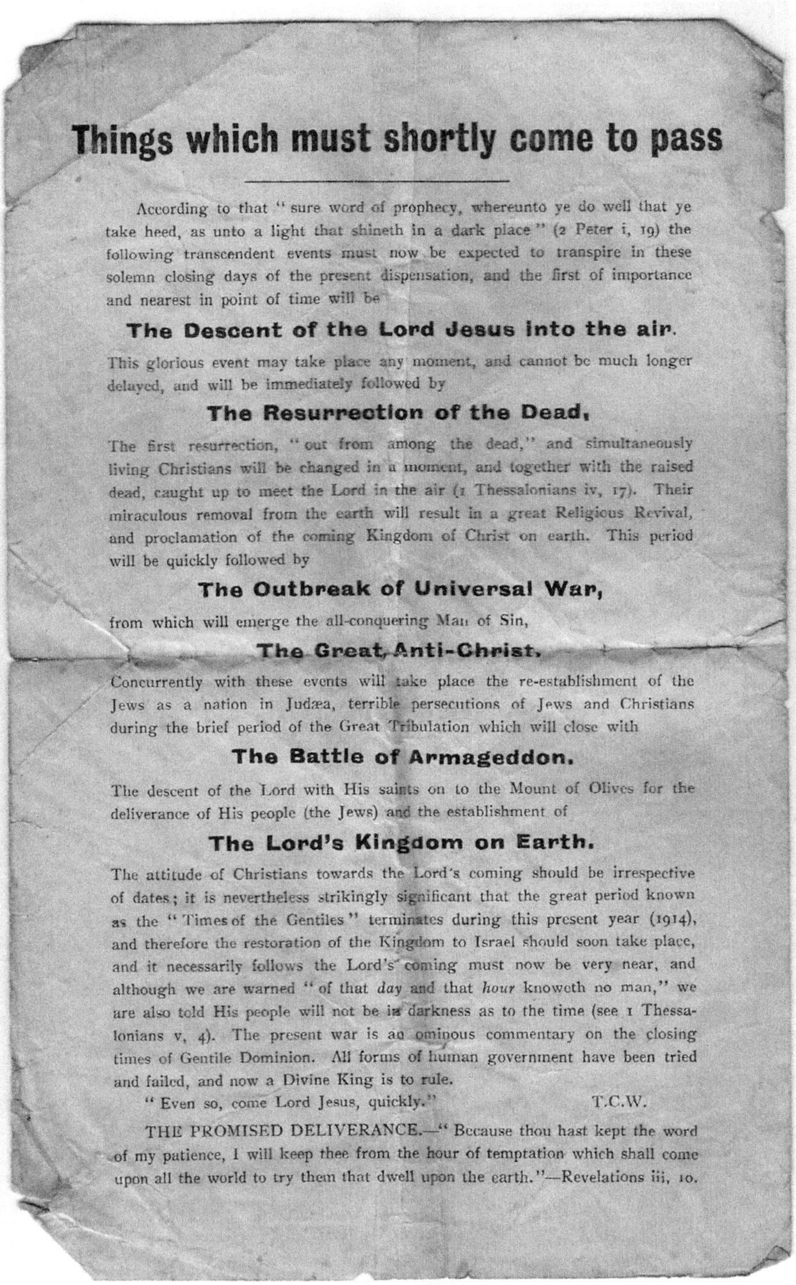

Things which must shortly come to pass

According to that " sure word of prophecy, whereunto ye do well that ye take heed, as unto a light that shineth in a dark place " (2 Peter i, 19) the following transcendent events must now be expected to transpire in these solemn closing days of the present dispensation, and the first of importance and nearest in point of time will be

The Descent of the Lord Jesus into the air.

This glorious event may take place any moment, and cannot be much longer delayed, and will be immediately followed by

The Resurrection of the Dead,

The first resurrection, " out from among the dead," and simultaneously living Christians will be changed in a moment, and together with the raised dead, caught up to meet the Lord in the air (1 Thessalonians iv, 17). Their miraculous removal from the earth will result in a great Religious Revival, and proclamation of the coming Kingdom of Christ on earth. This period will be quickly followed by

The Outbreak of Universal War,

from which will emerge the all-conquering Man of Sin,

The Great Anti-Christ.

Concurrently with these events will take place the re-establishment of the Jews as a nation in Judæa, terrible persecutions of Jews and Christians during the brief period of the Great Tribulation which will close with

The Battle of Armageddon.

The descent of the Lord with His saints on to the Mount of Olives for the deliverance of His people (the Jews) and the establishment of

The Lord's Kingdom on Earth.

The attitude of Christians towards the Lord's coming should be irrespective of dates; it is nevertheless strikingly significant that the great period known as the " Times of the Gentiles " terminates during this present year (1914), and therefore the restoration of the Kingdom to Israel should soon take place, and it necessarily follows the Lord's coming must now be very near, and although we are warned " of that *day* and that *hour* knoweth no man," we are also told His people will not be in darkness as to the time (see 1 Thessalonians v, 4). The present war is an ominous commentary on the closing times of Gentile Dominion. All forms of human government have been tried and failed, and now a Divine King is to rule.

" Even so, come Lord Jesus, quickly."   T.C.W.

THE PROMISED DELIVERANCE.—" Because thou hast kept the word of my patience, I will keep thee from the hour of temptation which shall come upon all the world to try them that dwell upon the earth."—Revelations iii, 10.

Fig 43. A religious tract written by Thomas Clark Westfield in 1914 upon the outbreak of the First World War.

these massive airships silently passed overhead on their way to drop explosives in London using the Thames estuary as a guide. Tom raised his fists to the sky at these monsters of destruction and death – he must have looked like a biblical prophet with his long white beard and balding head raised to the heavens in condemnation.[12]

In 1916, British Summertime was introduced by the government to assist the country in food production during this time of great tribulation. An hour extra daylight would assist farmers in gathering crops during harvest time with so many men away on the Western Front. Tom, now 74, dug his heels in and refused to move his clock forward an hour. He declared 'Our politicians not only lied themselves but were making the clock lie as well!' but in the end he had to give in as he was getting into all kinds of muddles.[13]

In 1917, Tom suffered a further blow when his sister Alice died at the relatively young age of 58 – the same age as his wife Fanny. She was buried locally at North Benfleet churchyard.[14]

Fig 44. Tom's sister Alice (second left) in this family group circa 1915 at Bowers Gifford. To her right are Beatrice & Grace Palmer with Herbert Clark. Far right are Beatrice's daughter Eileen with Rosie Hawkins (white ribbon in her hair) and Bea's husband Edmund. The girl on the far right is Edith Hawkins. In the centre is Barbara Palmer.

It may have been at this time that Tom attended a séance. The Great War had prompted interest in spiritualism with so many grieving families wanting to contact their lost young men who died so suddenly and violently, and seek some solace and peace. Tom, too, had over the last decade experienced a terrible loss. His daughter Beatrice's mother-in-law Louisa Palmer was a medium but it is not known whether she conducted the séance that he attended. He went and was rather sceptical about the meeting and finished up being asked to leave. He said that they asked him to go because the whole thing was false and they knew that he knew it! As ever, Tom had everything worked out himself.

Chapter 7

———

THE FINAL YEARS –
WHAT TO DO WITH PA?

———

1920 – 1927

On 9 December 1921, Tom reached the milestone age of 80. His six children had produced a total of 13 grandchildren born between 1895 and 1917. It is not known where Tom lived at the time of his 80th birthday, whether at Bowers Gifford still or elsewhere. Families were becoming smaller by the early 20th century; he was one of 12 children whilst he and his wife had produced seven. Of his five children who had gone on to have children of their own, each of these had only produced between one and three children each. Not only had families shrunk, but work and war had driven his children further from both Bowers Gifford and in some cases, London. It is not known how much contact, if any, he had with any of his surviving siblings, nieces and nephews.

His sister Matilda Bawtree must have been in touch at least in correspondence, as there were photographs in Tom's collection of her daughters (his nieces) taken at the family home, Clapham Lodge, in Sutton dating from the 1910s. By 1920, however, his brother Fred had been dead for almost 30 years, Lizzie had died in Australia in

1913 after having emigrated following her marriage in 1875 and of course, Alice died in 1917. His sisters Millie and Florrie had married but found themselves widows following the deaths of their husbands whilst Polly had remained single.

He probably did not see some of his children very frequently. Walter and Beatrice both living at West Ham were the next nearest in terms of distance. Percy had moved to Cheshunt, Hertfordshire, following his marriage and worked in London. Bertie had suffered bereavement in 1909 when his first wife died young leaving two young daughters. Perhaps following the pragmatic course of his grandfather, Bertie had remarried in 1911 to Emily Steer. The quest for employment during the Great War had sent them to Coventry where Bertie worked in connection with a munitions factory and they had made the Midlands city their permanent home.

What to do with Pa? That was a question that his children struggled with as he faced his final years. Tom had by this time become more like his father – difficult; perhaps a combination of nature and age which always accentuates traits. Tom or 'Pa' as referred to by his children, did go to various locations to visit or stay for extended periods with his family and they did visit him too. However, they all revealed that Tom was just too difficult a man to live with.

Beatrice's three daughters, Eileen, Grace and Barbara used to visit their Grandpa. Barbara's husband, Maurice Wood, later spoke of those visits as retold to him:

> *Grandpa Westfield suffered rather badly from constipation and when the girls visited, they used to get the giggles, hearing him cursing everything and everybody in a very loud voice from "the little room". I think it was the only excitement they had during their visit.*[1]

Pa also travelled to Coventry where he spent time living with his son Bertie, his wife, two daughters and son. Bertie's granddaughter, Patricia Cowley, remembered hearing about those times from her mother Muriel, Bertie's daughter:

Mother said he was well-spoken and frequently used to correct her speech. Apparently he wasn't an easy man to live with and eventually my grandfather asked him to leave, he frequently caused upsets.[2]

Herbert's marriage to Edith ended after almost 30 years in the early 1920s. Divorce at this time was still difficult to obtain and Herbert had moved out of the marital home and went to live at Old Buckenham, a small village in south Norfolk by 1923 where he set up his own independent business enterprise.

Herbert's daughter, Marjorie, was later told several anecdotal stories of her Grandpa during his declining years.

Pa used to travel up to Norfolk by train to Attleborough station. On one occasion, my father waited for the one train he was supposed to be on, then the one after, but no sign of Pa. My father did not return again and on eventually arriving at the station and without Dad to collect him by car, Pa had to walk the two to three miles to Old Buckenham.[3]

Herbert's youngest daughter, Doris and Marjorie's mother, Grace, shared Bertie's family's aversion to living with the disagreeable old man at Old Buckenham probably during the years 1923 to 1926, and they issued Herbert an ultimatum: either he goes, or we do! Still, they were but young women who were unable to cope with a difficult and perhaps slightly senile octogenarian.

Eventually, in need of care which his family could not or would not provide, Tom had to enter a nursing home. Central Home at Leytonstone was formerly the workhouse but had become known by its new name after the war. It was situated in an area familiar to Tom because he had lived at Leyton in the 1890s. Walter and Beatrice, living at West Ham were nearby. However, the decision to go to Central Home was not at all well received by Tom. The poor old man threatened to leave so his clothes were taken away from him. Herbert went to visit him and Tom said reprovingly, 'my place is with you' and Herbert replied 'if you had behaved yourself, you could have stayed with us'. Herbert was very unhappy to leave Pa at the institution but Doris and Grace had insisted if he came back again, they would leave. Herbert felt his hands were tied.[4] The often flighty nature of youth revealed itself in the fullness of time when both his daughter and his young love left Herbert to reflect on the way he rejected his Pa and by that time it was too late.

Tom passed away on Monday 31 January 1927 at Central Home. He was 85 years of age and his death was certified as caused by myocardial degeneration without a post mortem taking place. His son Percy, then residing at Hendon, London informed the registrar of his death on the very same day.[5] The certificate does not say that Percy was present at the end and so it is likely that Tom died alone without any family at his side. His usual address was given as 288 Green Street, West Ham the home of Beatrice and her family so perhaps he had only recently entered Central Home for the final time.

Tom was now reunited with his wife Fanny. More than 22 years after she had died leaving him bereft, Tom joined her mortal remains at Nunhead Cemetery on Friday 4 February 1927 when he was interred in the grave with her and their son Sydney.[6] A pedestal type memorial was erected over the grave. During the Second World War, this area of London sustained severe bomb damage. The grave is still there today, broken and damaged but with nature reclaiming its own, tree trunks growing through the centre and all around. At the front kerb where it is turned over slightly by the pressure of tree roots, the name "CLARK" is visible to those who care to look. The one remaining sign today of lives lived fully and people who loved each other dearly but lost to the world forever.

> *Nor can high heaven contain a greater bliss than our reunion, on that joyous day...*
>   *Oh! Come then death, in mercy bear me hence...*[7]

As one earthly life ended, a new one had begun. Tom's last grandchild, Marjorie, had been born at Old Buckenham just five months earlier. Perhaps he may never have seen her but Marjorie and later on, her

Fig 45. Tom in later life, his velvet jacket had seen better days.

daughter, would ensure that Tom would live on and his compelling life story and journey would be recorded for posterity into the 21st century.

PART THREE

THE CHILDREN OF THOMAS CLARK 1841-1927

Chapter 1

THOMAS WILLIAM FRANCIS CLARK

---

25 June 1866 – 28 April 1947

…he was always keen to demonstrate how strong he was and used to wrap a hankie round the back of a dining room chair and lift it up with his teeth.
(Maurice Wood, March 1990)

Tom and Fanny's first-born son was born on 25 June 1866, nine and a half months following their wedding.[1] There is no doubt then that the child was a honeymoon conception. Not only was he a first-born son but a first-born grandson too for both sets of his grandparents, Thomas and Mary Ann Clark and William and Jane Bailey.

Tommy, as we will call him to differentiate him from his father and grandfather of the same name, was born at 5 Palace Road, Penge, near to the Crystal Palace at Sydenham. The young family's stay at this address was of a short duration, eighteen months later, when he was joined by his brother, Ernest (Percy), the family of four were

Fig 46. Baby Tommy with his mother Fanny, circa 1867/8.

residing at Clarendon House, Coburg Road, Camberwell – a property connected to the Bailey family.

Sadly, Tommy's first year of life was marred by the sudden death of his Grandmama Mary Ann Clark who passed away in October 1866 when he was four months old. This event would have thrown his parents into deep mourning and they would have become immersed into wearing appropriate mourning apparel which had been widely encouraged by the death of Prince Albert, consort to Queen Victoria just a few years before. A photograph of baby Tommy taken with his Mama appears to show that she is in full mourning wearing a suitable black dress and black-jet jewellery (see Fig. No. 28).

However, in addition to mourning for deceased relatives which affected young, old, rich and poor alike, Tommy was born into a privileged world for a Victorian infant as he had every comfort and lacked for nothing. His Papa had joined his own father in partnership as a colonial broker shortly before his marriage and as traders they would enjoy glittering financial rewards for the importation of produce on an international scale. Not only were the financial rewards great, but his parents were ecstatically in love and life in the Clark household must have been largely extremely happy.

Fig 47. Tommy circa 1870.

Snaps of young Tommy show him as a fair-headed child with piercing eyes. In keeping with etiquette of the time, Tommy wore his hair long until the age of around seven and he would also have worn dresses too until he was 'breeched'. These photographs show a young child with ringlets and wearing dresses, easily mistaken for a girl in 21ˢᵗ century eyes. In another image, he appears alongside his brother Percy.

By 1871, the family of four were living at Claremont House, Brighton Road, Sutton, Surrey and the census that year reveals that the family had the help of two servants, one of whom was Charlotte Potter, a 16-year-old nursery maid. She was employed to care for Tommy and Percy thus helping their Mama to run the household in conjunction with the other general servant.[2]

Tommy was no doubt doted on by his paternal aunts, who were frequent visitors to their home in Sutton. On 2 April 1871, Alice was staying with the family. At 12 years old, she was a child herself.

Her older sister, Matilda (Tilly) recorded in her diary of 1872 some incidents involving her young nephews during her own three week stay. The year was noted for posterity for its unusual extremely wet weather and thunderstorms.

Wednesday 8th May 1872

Little Tommy and Percy have amused me very much today, they say such strange things, dear little things. Tommy said he saw the thunder, and it was so beautiful and the dear little thing could not understand that I did not want to see it. He jumped with glee when a flash came, while I trembled, and longed for his happy feelings. He called it lighting afterwards, and asked me "who made it?" I said God and he said "Why did God make it?" I said I did not know how, and he said "does he do it for fun?" Of course I told him no.[3]

On Wednesday, 25 September 1872, Matilda noted in her diary that her sisters Alice and Florrie were both staying with their brother Tom and family at Sutton.

The following year, Tommy had an important role to play at the marriage of his aunt Matilda to Alfred Bawtree on 10th May at St. Stephen's Church, South Dulwich. Matilda recorded that Tommy assisted his younger cousin, Annie Clark, as a 'groomsman baby and was dressed exactly like the bridesmaids, bouquet and all'[4].

Tommy's early years were probably spent happily as part of an extended Victorian family with lots of visits from his paternal aunts and for several years joined by his maternal grandparents, William and Jane Bailey, who seemed to have begun living at Claremont from 1874 if not earlier.

By 1879, when Tommy was 13, he had five siblings and his family base was at Tottenham, north London with his maternal grandparents. However, before 1881 Tommy and Percy were not living with the rest of the family as they had been sent to boarding school up at Chipping Ongar Academy in Essex.[5] These boys were the first boys in the Clark family to benefit from the wealth coming into the household at this time to be able to have a fine education as befitted the sons of City merchants. Perhaps the family's move from South to North London had even been made in the late 1870s to facilitate their Essex education.

Before sending his sons up to Ongar Academy, their Papa no doubt considered other schools and would have almost certainly perused many prospectuses in the process. Ongar seemed a totally suitable choice, as its prospectus highlighted the areas both academic and of a personal nature in which parents could be reassured that their children would receive the best possible tuition and that their every physical care would be catered for.

It was described as 'dry, 200 feet above sea level on gravel soil and close to the "famed" Epping Forest' – an ideal situation, it was claimed, for an attractive and successful school. Ongar was described as a 'delightful and charming country town, neat, picturesque, relaxed, neighbourly' and most importantly, it was within easy reach of London.[6]

The fees for the privilege of a good private education at Ongar Academy were £30 annually (for 'young gentlemen' under 12) rising to £35 for those over 12 years and the majority of boarders in the 1881 census stated they were born in London, Middlesex, but pupils came from far and wide areas.[7]

The subjects offered in the 19th century included all subjects felt to be required for a sound education including Greek, Latin, arithmetic, geography, history as well as elocution, grammar, composition, book-keeping, geometry, trigonometry and chemistry – these last subjects all being newly offered from at least the time of the 1875 Prospectus. New learning was also reflected in subjects such as astronomy and penmanship, both of which would have appealed to Papa's own inclinations. As indeed would the disciplines of algebra, merchants' accounts and land surveying. If Papa had wished for Tom and his brother Percy to learn French, German or drawing in pencil, another two guineas would be needed and four guineas was the fee for drawing in colours, dancing or music. Access to the school library was also available for a small annual charge.[8] The arts would surely have been a draw to an artistic family such as the Clarks. Money was perhaps no object during this period for the well-to-do family and to ensure that his sons had the best possible start in life – a thorough education.

As well as providing the annual fees plus extra money for extra-curricular subjects, Tom and Fanny would have to send them off with the items on the Principal's extensive list ticked off.

Three suits of clothes – best, second-best and 'school'.

Two caps, 'best' and 'playground' the best one was the college cap, black and with tassel and obtainable from the school for 6s 6d.

Pupil Boxes (height 14 inches maximum) containing:

Three pairs of boots, six handkerchiefs, a pair of slippers, six white or three coloured shirts (with pieces for mending) eight collars, six pairs of socks, bathing drawers, three nightshirts, four towels and four table napkins. A rug for the grass in summer was an additional item.[9]

Parents' wishes were decisive at Ongar and subjects were selected which would have been relevant to the student's chosen career. However, career advice was either deferential or non-existent.[10] As well as the curriculum outlined in the prospectus, there was very much a 'hidden curriculum' at the school with the task at hand being to instil values of serious industry, self-sufficiency and honour, so vital for sending good and worthy young men out into society.[11] These were values which Papa and Grandpapa would have endorsed as being necessary for the future success of their family and their honour, as important traders of Her Majesty's Empire.

There were 135 boarders in the 1881 census under the Principal Dr. William Chignall Clark who had been in post since 1859.[12] The relatively low number of pupils made it possible to adapt studies to fit each one of them '…with a special regard to the position he is expected to occupy in after life'. Dr. Clark promised he was able to employ enough qualified and trained teachers to allow every pupil a good deal of individual tuition.[13] In 1881, Dr. Clark's son, Oswald, is the 25-year-old headmaster and there are four youthful assistant masters too.[14]

Fig 48. Ongar Grammar School front view.

As well as the time spent in learning, Tom and Fanny would have expected their sons to receive care, kindness and personal attention. The prospectus gave a reassurance of Dr. Clark's personal supervision of work and welfare, the guarantee of individual attention and most importantly, a monthly report to them on their sons' progress, conduct and health.[15] In turn, Tom or Fanny could write in confidence to the Principal on matters concerning the treatment of Tommy or Percy and it may have been possible for them to visit outside of school hours which were Wednesday or Saturday afternoons being lesson free.[16]

Papa and Mamma would no doubt, like most parents, be glad that the school discipline was observed to be not harsh, but firm. Both boys attended church twice on Sundays as well as morning and evening prayers daily at school.[17]

In the 1881 census, Sarah Brunt is employed as wardrobe keeper at the school and may have been responsible for supplying well-aired clothing and bed linen as well as ensuring a bed for each pupil and an 'unlimited supply of the best provisions'. As well as the wardrobe keeper, the school had a full complement of domestic staff; there was a male cook and two further male servants, one working in boot care, the other in the scullery. There were also two housemaids and two laundry maids and the school kept its own dairy cows.[18]

To add that extra piece of personal service, the Principal accompanied his pupils to London and arranged for them to be met (…'at any of the London railway stations') at the start of each term.[19]

Tommy and Percy would have broken off their lessons for their daily meals. Breakfast was at 8.00am and consisted mainly of bread and butter with milk or coffee. Lunch was at noon and comprised of mainly biscuits with more bread, butter and milk. Dinner was an early 3.00pm and the main meal was beef or pork with a pudding served afterwards. Tea at 7.00pm was yet more bread and butter.[20]

The ethos of the school very much demonstrated the link between a healthy mind and healthy body and there was plenty on offer to engage those that were inclined. Rambles in the surrounding countryside were a regular occurrence in which the boys had an opportunity to learn about flora and fauna.[21] All manner of physical activities were encouraged, there was a football club which had formed in 1869 as well as other sports such as athletics, fencing and swimming instruction undertaken, presumably in the local river. During the winter months, more sedate indoor activities could be enjoyed including games such as chess and draughts. Advertisements in The School Gazette of 1869 show hobbies were catered for too including private circulating libraries providing all kinds of literature, stamp exchange and a mathematical society run by Dr. Clark as well as an elocution society.[22]

It is not known how Tommy progressed at school and the records have not survived, but later on in life, he was not remembered as someone particularly academically gifted. Future generations would recall that he definitely suffered from what would be termed over one hundred years later as learning difficulties, for he was not regarded as bright as his younger brothers.

A photograph of Tommy may have been taken on his 21st birthday in 1887 just like his own Papa had one taken in a studio for his own

Fig 49. Tommy as a young adult circa 1887.

in 1862. In this, he appears to have retained his fair hair and piercing eyes. The fair hair was an unusual characteristic as nearly all of his siblings had inherited darker hair from their parents.

By this time, Tommy would have been expected to have joined his Papa and Grandpapa in the City as a broker. Due to Tommy's ineptitude, this probably was not an option even though it may have been encouraged initially. However, in the 1891 census, when the family are all together again at Devonia, Queen's Road, Leyton, his occupation is that of mercantile clerk, rather than a broker so perhaps he was helping out in the business at this time.[23]

By late 1894, Tommy had met a young lady named Rose Carter and on 31 August 1895, they married at Edmonton Register Office.[24] Rose was eight months pregnant and their son, Thomas John William was born on 29 September.[25] On the marriage certificate, Tommy is described as having the profession of stockbroker. This is rather puzzling because his father is clearly stated as being a colonial broker on the same document. There is a clear distinction between a stockbroker (someone who manages a financial portfolio for clients) and a colonial broker (one who acts as an intermediary in selling produce). One explanation could be that his Papa had given him the task of handling the stocks and shares the family had inherited from Tom's father who had died in March 1895. However, the will had not been proved until July, so it is a possibility but really impossible to know. Tommy stated that he was residing at 69 Poynton Road, Tottenham, at the time of his marriage, the same location as that of Rose.

The marriage and the circumstances in which Tommy found himself did almost certainly not meet with Papa's approval but given that Rose Carter was pregnant, Tommy had to do the honourable thing and make sure his child was born in wedlock. Tommy and Rose produced two more children after Thomas. On 24 November 1896, their daughter Mabel Eveline Janet was born at 62 Bailey's Lane, Tottenham. At this date, Tommy is described as being a commercial clerk, certainly not a broker of any variety.[26]

On 24 August 1898, their son Leonard Albert was born at Walthamstow.[27] However, by this date the short disastrous marriage was over. Rose took the unusual step for a woman at this time – she left her husband. Perhaps this took place before Leonard's birth or if not, shortly after. At the time of the 1901 census, Rose Clark is living with her three children at 108 Leigh Road, Walthamstow. The stigma of separation is tangible as she falsely states she is a widow. She is not able to state anything different. To write on the form that she is single would be shocking for a woman with children and, as she is still married, it would be a lie too. To say she is a widow is much more respectable. Divorce at the turn of the 20th century was still hard and costly to obtain. Rose is just 24 years old and working as a dressmaker at home to support herself and her children.[28] Possibly Tommy sent her money to supplement her no doubt meagre income.

It is not known if Tommy ever saw or had contact with his children again. His whereabouts around 1901 are also unknown. How different his life had turned out from his own father, Tom, who enjoyed such a happy marriage and comfortable life surrounded by luxury by his age. Edith Hawkins, a niece of Herbert's wife Edith Reader, recalled as an elderly lady in the mid-1990s that 'Tom went to live in Clifton Avenue, off Pound Lane, with his father' following his 'divorce' from Rose. Indeed, in 1911, Tom appears in the census living with his Pa at Clifton Road, Bowers Gifford and Pa provides his status and occupation as a married fruit salesman.[29] In the meantime, his wife Rose had found a new man. She set up home at 25 Ashford Road, Walthamstow with Alfred Moss, a mason, taking her three children with her. Alfred Moss states that they are married and have had a total of six children, two of whom have died. Tommy's eldest son (Thomas John) with the name Thomas dropped perhaps to distance himself from his absent father, is known as 'John' and working as a French polisher at the age of 15. The three children now have a half-brother Alfred.[30] Rose and Alfred Moss did not marry until 11 April 1914; however, their union was almost certainly bigamous as there is no record of a divorce between Rose and Tommy.[31]

If Tommy's own marriage and family life became one of separation and alienation, he was affectionately remembered by the families of some of his siblings. Maurice Wood, who married Barbara Palmer (daughter of Beatrice) in 1937, reminisced about Tommy describing him as an 'entertaining personality' when as a young man, Maurice was getting to know Barbara's family at the time. Recalling visits made by Tommy to Ilford and the Palmer family home, Maurice recalled:

> *He used to turn up and was always keen to demonstrate how strong he was (goaded on by three giggling girls)* [Barbara and her two sisters] *and used to wrap a hankie round the back of a dining room chair and lift it up with his teeth. He was getting on a bit, but I was told not to applaud until he turned from pink to red, and then on to purple. It was at the purple stage one clapped, while others grabbed him to save him falling whilst still giddy.[32]*

Herbert's daughter, Marjorie, also remembered her Uncle Tom paying a visit to Old Buckenham during the 1930s. Her childhood recollection was of a slightly overweight man who was kindly and took an interest in her colouring book and pencils.

Uncle Tommy was evidently unable to look after himself later on and the memory of Eunice Bridge, née Croisette, (Herbert and Edith's grand-daughter) born in 1918, was that:

> *Uncle Tom lived rough at times in a tent etc. I knew him when he had a little house or room in Benfleet. My mother* [Winifred] *and grandma* [Edith] *used to keep him clean and get food for him*[33].

In spite of his unconventional lifestyle, Tommy lived to his eightieth year and perhaps it is worth remembering him at this point, as that small child back in 1872 when he entertained his aunt Matilda during a thunderstorm through all the years to the 1930s when he continued to entertain his own nieces.

Tommy died on 28 April 1947 at Southend Municipal Hospital, Rochford.[34] His sister Beatrice gave the details of his passing to the registrar and his address as Gibbold Brook Road, South Benfleet and his occupation – formerly a nurseryman. The cause of death was stated as cardiac failure and arteriosclerosis; he was later buried at South Benfleet.[35]

Chapter 2

ERNEST PERCIVAL
FREDERICK CLARK

---

5 March 1868 – 28 October 1938

*Little Percy fell down on the steps and cut his head very badly
and he lost a great deal of blood. The doctor when he came sewed
it up. He was a brave little fellow and never cried even when the
needle went through or when the stitch was taken out.*
(Matilda Clark, Percy's aunt – June 1872)

A lthough named Ernest Percival, it seems that the young child
was named 'Percy' early on by his family; perhaps they felt
it suited him better than Ernest, rather a formal name for a
child.

Percy was born on 5 March 1868 at Clarendon House, Coburg
Road, Camberwell.[1] This was a residence associated with his mother's
family. Her father's brother-in-law Charles Vizer was living here at
the time of the 1861 census whilst his relatives, the Baileys, lived next
door.[2] Young Percy probably did not live here long enough to form
any memories of the house or the locality. By 1871, he was living at

Claremont House, Brighton Road, Sutton, with his parents and older brother.[3] Here, the youngsters had a nursery maid to help care for them at the time of the census that year and by the end of the year, the two boys had a new brother, Herbert.

Matilda, Tom's sister, recorded in her diary in 1872 that four-year-old Percy had a serious accident at Claremont whilst she was staying with the family.

1st June 1872

Little Percy fell down on the steps and cut his head very badly and he lost a great deal of blood. The doctor when he came sewed it up. He was a brave little fellow and never cried even when the needle went through or when the stitch was taken out. Two days afterwards, we were all in a great way about him and two or three days after, he fell upon the same place in the nursery and made his head bleed.[4]

Photographs of Percy as a child depict him already with a debonair air about him for which he would become strongly associated. Also perhaps, he was a precocious child very unlike his brother Tommy.

Fig 50. Percy circa 1878.

Fig 51. Percy was a model pupil.

He was very likely academically gifted and studious. Photographic images show him intently looking at books to highlight his love for learning. No doubt Papa and Grandpapa were pleased with his progress and looked forward to the day when he would use his mind to assist in the family business and join their ranks as a broker.

Like his brother Tommy, he joined Ongar Academy as a boarder and he was a member of the Cadet Corps at the school. Another photograph shows him in the distinctive costume of the Cadet Corps which actually looked quite French. Family myth in the 20th century had it that Percy was educated in 'Onge, France'![5] However, it was subsequently discovered to be somewhere not quite so exotic – Chipping Ongar, Essex. Formed from 1860, the Cadet Corps was an organised expression of the ideals of discipline as well as development and corporate spirit. The 1875 school prospectus stated that participation was optional but encouraged as it '...advised as being producive [sic] of great benefits'.[6] It was clearly something to which Percy was proud to belong. His photograph portrays him in the uniform that was considered every day for participating pupils, for the second best suit of essential clothing required on entry could be used to join the Cadet Corps which should consist of tunic, trousers, shako and belt.[7]

Whilst at the Academy, Percy would have learnt languages amongst all the other subjects considered appropriate for sons of men in business and commerce. Also he would have rubbed shoulders with other students, some of whom may have been foreign nationals.

Percy's grandson Robert later recalled hearing tales that his grandfather had been taken to Grandpapa's warehouses (most likely in the 1870s or 1880s) which were stacked with ivory and animal skins, an outing which evidently left a strong impression on him.

By the late 1870s, Percy, his parents and siblings had moved to Tottenham, North London. There would have been easy access to the school by railway from here, the line to Ongar having opened

(Left) Fig 52. Percy wearing the Cadet Corps uniform of Ongar Academy circa 1880. (Right) Fig 53. A suave young man circa 1885.

in 1865. Robert reported hearing that some kind of financial crash had occurred causing loss of income for the family and instead of the career he had hoped for, by around 1890, Percy was working for the Midland Bank in the City of London. The 1891 census of all the family together for the last time at Devonia, Queen's Road, Leyton, shows this to be the case as Percy's occupation is bank clerk.[8]

Percy had to work to provide income for himself but like some of his other brothers and cousins he had a great love of photography which turned out to be a life-long passion in his case. Percy inherited the artistic side of the family as he also painted and played piano. The young child turned into a tall and distinguished looking man sporting a fashionable moustache in the 1890s and beyond. He also demonstrated he was more careful than his younger brother Herbert who married at the youthful age of 21 and he was not going to rush into marriage.

Percy married Gertrude Susie Clarke on 14 August 1900 at St. Botolph Bishopgate, in the City of London.[9] He was then 32 whilst his wife was just 23. His base before the ceremony was the family home 27 Springfield, Clapton, whilst Miss Clarke lived in the neighbouring parish of Waltham Cross. Her father was a respectable farmer, gent and employer so the marriage must have been perfectly acceptable to Papa. It was a coincidence that the couple both had the same surname – they were not related. Moreover, they were both known by their second names. After the marriage the couple settled in the town of Cheshunt, Hertfordshire, which was just twelve miles north of central London and located in the peaceful and lush Lea valley.

In the 1901 census, the couple are together at their home named Pevensey situated in the road Churchgate, so called as it was located near to St. Mary's church.[10] Percy was occupied as a bank clerk, undoubtedly leaving Churchgate and commuting daily into the City by train. Their neighbours – at Hillside were Charles Eglington, a 39-year-old man living on his own means who had been born in Islington, with his wife Emily (27) and two children, whilst at 3 Pengelly Terrace were Arthur Vince, a 31-year-old worker at the Royal

Fig 54. Percy's portrait at the turn of the 20th century.

Small Arms Factory with his wife, 31-year-old Annie, their daughter and his brother-in-law and wife.[11]

On 24 April 1904, Susie Clark gave birth to their first and only child, a son whom they named Stanley Randell. The name Randell was used to perpetuate the surname of Susie's maternal grandparents, John and Kezia. However they were not happy or settled on their boy's first name and it was changed to Maurice by the time it was registered on 2nd June.[12]

By 1908 the family had moved to a new address in Cheshunt, a house named Vista in Albury Ride.[13] The north side of Albury Ride was a new development of the late 19th century and was built as an access road to Theobald's Estates.[14] On census night 2 April 1911, the family is still at this address and Percy remains working as a bank clerk. His income was sufficient enough to afford the services of a live-in 16-year-old general domestic servant, May Frost, born locally in Edmonton.[15]

By 1912, the family had moved from Cheshunt to 146 Crossbrook Street in neighbouring Waltham Cross. Percy's grandson, Robert, takes up the story:

The family continued living at Waltham Cross into the First World War days. My father used to tell me a story about his father. Percy was issued with a revolver by the bank he worked for as a manager. There was a heavy Zeppelin bombing raid and my grandfather recognised that street lighting was acting as a target so he went out and shot out the street lights near their house. Their maid named May happened to be the local policeman's daughter and there was some embarrassment as he had to arrest my grandfather for vandalism or whatever the charge was. Once the authorities realised he was correct in creating a 'black out' he was of course exonerated.

Whilst living at Waltham Cross, my father witnessed the aftermath of the first Zeppelin being shot down as it crashed quite near them in a local park. My grandfather took my father with him to see what was happening, apparently there were burning bodies hanging from trees, the sight and smell which made a terrible impression which stayed with him all his life.[16]

This incident refers to the shooting down of a German Schutte-Lanz SL11 airship during the night of 3 September 1916. The ship had taken off near Cologne with 16 men on board with its mission to bomb London. The ship, as it flew over Enfield that night, was shot down by Lt. William Leef Robinson firing incendiary ammunition from his BE2c aircraft. The ship crashed at Cuffley, Hertfordshire, and illuminated the sky for miles around and as the stricken vessel broke up, it rained bodies and debris. All 16 men on board died and it was widely recorded that people descended on the crash site to see the burnt out remains in their droves.[17] It must have so happened that Maurice accompanied his father Percy and formed a part of these vast crowds.

As the blazing wreckage of SL11 slowly fell to earth in a field in Cuffley, before it even reached the ground, London was celebrating in a boisterous fashion; long before dawn hundreds of sightseers set out for Cuffley to view the wreckage. Over the next two days 10,000 people travelled to the tiny village. Special trains were laid on from Kings Cross and extra ticket collectors were sent to the village station to help deal with the crowds. The Plough Inn nearby had sold everything that could be eaten or drunk and had to bolt its doors to keep the crowds out. The field in which the airship lay was turned into a quagmire as thousands of boots tramped through the wet soil. The roads leading to the site were jammed with cars. Police and troops were called in to control the crowds. There was a scramble for souvenirs, even though keeping pieces of an airship was a punishable offence. There was also much morbid curiosity over the charred bodies of the German crew.[18]

Robert continues the narrative of the Clark family of three:

Not long after this, Maurice and Susie [Percy's wife] moved to Torquay to escape the bombing leaving Percy behind in London. My father was then enrolled in Torquay Grammar School.

After the War ended, my grandfather was transferred to work at the Midland Bank in Dawlish, Devon and the family were reunited. Whilst living there, Percy arranged for my father to be given an engineering apprenticeship with the Dawlish Electric Light Company starting from October 1922. After completing his apprenticeship, the family moved back to London. Maurice was then employed at Selfridges in the electrical department. In 1927 he witnessed the Welsh miners marching and being broken up by mounted police from the roof of Selfridges.

Maurice my father hated living in London and longed to go back to the south-west. Then, for whatever reason, my grandmother [Susie] and my father left London to live at St. Austell, Cornwall. My father joined the St. Austell Electric Light Company which was owned by the engineer whom my father had been apprenticed to at Dawlish. He built a bungalow at St. Austell where he lived with Susie. After this, they moved back to Torquay. My father then designed and built an all-electric house named Suncourt and my father lived there with his mother until he married my mother [in 1939].

Percy had not accompanied his wife and son back to Cornwall but remained in London which inevitably led to a separation from that time onwards.

My grandmother Susie basically forbade my father to keep in contact with his father. She was a very domineering character and I think my father was terrified of her and very much under her thumb. She believed her only son's duty was to look after his mother. There was a huge bitterness on my grandmother's part towards my grandfather. Of the little correspondence from my grandfather, he sounds a very kind man.

Before retirement between 1925 and 1930 Percy's address was 22 Shirehall Park, Hendon.[19] In 1930, Percy turned 62 and thoughts turned to retirement from life at the Midland Bank. Due to the estrangement from his wife and son, Percy's concern for his future years perhaps focused on the companionship of his brother Herbert to whom he had been particularly close. Herbert had moved to the village of Old Buckenham in Norfolk during the 1920s after the breakdown of his own marriage to Edith. There, Herbert had taken on a successful business serving the local community as the proprietor of a general shop where he also carried out cycle repairs and sold petrol.

A house named Sunnyside Villa became vacant immediately next to the shop and Percy took up residence. Old Buckenham was an attractive village with an exceptionally large green and was a restful setting for someone retiring from city life.

Herbert's daughter Marjorie later on held clear recollections of Percy during her childhood in 1930s and her memories were recorded of those times.

The two houses were separated by a fairly large garden belonging to us and a garden path between the two residences brought Percy into our home where he would enjoy meals cooked by Elsie [Herbert's wife]. Percy enjoyed his food and had quite an appetite because he finished eating not long after everyone else had started! Elsie would exclaim 'where is your meal, Percy?' in surprise that it had been consumed so speedily, and he replied 'I've eaten and enjoyed every bit of it!'

Fig 55. Percy (far left) with Elsie, Marjorie & Herbert at Great Yarmouth, circa 1930.

Percy was a motor car enthusiast and he was always working on his car. Any watch he owned was never kept for long as something always seemed to go wrong with them.

Percy dressed very smartly and wore trilby hats. He loved socialising and did quite a bit of this in the community. He became friendly with the Beales family who lived adjoining the old village school in Church Lane. They had a daughter, Alma, and were regulars at The White Horse public house not far from the shop and were a very working class family. Mrs. Iris Beales was recalled as being an excellent cook.

Percy was also acquainted with another girl Stella Gedge, who also lived in Church Lane close to the Beales family. Percy would take her out for rides in his car and like the Bealeses the Gedges were an ordinary working class family.[20] He used to take Mrs. Petley out sometimes too.

Then there was the occasion when he raided the box of face masks kept at our home, put one on and walked up the road near the pond to meet someone off the bus to give them a nice surprise!

Percy's personality is revealed as gregarious and he craved for and loved company, especially female but also he indulged in many hobbies including photography, cars and gadgets. In addition, he enjoyed gardening and was remembered for growing lovely sweet peas for which he won awards.

Marjorie remembered her uncle going away for days at a time and was aware he liked to visit Dawlish in Devon. He took his young nieces Eileen, Grace and Barbara Palmer with him on these trips which probably took place during the 1930s following his retirement. Seemingly, he had an ulterior motive for requesting their company, as retold later by Barbara's husband, Maurice Wood:

> *He was a very keen photographer and had a huge camera, stand, boxes of lenses and he used to take the three girls on holiday to Devon, mainly so they could carry all the equipment. I know 'Bar' said they walked miles and were worn out at the end of the day, carrying all that equipment. There was a bioscope and glass covered negatives at Green Lane of those holidays.*
>
> *I met Percy on several occasions and found him an entertaining personality.[21]*

Marjorie recalled too, like her older cousins whom he took to Devon, that he was an excellent photographer and took portraits of her and Elsie. She remembered the seriousness of the occasion, with Percy donning a cloth over his head and shoulders whilst the task was performed inside his living room. Whilst there having her portrait snapped, Marjorie admired his art work which adorned the walls and the piano too, indicating his artistic leanings like so many of his close relatives. She could not recall ever hearing him play the instrument though. Marjorie was the recipient of gifts given by her uncle including some pencils bearing her name. Even as a child, she perceived that Percy loved life, he was so full of enthusiasm for many subjects and he loved living life to the full. One day, whilst out driving with Mrs. Petley, he became unwell and it turned out to be a mini-stroke. Mrs.

Fig 56. Percy's son Maurice.

Petley was concerned about him and the fact that he had been driving at the time.

On 5 March 1938, Percy turned 70. Sometime that year, he retold a story to his relatives next door of a strange experience he had in the early hours of the morning. He was awoken by loud knocks at his front door, he went downstairs, unlocked the door, looked outside but no one seemed to be there. He remarked 'If anything should happen to me, remember this'. Perhaps it was because he had already suffered a mini-stroke that made him think about his own mortality but his thoughts clearly were that this was a premonition that the 'grim reaper' had knocked to call him away from the world he loved.

In the second half of October, Percy suffered a severe stroke and was brought into Herbert's home at the shop next-door, where he was cared for by Elsie; a week later he passed away. Just before all this happened, he had a photography commission from Mr. Twiddy, the headmaster of Old Buckenham Area School, to take several photographs of the harvest festival celebration when the stage at school was laden with fruit and vegetables. He did take the photographs, but Marjorie wondered what happened to them as she never saw the finished work.

Percy died on 28 October 1938 and he was buried in the tranquillity of Old Buckenham churchyard alongside the left of the grassed path edge which ran parallel with the north side of the church. Percy's son Maurice came up from Devon to attend his father's funeral. He was smartly dressed, like his father, and arrived in a raincoat. He thanked Elsie most profusely for the care she had given to his father and then he departed to take up his life again in Devon.[22]

Percy had made his will on the 5 September 1935 at Old Buckenham.[23] He appointed his sister-in-law, Elsie, as his executor and legacies were given to her, his son Maurice and his brothers Walter and Bertie. It was his wish that his home at Old Buckenham should be sold or auctioned along with his possessions including his car, furniture, lathe, tools and photographic apparatus and the proceeds to be joined to the one hundred pounds from his life policy.

Fig 57. Percy riding a bicycle, probably built by his brother Herbert, who is seated at the front with their brother Bertie, at Pound Lane, Bowers Gifford, circa 1910. A closer inspection of the window behind Bertie reveals the face of a young girl, probably that of Herbert's daughter, Violet.

The residue after the legacies, debts and funeral expenses had been settled should be divided equally between his brothers Herbert and Thomas and his sister Beatrice, indicating where his loyalties lay. His older brother Thomas had been his companion through school days at Ongar and undoubtedly was seen as a vulnerable character by his brother.

On 2 December 1938, probate was granted at Norwich.

Chapter 3

HERBERT LIONEL
ALEXANDER CLARK

---

4 December 1871-20 March 1955

I can see him serving petrol holding hat or mac in gusty wind
or sitting in the chair discussing politics or worldly scene and
in the mornings not in bed asleep or waking from a dream but
looking after car or wireless batteries in garage or shed out back
always busy, always active, never ever slack.
(Marjorie Walshe nee Westfield 'Dad' 1976)

erbert, the third son of Thomas Clark and Frances was born on Monday 4 December 1871.[1] He was a baby of a few months old when the diary was written by his aunt Matilda, his father's sister, who was a regular visitor to his birthplace, Claremont House, Brighton Road, Sutton. She stayed there during the spring of 1872 and she would have assisted Fanny in Herbert's childcare.

He would join his two elder brothers, Tommy and Percy, in the nursery at their home. Photographs of young Herbert show him to be often wearing a cheeky expression and sporting tousled curly

Fig 58. A young Herbert, circa 1876.

hair. These curls he would retain all his life, as his daughter Marjorie recalled that as a child, she would curl his hair around her pencil.

His formative years would have been spent at Sutton in the two separate addresses they were known to have lived at. After 1876, the family moved to Tottenham and Herbert was living at 2 Lansdowne Road at the time of the 1881 census when he was 9 years old. Both of his older brothers were away at Ongar Academy as boarders.

It is assumed, although by no means certain, that Herbert also went on to school at Ongar during the 1880s. There are no records in existence which reveal that he was educated here. Indeed, family lore held that Herbert may have been sent to school in France, merely on the strength that he could speak a little French, and notably, a tale he told Marjorie, that he had got into a fight with a French boy at school. As a punishment, he had to hold a steak over the pupil's swollen black eye, an old remedy for this type of injury – it was believed to reduce swelling. However, it could well have been the case that there was a French pupil at Ongar Academy as the school had students who

(Left) Fig 59. Herbert in a sailor suit, circa 1883.
(Right) Fig 60. Herbert lying on the grass with his mother, Frances to his
right. The identity of all the other people in this image is unknown. It
is a possibility that the other lady is Frances' elder sister, Jane.

joined not only from all parts of the British Isles, but occasionally from overseas.

At the age of 19 at the time of the 1891 census, Herbert was employed like his two brothers in the commercial world as a merchant's clerk[2]. He could well have been working in the family business. However, just over two years later, Herbert married the family servant Edith Reader, a 17-year-old labourer's daughter. This probably did not go down well with Papa who would have hoped and expected that due to his son's middle-class status and excellent private education, he would aspire to marry a young lady of equal background.

Herbert would always do things his own way and the rather cheeky young lad grew to adulthood, not it would seem, with any great aspirations in mind. Here was a young man who was a combination of many facets of his family. He was deeply cultured but also very practical, interested in technology and innovations of the day. Times had changed since his Grandpapa's day; he was considered a gentleman because he worked in an office, not as a manual worker. Young Herbert enjoyed using his hands in a practical way as well as his mind. Alongside the working-classes, Herbert enjoyed going to the theatre sometimes, especially the Music Hall and perhaps he saw Marie Lloyd and Vesta Tilly amongst other popular artistes of the era.[3]

Marriage and Family Life

Upon his marriage to Edith on 4 September 1893, his occupation was described as a photographer. It is not known where the couple lived immediately after their controversial marriage. Their first daughter, Violet Frances Dorothy, was born on 7 February 1895 at West Ham and she was baptised on 10 March at Holy Trinity, Harrow Green.[4]

Another daughter followed, Winifred Edith, born on 6 October 1896, also at West Ham.[5] However, it would seem that Winnie did not follow her sister to the baptismal font as a baby. She was not baptised until she was 16 years old; perhaps an indication of Herbert's lifelong aversion to infant baptism and in that, he was influenced by the non-

Fig 61. Possibly Herbert's 1893 wedding portrait.

conformity of his father Tom who disapproved and had none of his own children christened.

At the turn of the 20th century, Herbert moved out of London to the countryside and settled in Bowers Gifford, a village in south Essex close to modern day Basildon. His youngest daughter, Doris, was born here in February 1900 and the 1901 census confirms his address of Clifton Road New Estate.[6] Herbert had purchased a plot of land on which his new residence with six rooms had recently been completed.[7] Herbert himself may have had a hand in building his home.

Herbert was still a self-employed photographer whilst Edith too was an enterprising new woman of the fresh Edwardian era – a married woman with an occupation as a provisions dealer, which was a job to run alongside raising her three young daughters. Herbert's brother, Walter, was staying on census night and describes his occupation as a photographic traveller, perhaps indicating that they worked as partners in this venture.

The three girls went to school locally at North Benfleet and probably all left by the time they were 14 years, which was the age at which education finished at this time. The school log book makes reference to daily life at the school and contains remarks made by the teachers about the 'Westfield' sisters.

> *June 19, 1905 Winnie Westfield absent.*
> *February 17, 1908 Violet Westfield has left the school.*
> *June 25, 1909 Winnie Westfield is in London.*
> *July 16, 1909 Winnie Westfield is still away in London.*
> *July 20, 1909 Winnie Westfield has returned to school.*
> *May 27, 1910 Doris Westfield has left this school, she is 10 years of age and attending no school.*[8]

Although the 1901 census describes Edith as a provisions dealer, it seems likely that whilst working as a photographer, Herbert was actually engaged in several other occupations to forge a successful standard of living. In the 1902 school register for his two eldest girls, he is described as a shop keeper whilst in a 1908 trade directory as a grocer.[9] By 1910, he has picked up another job as an assistant overseer.[10] Nevertheless, he and Edith were working jointly as shop keepers in Bowers Gifford. Winnie's daughter Eunice later recalled that the family were purchasing and eating food containing spices like ginger and other exotic produce which was very new to people at the time but perhaps accessible to a provisions dealer.[11]

Apart from holding a variety of jobs, Herbert had several hobbies. As an engineer, he was keen on new technologies and transport models and he built his own bicycles and motorised vehicles. Three surviving photographs, taken circa 1910 outside the family home, show some examples of his engineering work. What is clear is that Herbert very much liked the freedom of being his own boss and largely was a self-employed man his entire working life.

In the 1911 census, Herbert is described as both a shop keeper and grocer whilst his wife apparently does not have an occupation.[12] Eldest daughter Violet has left the family home and his treading the same path

Fig 62. Win and Doris (front), Edith at the wheel and a moody-looking Violet, pictured on one of Herbert's motorised vehicles outside their home at Bowers Gifford, circa 1910.

as her mother did 20 years earlier in the same neighbourhood; she is a 16-year-old domestic servant for John and Mary Ann Hawkins at Leytonstone.[13] It was rather ironic that just a short time ago, Herbert's family were employing servants and now they had family members who needed to work in this sphere themselves! It could be that this couple were relatives in Edith's family, as the girls had cousins on her side of the family with this surname.

The arrangement may have been amenable to all parties. John and Mary Ann Hawkins, 64 and 59 respectively had help around the home, Violet had gainful employment and the rest of the family had a daughter who was making her own way leaving them with more room at home. Middle daughter Winnie, then 14, had probably left education whilst Doris, 11, had either returned to North Benfleet school to continue her education or joined another school.

Three other members of the family were also staying at the time of the 1911 census. Herbert's brother Bertie had tragically lost his wife Ethel just two years earlier leaving their two young daughters, Rita and Muriel, motherless. Bertie had remained in London to stay in employment and had to pass the girls on to relatives. Six-year-old Rita is either visiting or staying on census night. Also in residence at Clifton Road, were Edmund and Louisa Palmer, the parents of Herbert's brother-in-law, Ted Palmer. The 1910 electoral roll reveals that Edmund Palmer was renting two unfurnished ground floor rooms from Herbert at his Clifton Road house. It is not clear whether the rental was done by the senior or junior Palmer. The family had a musical instrument business and father and son were piano tuners. As Herbert himself was an accomplished pianist with a wide classical repertoire, the families had much in common.

The First World War

With the outbreak of the Great War in September 1914, Herbert was probably relieved that at 42, he was considered too old to volunteer.

However, once conscription was introduced in 1916 to satisfy the demand for more men at the Front, the age was raised to 51, thus meaning that unless Herbert was engaged in essential work on the Home Front, he was at risk of being drafted.

Herbert was invited to attend a medical as a preliminary to being conscripted and the doctor asked him if there was 'anything else we ought to know about you?' Herbert replied 'yes, I've had an epileptic fit'. This of course disqualified him straightaway. It would appear that earlier on, he had been working on his car and thought he had been overcome by fumes but the doctor who attended him diagnosed an epileptic fit, though Herbert was sceptical about this. However, it came in extremely useful and stopped him moving towards the Western Front. He told his daughter Marjorie of this brush with the military life decades on and as he recalled the incident, it was his view that being over 40, he knew of some younger men who hadn't joined up to 'do their bit' so he thought, why should I.

Another aspect of the War that he must have been grateful for was that his children were all female and although his two eldest were contemporaries of many young men facing the horrors of the trenches, his girls were at least safe. In fact, Winifred was lucky to be alive at this time as Herbert had saved her from drowning head down in a water butt and found her just in time to pull her out during her childhood years.[14]

During these turbulent years of war, both Violet and Winifred married but fortunately their husbands seem to have escaped active service although they were of prime age. Violet married Harold Rand at St. Margaret of Antioch church, Bowers Gifford, on Saturday 1 July 1916.[15] It was a beautiful summer's day but the date would go down in history as the bloodiest day of the Great War for the British Army. It was the first day of the Battle of the Somme and whilst the young couple were celebrating their wedding in south Essex, slaughter on a massive scale was taking place across the Thames estuary. Violet and Harold's youngest son, Laurie, later

Fig 63. Violet Clark-Westfield married Harold Rand on 1 July 1916, the first day of the Battle of the Somme.

recalled how the wedding party heard the thud of the guns and no doubt the explosion of the mine under the German lines which launched the battle at 7.30 that morning as the awful noise drifted across the water.[16]

Harold Rand was a market gardener and due to his involvement in food production, which was considered an essential job at home, he was not sent to the battlefields. It could have been that the couple met through Harold supplying fresh produce for Herbert and Edith to sell at their shop or market stall which Herbert ran at Vange or Pitsea.

Young Winifred followed her sister, to marry in October 1916 but not at St. Margaret's church. Instead, this took place at St. Mary the Virgin, South Benfleet, when she wed Alfred Marc Croisette, nine years her senior.[17] Known as Mark, he was a draper by trade and came from French Huguenot descent having been born in Brixton.

Both girls' wedding photographs show them in wartime austerity attired in white plain dresses.

Fig 64. Winifred Clark-Westfield married Mark Croisette in October 1916.

The end of his marriage and the move to Norfolk

In the years after the War, Herbert continued diversifying his jobs having now taken on a new employment as a cycle agent in Vange and Pitsea.[18] He told Marjorie that he worked as a postman for a while and had the usual trouble with dogs! He is also known to have managed an ice-skating rink in the Southend area; perhaps it was here his path crossed that of some young ladies. Herbert always had a wandering eye for an attractive lady and in 1923 he had been married to Edith for 30 years. It was around this time that his youngest daughter, Doris, may have introduced him to a friend of hers – or it was also possible that they met entirely independently. Grace Emily Hilton was a smartly dressed young lady who was born in Westcliff-on-Sea, Essex, in 1904 and was therefore four years younger than his youngest daughter Doris.[19]

Herbert fell for Grace and they embarked on an affair which brought his marriage to an end. Before the close of 1923, Herbert had

Fig 65. Doris and Grace Hilton, dressed as Pierot and Pierette, the French clowns, circa 1923.

left his home and family and had moved north to the small village of Old Buckenham in south Norfolk. He had seen (perhaps advertised in the paper) that the old reading room was up for sale and he saw a business opportunity to convert it to a shop and garage. He was already established in Norfolk by that year as his name appeared in the local press for an offence that autumn.

Attleborough Petty Sessions – Monday
Before Lord Albermarle (chairman), Messrs. W.B. Colman and H. Phoenix.

Herbert Clark WESTFIELD, shopkeeper, Old Buckenham, was summoned for driving a motor-cycle without a licence. – Defendant pleaded guilty, but said he had not needed the cycle for some time, and had sent the money for the licence the day before he was stopped by the police. – The magistrates' Clerk said the money was not received until the 28th, the day after he was stopped, and pointed out that the licence had run out over eighteen months. – Defendant was fined 3/6.[20]

In 1925, Edith took advantage of new divorce laws which empowered women to divorce their husbands on the grounds of adultery and she took Herbert to court that year whilst retaining control of the businesses that they jointly held in Essex.[21] This ultimately led to Herbert becoming bankrupt. His daughter Doris, Doris' husband Harold White and Grace, all then moved into the shop at Old Buckenham. Herbert's father, Tom, also came to stay at Old Buckenham but this was challenged by the young ladies who resented the old man's presence. They both insisted that if Pa did not leave, they would![22]

Grace became pregnant with Herbert's child in the snowy winter of late 1925 and their daughter arrived in the hot weather of the following late August.[23] Pa died in a home in Leytonstone in January 1927 a situation that caused Herbert both grief and remorse. Doris (his daughter) left the shop, and so did Grace in 1928, the latter to embark on a new life in Canada but that is another story.

Westfield's Stores, Old Buckenham

After Grace's departure, Herbert advertised for a housekeeper to help him keep the business afloat and to assist in raising his daughter. Elsie May Cubitt was the successful candidate. A Norfolk lady, born at Scotow near North Walsham in 1899, she had spent the preceding years in service in London prior to taking up the post with Herbert. She had known hard times as two of her brothers had been killed in the Great War. She helped him get back on his feet financially as well as emotionally and they married in 1930. Elsie was possibly not the type of woman that Herbert would have found physically attractive but the marriage was perhaps based on convenience and social respectability more than love. Herbert undoubtedly respected and admired Elsie for her business capabilities and tough demeanour.

During almost 30 years, Herbert built up a successful business in Old Buckenham serving the community with a general shop, petrol and cycle repairs. He may well have been one of the pioneers in Norfolk supplying the public with fuel for the first motor cars on these country roads (an Old Buckenham resident described him as 'the first man in Norfolk to sell petrol' although this cannot be qualified). Locals knew him as Mr. Westfield.

One such local was John Loveday who was born the same year as Marjorie. The Loveday family were well known in Old Buckenham and John, recalling his childhood in the 21st century, said that Herbert was secretly known as 'Wiggy' Westfield to him and his pals as they had heard that he wore a toupee! John admitted to having little knowledge of the elusive 'Wiggy' because 'he was always at work, hidden his garage, only coming out at the occasional pulling up of a car beside his petrol pump.'[24] The boys were, however, grateful for his shop where they would purchase sweets, batteries or cigarettes and tobacco for

Fig 66. Pencil drawing of the shop and garage at
The Green, Old Buckenham in 1947 by Maurice Large.

their parents, and were served by Elsie or Marjorie. In a poem written in the 1970s, Marjorie would also recollect the industrious nature of her father – *always busy, always active, never ever slack.*

The narrative of Herbert's life will end here in the 1930s. His daughter Marjorie's voice will now dominate with her reminiscences of her father, encompassing all aspects of his life: his personality, his likes and dislikes, his views on religion and philosophy of life. This offers a unique window into the soul of a man who was extremely knowledgeable, well-read, cultured, thoughtful and sensitive.

Reminiscences of Herbert from his daughter

"When the old woman sneezed, everyone paid attention"

These words were spoken by Herbert concerning Queen Victoria, and as he was 29-years-old when she died in 1901, he grew up in a world dominated by her presence and influence.

He was a Victorian and held middle-class views about politics and society. Marjorie described her Dad as 'an out-and-out Tory' who was very interested in politics and the world scene. He always came down hard on the Labour Party and he read that well-known Tory tabloid, The Daily Express, daily, for many years. He held a great admiration for Winston Churchill and was very upset when he lost the election following the war.

Herbert was a man of his time and was born into a Great Britain that was the head, and at the height, of the Empire and he had no sympathy for the cause of Irish independence that raged at the time of the Great War and afterwards. He thought the Irish dissident Eamon de Valera 'should have hung' but because he was an American national, he was spared. Herbert felt that the Irish had always 'been a prick and thorn in our side' which was a biblical quotation (Numbers 33:55). He believed that the whole question of Irish independence was being raised because the south wanted to benefit from the industrious and prosperous north.

Herbert's dim view of the Irish cause may have had its roots back in his youth of the 1880s when he would have been aware of the Fenian bombing campaign orchestrated by Republicans against the British Empire from 1881-85. Many prominent London landmarks were targeted including the Mansion House twice; in March 1881 a bomb was diffused and just over a year later a bomb actually exploded. No doubt the campaign of violence was reviled by Herbert's Papa Tom who as a city merchant attended the annual Lord Mayor's banquet at Mansion House. Bombs were also planted at other locations in the City including Whitehall, the offices of *The Times* newspaper and the London Underground, leading to 70 people being injured at Paddington.

Later on, at the time of the Second World War, he distrusted the Russians as much as the Germans declaring, 'It would be a good thing if the Russians and Germans fought each other until both were beaten'.

A more compassionate side of Herbert's nature was glimpsed in his affection for the animal world. He loved dogs and always had a dog at home. He particularly liked spaniels, and he kept budgies.

Whilst growing up in a society where a usual diet was heavily meat-based, Herbert looked upon animals as equal to man in their right to life and their capacity to suffer. He told his family 'if the lady who likes her lamb chop had to go out and kill the lamb herself, she would go

Fig 67. Herbert in the 1940s with Elsie his wife and her sister Emily.

without her chop'. At Christmas, his thoughts turned towards the fate of that unfortunate 'festive' bird – 'not a very good Christmas for all the poor old turkeys' he remarked.

Yet, it was not only human-kind's consumption of animals that Herbert questioned whether was necessary – he thought too that the animal kingdom was flawed because predator species had the instinct to kill for survival. He considered this a 'blot' on creation. The man who ran Old Buckenham Post Office once remarked that we lived in a wonderful world and that mankind was the cause of all the trouble. Herbert replied that although this was right, in the world, under the sea, in the deepest forests, everywhere, animals were preying on each other and this definitely spoilt the world as far as he was concerned.

Conscious since his childhood days of his father Tom's views and book of essays on the origins of the universe, Herbert spoke of the natural rhythm of the world that existed and the marvel of the sunrise each day since the dawn of time, never a second out of time. He likened the universe to a complex clock which could not possibly exist without a divine creator.[25]

The greatest love of Herbert's life which proved constant, unlike his romantic relationships, was his love of music, good music. At home in Old Buckenham, he played the piano most evenings for up to two hours and Marjorie would hear him play from her bed as she drifted off to sleep. He had a radio and record player combined and a large record collection, which the family often listened to in the evenings or whenever there was an opportunity. Joe Petersen (a boy singer of the late 30s / early 40s) was one of his favourites and he had lots of his recordings.[26] He also had Gracie Fields and other humorous ones in his collection.

Classical music was without doubt his favourite genre, especially the romantic composers – Ludwig van Beethoven, Frederic Chopin and Franz Liszt amongst the greats. One day, when listening to the Intermezzo from the opera *Cavalleria Rusticana* by Pietro Mascagni, Marjorie noticed him sitting in the chair with tears in his eyes. She was young and did not understand the context for his tears and she asked him what was troubling him. The music is very powerful emotionally and had the ability to stir deeply the soul of Herbert who found it very moving. Along with *Tannhauser* by Richard Wagner, these were the pieces he found most profoundly emotional.

As well the effect of music on the mind, of course Herbert was an engineer and in addition to building motorised vehicles and cycles, he took on other projects. He built up wireless sets and carried out electrical repairs and wiring. He generated his own electricity. He was quite good at water colour painting. Like his brother Percy, he wore a trilby when out and boots on his feet rather than shoes. Perhaps seeking nostalgia from his childhood, when his Pa and Ma used to take the family for holidays to the South Coast resorts of Hastings and Brighton, he also came to appreciate the Norfolk resorts of Cromer, Sheringham, Hunstanton and Great Yarmouth. Also he shared with Percy a love of food and amongst his favourite dishes were mussels and other shellfish. He also liked celery and watercress.

Herbert lived through the era of the earliest moving pictures and witnessed the transition from silent films to 'talkies'. He loved the antics of Charlie Chaplin and he had his own collection of silent films and a projector. Marjorie remembered a lovely film he watched known to her as 'The Legend of Sister Beatrix'.[27] He combined his love of music and appreciation of silent films by accompanying them on the piano at the cinema, as the backdrop to the dramatic moments, during the years before moving to Norfolk in 1923. Although Herbert had a serious nature, he enjoyed humour in good taste and at times would laugh uncontrollably. However, he found the poor jokes of the comedians of the day in poor taste and disliked how audiences laughed. He described this in biblical terms, 'they were like the crackle of thorns under a pot' (Ecclesiastes 7:6).

He enjoyed dressing up as Santa Claus for Marjorie to surprise her – the illusion being shattered when she found his costume hidden behind some furniture at home.

He was very interested in the supernatural and talked about ghosts and ghost stories. Marjorie remembered that he had a supernatural experience when he saw someone go into the side of the road and disappear. On another occasion, he heard a noise like animal footsteps or panting but as it was dark, he could never establish the source of the noises.

It was perhaps inevitable that Herbert should inherit many views and opinions that his father held in relation to Christian faith.

Perhaps revealing or reflecting the non-conformist beliefs of his father and grandfather he thought that infant baptism was wrong and that adults should be baptised at the time when they understood enough to find it of value. He claimed that there was no record of infant baptism in the New Testament. Like his views on Ireland, Herbert grew up in a Protestant country that was largely still hostile to the Roman Catholic faith. His father after all, had written a pamphlet entitled *England's Past, Present and Future, in Connexion with Rome*.

He did not approve of the Roman Catholic dogma of the adoration of the Virgin Mary. He upheld the traditional Protestant view that the Old Testament teachings were that man should not bow down to images or idols and accused Catholics of this fault by their veneration of the Mother of Christ. He said that the Gospels revealed that Christ himself spoke rather unfeelingly to his mother and that Mary was not mentioned very much in the New Testament books following her son's death and resurrection.

However, there were signs that attitudes towards Catholicism were shifting at this time. Herbert owned a book which meant a great deal to him. He told Marjorie that the author asked the questions 'who am I?' and 'what is the real me?' considering every part of the body completely changes in the course of six or seven years. The book argued that the soul embodied the real person.[28]

He preferred prayer to be spontaneous and from the heart rather than read verbatim from a book and he had an aversion to high church services which were sung in plainsong, when broadcast on the radio.

His knowledge of the Bible was extensive and he was particularly interested in the Book of Revelation and the prophecies of the end of the world this contained. He mentioned the huge hailstones which would fall and kill men and was taken up with the idea of the beast to appear with the number 666. During the War, he believed it was Hitler.

To him, the prostitute woman in Chapter 17, and the one with whom all the kings of the earth had committed fornication was Rome, because world leaders made their way there to bow down to the Pope.[29]

When his only son Raymond died in 1936, he admitted to praying in earnest but his prayers had not been answered. Of his own faith, Herbert simply said 'I'm one who doesn't know' which was quite a humble response considering his sense of spirituality.

During the War, Herbert built an air raid shelter in the garden at Old Buckenham. The village became home to the Americans who had an airbase there between 1943 and 1945. 'The Yanks' were frequent visitors to the shop. Marjorie recalled that during the War years, one evening someone was feeling all-round the glass door to the shop and he could be seen in the porch way as a shadow could be discerned. Herbert took a poker and went round the back to approach from the front to see what was going on. It was a drunk American looking for shelter and after talking to him, Herbert fetched a pillow and blanket and gave them to him. He consented to him remaining in the porch to sleep off his hangover, satisfied he meant no harm.

Both before and after the War, Herbert's sister Beatrice and her three daughters Eileen, Grace and Barbara were regular visitors to Old Buckenham from their home in Ilford. Marjorie remembered the musical evenings that the family enjoyed together, as the girls were all talented musicians. Later on they were accompanied by Barbara's young son, Barrie.

Herbert's last years

In the early 1950s, Herbert reached the age of 80 and he retired with the family a short distance to a house at Foundry Corner on the Old Buckenham side of Attleborough. Here, Herbert built a workshop fitted out with tools in which he occupied his time by making useful things. However, his eyesight was rapidly fading.

Elsie would make ginger beer herself which Herbert enjoyed

drinking. One evening whilst alone, Herbert went to look for his favourite tipple and what he thought was the beer was in fact neat acetic acid use as a component of the beverage. He drank enough to cause severe swelling to his throat. A doctor was called but underestimated the seriousness of the situation although at the time, Herbert was already having breathing difficulties. The doctor commented that he seemed unduly anxious. A tracheostomy should have been performed but it was not considered.

To the great shock and sadness of his daughter and wife, Herbert died on Sunday 20 March 1955. He was 83-years-old. An inquest was held and the verdict: misadventure. Herbert Clark Westfield was buried in the same churchyard at Old Buckenham as his brother Percy in 1938 and his infant son Raymond in 1936. Every spring, daffodils planted on his grave still bloom.

Fig 68. Elsie, Herbert and Marjorie in front of the garage, The Green, Old Buckenaham, late 1940s.

Chapter 4

————

BERTRAM ALLAN
LESLIE CLARK

————

29 June 1875 – 26 August 1944

*Mr. Clark was a quiet man… on Sunday afternoons he would
take us out for nature walks and then he really came alive. I
remember those walks with great affection.*
(Constance Hirons, 1995)

When her new baby arrived, his mother Fanny must have been exceedingly disappointed that he was yet another boy and not the longed for daughter. After all, she herself had been the youngest of four daughters and had no brothers!

If Percy was the academic one, Herbert the rather cheeky practical son, Bertie, as he was known, was the exceptionally attractive boy with an angelic face who would grow into a handsome man and much more besides.

Until he was four or five years old, Bertie's early years were spent at Sutton. Firstly at Claremont House, Brighton Road and afterwards at Hill Side, Sutton (road name unknown). Following this, the family

(Left) Fig 69. Bertram circa 1881; (Right) Fig 69a. With childhood toys.

moved to 2 Lansdowne Road, Tottenham and this was his home at the time of the spring census of 1881. Bertie's older brothers, Tommy, Percy and probably Herbert too, all went to boarding school at Ongar, Essex, but it is unlikely that he was able to follow in their footsteps to such an excellent school. By the time Bertie was 10 or 12 years old, it was the mid-1880s. Times had changed and the family wealth in all likelihood had taken a decline.

Bertie's daughter Muriel recalled that her father had a governess until he was 12 and then he went to college, possibly at Leytonstone, although she was uncertain.[1] Bertie had his younger siblings, Walter and Beatrice, as companions at home. By 1891, the family had indeed moved to Leyton and Bertie, 16-years-old that summer, was likely to have completed his education in that district.[2]

It was probably around this date that an informal photograph was taken of Bertie, Beatrice and Percy either sitting or reclining in a relaxed pose near shrubs and a winding pathway in the background.

Their laughter seems infectious, seen through the happy, smiling and carefree faces.

In 1901 Bertie is with his parents, Tom and Fanny, on census night at their address, 27 Springfield, Upper Clapton, Hackney. In spite of a probable lack of a prestigious boarding school education, Bertie was able to accompany his older brothers into the world of employment as a commercial clerk.[3]

Life was shortly to change for the family core and probably the biggest part of that future was influenced by the move to Bowers Gifford, a small village in South Essex, which had already been undertaken by Bertie's brother, Herbert, and his young family by 1901 and was something which Pa and Ma would complete themselves within a year or so.

Fig 70. Bertie relaxing with his siblings at Leyton.

Marriage and Widowhood

Although Bertie almost certainly worked in London he undoubtedly spent time with his parents out in the countryside of Essex and came to appreciate the rural pace of life and the unspoilt countryside. Whilst his parents were moving, Bertie was probably conducting his courtship of a young lady named Ethel Maud Mary Lamerton. Ethel had been born in Gloucester in 1879.[4] Her father, Walter, was a commercial traveller and her parents and elder sibling had been born in London. However, the family settled in Gloucester for some years, as they were still there at the time of the 1891 census. Walter had then changed occupation to that of a cabinet manufacturer.[5]

Fig 71. Portrait of Bertram Clark around the time of his marriage to Ethel Lamerton in 1902.

Before 1901, the family had returned to London. Ethel's mother, Ellen, having died sometime earlier, her father remarried. Ethel is working perhaps in the family home at Dartmouth Park Hill, St. Pancras, as a milliner to supplement family income.[6]

Most likely the couple met whilst Bertie was working in London. They were perhaps attracted to the idea of a peaceful countryside wedding near to Bertie's folks' new abode and they married at All Saints' Church, North Benfleet, on 27 July 1902.[7] Bertie stated his home address as at St. Columb, Notting Hill, whilst Ethel gives her residence as North Benfleet, which could have been a requirement for at least one party (usually the bride) to have resided in the parish before marriage. Ethel's brother, Vernon, was a witness in the register and Bertie's sister Beatrice, acted in the same capacity.

The couple returned to the bustle of London life and their first daughter named Rita Ethel Beatrice, was born on 3 July 1904.[8] The name Beatrice was chosen in honour of Bertie's sister. The family home at the time of Rita's baptism that September was 92 Kemp's Road, Kensal Rise.[9]

Two weeks before Ethel gave birth Bertie left his heavily pregnant wife to join the midsummer nuptials of his sister Beatrice on 22 June at Bowers Gifford where he had returned the duty of signing as a witness in the register upon her marriage to Edmund Palmer.

Four years later, Rita's sister Muriel Lamerton (Lamerton being her mother's maiden name) was born on 19 July 1908 at 55 St. Ervan's Road, Kensington.[10] Bertie is still employed as a commercial clerk at this time.

All was not well in the weeks and months after Muriel's birth. It was possible that Ethel lived isolated from family and after her husband left each morning to start his job, she was alone all day with her four-year-old daughter and the new baby. By February 1909 Ethel's mental health had declined to the point that on the 26th of the month she was admitted to Colney Heath Asylum.[11] It was likely that the move to institutional surroundings and the separation from her family must have added to her mental anguish and just five days later, Ethel died. Her death certificate cited the cause of death as exhaustion from mania which had lasted 11 days and a secondary condition of pulmonary congestion lasting two days.[12] Due to the suddenness of her death, a post mortem was carried out which found it was due to natural causes. The news must have been a terrible shock to Bertie as well as Ethel's family, especially her brother Vernon to whom she was very close. The cause and exact nature of her mental illness is unknown and the asylum records seem not to have survived for this period. However, it cannot be ignored that she had, a few months previously, given birth to her second child, and the description of 'mania' could indicate she had been suffering from postpartum psychosis. Today, mania is defined as a severe form of over-active and excited behaviour that lasts more than a week and impacts on the sufferer's ability to carry out day-to-day activities, a very serious condition needing hospital treatment.

Her funeral was held on 8 March and she was buried at St. Pancras.[13] She was just 29-years-old and left behind two young girls, one just a baby of a few months old. Perhaps it accounts for the absence of Herbert's daughter Winnie, recorded in the North Benfleet school log book of June and July 1909. It is easy to suggest that Edith had gone to Kensington to assist Bertie to care for his young girls, as it remained necessary for him to earn a living at this difficult time, and the family may have rallied round. However, circumstances often dictate how life will pan out and in the dreadful aftermath of the loss of Ethel, Rita and Muriel were 'farmed out' to their Lamerton relatives during Bertie's widowhood. Rita went to Aunt Jemima whilst Muriel to Vernon and Alice (Ethel's brother and his wife). The sisters were separated for four years.[14]

Bertie, like his brothers Percy and Herbert, was very interested in engineering and having a creative mind led him to becoming an inventor; perhaps to distract himself following his bereavement, he created a bullet which he termed as a flaming bullet. He contacted the War Office at the time suggesting to them that it might be useful for signalling purposes but as he did not receive an encouraging response, he abandoned the project.[15]

Remarriage to Emily Steer

Just like his Grandpapa, Bertie remarried following the family tragedy and so his daughters came to have a step-mother. Once more, he returned to rural Essex to marry Miss Emily Steer. Emily was 10 years younger than Ethel and had been born in Canning Town in 1889, but by 1891 her family lived in Greenwich.[16] However, by the turn of the new century, the family had moved out of London to Southend Road, Vange, Essex, bringing her inevitably closer to the fate of meeting her future husband.[17] It was at this location that her father ran the Vange Post Office with all the family living on the premises. During the evening of 27 February 1902, at closing time, a fire broke out which was believed to have been caused by a lamp exploding when being extinguished. Mr. Steer and all the family escaped unharmed but the premises were destroyed. Not only did Emily's father run the post office but also had a drapers and boot and shoe warehouse on the site which were all owned by a Mr. Humm who lived in a wing of the building which was also burnt that night.

On 3 March, the vicar of Vange, St. John Methuen, wrote a letter to the editor of *The Newsman* paper in support of the family who had lost their home and all the contents which were only partially insured; this meant a certain loss of at least £100. George Steer had been gradually building up his small business here and the loss, the vicar felt, would be disastrous especially as he had been suffering recently from a bad attack of erysipelas and at the time of the fire was ill in bed. To avoid certain ruin, the vicar wrote to encourage financial support from well-wishers and neighbours to give him a fresh start and he personally took on the responsibility of collecting donations to the Rectory 'to help this very deserving and afflicted family'.[18]

Fortunately one way or another, the post office and business rose from the ashes and in the year 1911 George Steer was still running the general stores and post office from High Road, Vange.[19] Emily was working as a shop assistant and it is probable that she met Bertie when he visited the store for purchases or transactions; what began as a flirtation developed to a romance springing up between the handsome widower and the daughter of the proprietor.

They married on 29 October 1911 at St. Mary the Virgin, Woodham Ferrers.[20] The bride, just 22, her new husband 36, made their home in Kensington, London eventually reuniting Bertie's two daughters in the process and welcoming them back into the family home. It is perhaps not surprising that the couple delayed having a child of their own for a couple of years as the family adjusted to the new circumstances. Muriel recalled later how pleasant her stepmother was and said she couldn't have had a better or more pleasant person to be her stepmother; she was a very kind person.[21]

Emily's first pregnancy progressed in 1913 but there was more misfortune and heartache around the corner for Bertie and his new wife. Premature twin boys were born in the spring of 1914. They were given the names George (after Emily's father) and Bertram, but both died shortly afterwards.[22]

Fig 72. Bertram at Clifton Lane, Bowers Gifford, before his departure to Coventry in 1915.

The Coventry Inventor

With the outbreak of the War in September 1914, life for everyone in the country would change. The Clark family were no exception and they left London before the beginning of 1915. The move to the Midlands was for purposes of employment as Coventry was the centre of ammunition production and military vehicle manufacture, an industry in which Bertie had both knowledge and practical skills. He perhaps keenly felt and hoped that his skills as an amateur inventor may have been of use to the city and the country. Bertie may have perhaps been at risk of being drafted once conscription was introduced in 1916 and this may have helped him avoid entering the conflict in the field.

Thirty thousand people were drafted into Coventry from all over the United Kingdom to join the local workforce. They were making military vehicles, motorbikes, lorries, tank engines, submarine parts and naval guns alongside the weapons of mass destruction for the battlefields such as artillery shells, fuses, bullets and grenades. It was an extremely dangerous occupation as the materials handled for explosive manufacturing caused lifelong health problems and in many cases, workers died from the poisonous after effects.[23]

In early 1915, probably shortly after moving to Coventry, he experimented with small rubber balloons filled with hydrogen and brought them down in flames using the bullet he had invented six years before. After contacting the War Office with his discovery, it was his opinion that if the bullet penetrated the German Zeppelin gas bags, it would result in bringing them down in flames. The government office responded that it would not be possible to achieve this with rifle fire as the Zeppelin would travel out of range. In late March or early April of that year, Bertie spoke to a Mr. McCartney of the Coventry Ordnance Works about his invention and left a prototype bullet with him. McCartney seemed interested and promised to let him know the result of the examination into his invention but he never heard anything more and did not pursue it either. Bertie was not aware until July 1919 that the 'tracer bullet' used in the Great War was a phosphorous one similar to his own invention of 1909. This discovery led him to write to Winston Churchill who was at the time Minister of Munitions. His letter was acknowledged but eighteen months later, he still had heard no more.[24]

In early 1917, Emily fell pregnant again and their son Roy was born on 21 October.[25] This new baby was Bertie and Emily's only living child together. Emily was very protective over her baby and would not take him out anywhere until he was six months old.[26]

My grandfather used to work in an ironmonger's, recalled Pat Cowley and although we don't know the timeframe for this, it seems likely it was one of his first jobs in Coventry.[27]

In January 1921, a Coventry inventor was rewarded for the invention of the incendiary tracer bullet which brought down Zeppelins during the war, and given a sum of £10,000 for his outstanding design. However, this inventor was not Bertram Clark as you might expect from Bertie's staggering claim that he was the first person to invent the bullet. It was James Frank Buckingham who took the credit for this achievement in his factory at the rear of Spon Street in Coventry. In this 'unpretentious factory in the heart of the city' stated the newspaper, more than 26 million bullets were produced and the tracer bullet played a very important part in deciding the air supremacy of the allies. It went on to defeat the Zeppelins as they crashed to earth in flames when struck. Apparently, Buckingham did not create the bullet by accident or chance discovery – it was the result of deep and careful research. In an interview for the paper, Buckingham revealed that the material he used for the incendiary part was, like Bertie's, a phosphorous one but he acknowledged that there were many obstacles and one of the biggest difficulties was to find a satisfactory method of working. Like Bertie, he conducted experiments using the bullet; some resulted in accidents but in the end success was achieved. The discovery was first revealed to the government in December 1914 but it was not until April 1915 (the same time that Bertie approached the works with his own invention) that a demonstration was given on the Range at Wedgenock Park, Warwick, where Buckingham set fire to balloons at 400 yards range and then further trials were conducted at Woolwich.

More experiments by Buckingham produced a bullet of .303 dimensions which had the capability to be fired from any gun and the first contract was given to the Admiralty in October 1915. The bullet was different in appearance to other types and aviators who fell into enemy hands with those particular bullets in their possession were severely punished. Buckingham eventually produced one exactly like that used in an ordinary rifle.

The first success in action was on 29 February, 1916 over the Belgian lines when a German aeroplane was shot down in flames. The Ministry of Munitions subsequently ordered the bullet in April 1916. The second use of the bullet was for the destruction of kite balloons, which was of even greater military importance than the bringing down of Zeppelins because the whole work of British batteries depended on their being kept from enemy observation. The Buckingham bullet was the only thing available to neutralise the German kite balloons before any large operation was conducted.

The allies found the bullet of invaluable use and it was manufactured in Coventry to the rate of 100,000 per day. At the height of its production 500 people worked specifically on it.[28]

Bertie read the paper bearing the history of the bullet and, surprised by the revelation that something sounding very like his own design may have been used for this significant development in the war, wrote to the editor of the local newspaper:

THE INCENDIARY BULLET *Sir,—With reference to your article in today's Midland Daily Telegraph "re the incendiary bullet". Whilst I have no desire in any way to challenge Mr. Buckingham in this matter, yet I certainly do refute the suggestion that the Government first became acquainted with the incendiary bullet in 1914. In the year 1909 I invented a bullet which I termed a flaming bullet, and I wrote to the War Office at the time suggesting it might be useful for signalling purposes, but the reply they sent me did not induce me to go further into the matter. In the early part of 1915 I experimented with small rubber balloons filled with hydrogen and brought them down in flames. So I wrote again to the War Office explaining that if my bullet, penetrated the Zeppelin gas bags it could not help bringing them down in flames, but they replied that it would not be possible to do this with rifle fire, as the Zeppelin would travel high up out of range. I next interviewed Mr. McCartney at the Coventry Ordnance Works—that would be about March or beginning of April, 1915—and I explained the whole matter to him and left a model of my bullet with him. He seemed to be 'very interested' in the matter and promised to let me know further about same, but I never heard anything more until I became acquainted with the fact that the tracer bullet was a phosphorous bullet similar to mine. That was in July, 1919. I then wrote to the Right Hon. Winston Churchill re the matter and received a letter stating I should hear further, but so far nothing else has happened.— Yours faithfully, B. CLARK. 98, Broad Street, Coventry, Jan. 26.*[29]

Meanwhile, after the war too, Bertie was perhaps pre-occupied with the health and welfare of his ageing father. Of family visitors to Coventry after the war, his father Tom stayed for a time which wasn't a success, as Muriel's daughter Pat recounted:

> *Mother said he was well-spoken and frequently used to correct her speech. Apparently he wasn't an easy man to live with and eventually my grandfather asked him to leave, he frequently caused upsets.*

Also Muriel could remember that Uncle Walter stayed with them when she was young but she had no recollection of her other uncles or aunts on her father's side.[30]

The memories of neighbours and friends

Decades later, Coventry residents who were children and young adults in the 1930s and 40s imparted their vivid memories of Bertram. Vincent Ball was born in 1928 and lived with his family at 106 Broad Street. Local knowledge of a time before he was born informed him that the nearby No. 98 Broad Street operated as a fresh fish retail business. 98 Broad Street was home to the Clark family certainly by early 1921 as Bertie's letter to the paper that January was written from this address.

Ron Brookes, resident at 94 Broad Street as a young boy, recalled that Bertie's shop backed onto his grandfather's house. He described the houses as late 18th or early 19th century terraced cottages of poor quality, originally one-up, one-down.[31]

Bertie was, however, not at that time the owner of this cottage. In 1923 whilst his family was in residence, the property was to be sold at auction on 6 February to a new owner whilst Bertie would continue to hold the leasehold. *The Coventry Herald* carried details of two roomy freehold houses and shops, formerly several tenements, now numbered 98 and 102 Broad Street, with spacious yards and right of cartway to the rear let on leases to a fish dealer and beer agent and producing £41 12s. per annum. The following month, another advertisement announced that the houses had been withdrawn from auction to be sold privately – the new owner's name being unrecorded.[32]

Constance Hirons was born in 1913 and her parents kept a general shop at 102 Broad Street, the one which would be sold at the same time as No. 98 in 1923. She recalled life in Broad Street between the wars:

I was friendly with Muriel and when we wanted her to come out and play, I and another friend helped her to 'eye' tubs of potatoes which was her task – the water was icy cold! Rita went out to work so wasn't expected to do any chores. Roy was very fair and pale and a mardy child and as far as we girls were concerned – a pest.[33]

Vincent Ball recalled that the potatoes were imported from Ireland, many covered with thick red clay. Bertie allowed the youngster and his friends access to the potato store (a garden shed to the rear of the shop) to remove the clay which they moulded into small figures and animals and then placed in the sun to harden.[34]

Bertie had grown up in a household with a father who valued the natural world and had acquired an immense store of knowledge. On the practical side, gardening and botany were enjoyed at the Clark home in Sutton, where the young Bertie spent his early years, as evidenced by the number of potted plants placed in bays next to the front windows at Claremont House, the glass houses visible to the rear and surplus plants given out to other family members.[35] When the business of the day was over and especially on Sunday afternoons, Bertie would take his daughter Muriel and friend out for nature walks as her friend Constance remembered:

Mr. Clark was a quiet man, he didn't seem to go out to work, but on Sunday afternoons he would take us out for nature walks and then he really came alive. I remember those walks with great affection.[36]

Muriel also recollected this deep love and interest in nature always held by her father as the Sunday afternoon walkers would study butterflies, insects and lizards.[37]

Bertie closed the fish and chip shop when his wife Emily became ill and he re-opened as a shoe repairer. Emily's brother, George Horace Steer, had also re-located to Coventry and was self-employed in the trade so it is easy to speculate that George was able to assist his brother-in-law in his new project. George lived with them for a time at Broad Street.[38]

By the mid-1930s, Bertie and Emily had several grand-children whilst youngest son Roy still lived with them. Muriel had three daughters, whilst Rita had a son, Lawrence. His granddaughter Patricia remembered her grandfather as friendly and welcoming to her and her two sisters and he liked to show them his hobbies. Other than his enthusiasm for nature and plants, Bertie had a talent for painting, like other family members, most notably his father. Muriel wished decades later that she had retained some of his work. Bertie was well-read and knowledgeable on many subjects and Muriel's husband Tom Cowley enjoyed conversing with him.[39]

The Second World War years in Coventry

During the years of World War II, Bertie and his family experienced the dark days and hardships of the Blitz of 1940-1 which destroyed lives and dwellings all around them. During those years, Bertie corresponded with his brother Herbert living far away in Norfolk.[40] Both brothers were very keen on current affairs so one can imagine the lively exchanges of views which took place on paper! He also wrote a letter to the *Coventry Evening Telegraph* in 1942 in which he gave his forthright opinion:

Sir – we heard a good deal of the German slogan "guns before butter" during the preceding years of the present war.

Now that Germany is presenting our Russian ally with a preponderance of guns, to say nothing of vast quantities of other useful war equipment, one may well wonder if this misguided people are still satisfied with their slogan. – Yours, B. CLARK, 98 Broad Street, Coventry, February 2.[41]

It was a time of transition and change not least because Bertie was growing older and his hearing became impaired with his family having to shout for him to hear them.[42]

Ron Brookes, who grew up at 94 Broad Street, recalled that Bertie introduced his grandfather to the art and mystery of growing cacti. Ron remarked that it was an unusual hobby at this time and in this locality. Bertie corresponded with people all over the country, and Europe too, who were also enthusiasts.[43] An advertisement in the *Coventry Evening Telegraph* in May 1942 promoted the sale of cacti and succulents from those he had grown and nurtured and those interested could apply to him any evening after six.[44]

On 26 August 1944, two months after his 69th birthday, Bertie died from pancreatic cancer. Ron Brookes, the boy from 94 Broad Street, remembering the event decades later, disclosed how it was rumoured that Bertie took his own life rather than suffer a lingering death but he could not vouch for this.[45] The truth was revealed in Bertie's death certificate which confirmed that he did have a natural death.[46] His grieving family placed a Notice in the *Coventry Evening Telegraph* on 30 August 1944 stating he had undergone 'much suffering' but had died peacefully.[47]

This talented, knowledgeable man who had been an unrecognised or unrewarded inventor, a naturalist, artist and a father to name a few of his achievements, was buried at Foleshill cemetery following a funeral service at nearby St. Paul's Church.[48]

Chapter 5

———

WALTER VIVIAN
HAROLD CLARK

———

15 August 1876 – 6 November 1957

*Walter had a huge magnificent model ship in his front room
at Thorold Road. When he saw me admiring it, he explained
that it was magic. He did something to it which caused it to
automatically roll a herbal cigarette somewhere below decks
which when completed was popped out of one of its funnels.*
(Peter Taylor-Wood, 1991)

W alter was born at Hill Side, Sutton and was the final son
in the family.[1] Walter spent his first few years of life in
Sutton before the family moved to Tottenham where his
sister Beatrice was born in 1879.

Like his brother, Bertram, Walter may have been educated at
home until he was of an age to go to school. When we see Walter at
the time of the 1891 census, his family had moved to Leyton and he is
described as a scholar.[2]

On 12 May 1900, Walter took the unusual step at the age of 23,
to be baptised in the Church of England. It would appear that he was

the only one amongst his siblings to take this step, as his parents and paternal grandparents had not baptised any of their children as babies. Walter's baptism took place at St. Matthew's Church, Upper Clapton, being the parish where the family resided at the time.[3] Clearly, Walter had an inspired religious reason for embracing baptism as a young adult and possibly a profound experience led him to the sacrament.

Around the turn of the century, the family had moved to a house at Springfield, Upper Clapton and in the census of 1901, Walter is absent from his parents' home. He is staying with his brother, Herbert, and his family at Bowers Gifford. Herbert is working as a self-employed photographer whilst Walter assisted the business as a photographic traveller.[4] This may have been in connection with a business Walter had founded from the parental home at Springfield. A surviving photograph of an unknown London drawing room is stamped on the reverse 'W. Westfield – Fine Art Dealers, 27 Springfield, Upper Clapton'.

It would appear that photography was not the only creative occupation which Walter participated in. He may have followed in

Fig 73. Walter Clark-Westfield with his phonograph; he inherited the Clark musical talents.

the footsteps of his uncle Josiah Fountain Meen to become a musical composer. The Second Boer War ended on 31 May 1902 with the signing of the Treaty of Vereeniging. *Lloyd's Weekly Newspaper*, a month later, carried a review of a composition entitled *The British Victory March* which was written by a certain Walter C. Westfield – surely our man.[5] It would seem likely that Walter felt inspired to express his feelings about the end of the war in music. The musical journalist wrote that 'the spirit of the measure is infectious' and advised the readership that it had been published by The Lyric Music Publishing Company.

A short while later, Walter's parents Tom and Fanny had themselves permanently joined Herbert out at Bowers Gifford but it is not known if Walter also lived here. On 22 June 1904, he is present for the big family gathering at St. Margaret of Antioch Church, when his sister Beatrice married. No doubt, like everyone else, Walter was shattered by the sudden death of his Mama just a few months after the happy summer wedding of his sister.

Photographic images of the young Walter show a slight young man without any facial hair at a time when moustaches were extremely popular and at least three of his brothers sported them. Indeed, Herbert remarked to his daughter Marjorie much later, that Walter was delicate, almost effeminate and never had to shave.

Fig 74. These elegant unknown ladies, may have been photographed by Walter at Clifton Lane, Bowers Gifford, on a family occasion. The location can be identified by the arch behind them.

Four years later, at the age of 31, Walter married Grace Gertrude Dennis at the church of St. Mary the Virgin, Little Ilford.[6] His wife was always known by her second name, which was shortened to Gert or Gerty. She had been born in 1883 at Manor Park so was a local lady. At the time of the 1901 census, she was living in the parish of Little Ilford with her family. Her parents were William and Agnes Dennis and her father stated his occupation as a plumber and gas fitter; he hailed from St. Luke's parish in the City. Young Gert was then working as a 17-year-old paper mill folder and two of her other sisters were also in employment.[7]

Just three years after their wedding, Walter and Gert had settled down to married life. Walter liked to try a variety of jobs and at the time of the 1911 census he is working as a pianoforte shop manager. Perhaps this is in conjunction with his brother-in-law Edmund Palmer who helped to run his family's piano shop business. The couple then lived at 1 Brancaster Road, Manor Park. Gert's unmarried sister Florence is living with them and she has a job as a shop manageress for a corset maker.[8]

Unable to have children of their own, Gert and Walter adopted a child, probably not long after he was born. Donald Charles Lamble was born on 4 March 1914, his birth being registered in Leicestershire.[9] Walter and Gert lived their entire lives together at Manor Park, West Ham and then Ilford.

Walter's brother Percy was the first of the adult Clark siblings to pass away in 1938. It was said that Walter was upset that he was not a major beneficiary in his brother's will, receiving a bequest of £5 which was exactly the same as what his brother Bertram received.[10] Meanwhile, the other siblings fared better, notably Herbert, Thomas (Tommy) and his sister Beatrice, and this reputedly caused some ill-feeling.[11]

In the 1939 Register of the population taken in September just at the outbreak of the War, Don (Walter and Gert's adopted son) was by the time a successful 25-year-old journalist living with them at 106 East Ham Grove, West Ham.[12] However, in all probability war would displace him from the area and in 1945 he married Gladys Drinkwater in Wallasey, Cheshire.[13] They later settled in Wales and Don stayed in contact with his adoptive family.[14]

By the 1950s Walter and Gert were living at 17 Thorold Road, Ilford and their home was only a mile away from his sister, Beatrice, and her husband Ted Palmer, who lived at Green Lane. In 1937, Beatrice and Ted's daughter, Barbara, had married Maurice Wood and during the 1940s they would have two sons. Grace, Barbara's sister, would take her young nephews to visit their great-uncle Walter and his wife.

Peter Taylor-Wood, the younger of Barbara's two sons, recalled a particular visit to Walter and Gert:

Walter had a huge magnificent model ship in his front room at Thorold Road. When he saw me admiring it, he explained that it was magic. He did something to it which caused it to automatically roll a herbal cigarette somewhere below decks which when completed was popped out of one of its funnels. He then, much to my embarrassment, insisted that I smoke it. Ah! What halcyon days.

Peter recalled this occasion being the one also when Walter persuaded him to have his first cigarette when he was just nine years of age![15]

Walter was the last of the siblings to pass on, dying on 6 November 1957 at his home, 49 Thorold Road. His occupation on his death certificate stated he was a retired clerk with the county borough council. His cause of death was acute bronchitis.[16]

His wife Gert (Plate iv) lived on until 1980 and continued to receive visits from Barbara weekly and no doubt others in the Palmer family too.[17]

Chapter 6

———

BEATRICE FRANCES MARY CLARK

———

29 April 1879 – 14 March 1955

She was a lady with a lovely, kind and gentle disposition in whose company one felt quite at ease and comfortable with and who was a delight to know and be in the presence of
(Marjorie Walshe, nee Westfield – niece).

The long awaited baby daughter of Thomas and Fanny, Beatrice, was born on 29 April 1879 at 2 Lansdowne Road, Tottenham.[1] She was the youngest of seven children and the final child born to the couple.

Beatrice was given middle names reflecting her family: Frances after her mother, Mary after Tom's mother (Mary Ann) and also after Fanny's own sister, Mary. Bea, as she was affectionately known, probably grew up rather spoilt with lots of attention from her doting parents and older brothers. She may have been particularly attached to the youngest boys, Bertie and Walter, when she was very young and would have joined them in the nursery.

Fig 75. Beatrice was the long awaited daughter of the family.

Her brother, Herbert, later remarked that Bea was exceptionally pretty when a young woman. Like many of her brothers, she excelled in creative pastimes, particularly needlework. She could also paint on canvas and incorporated her brushwork onto handkerchief sachets, cushion covers and the like, painting lovely roses and other floral designs. Bea loved cats and in surviving photographs she appears often with a cat in her lap, perhaps an inherited love shared with her mother.

In the 1901 census, she is a 21-year-old, living with her parents, Tom and Fanny, and her 25-year-old brother, Bertram, at their home, 27 Springfield, Hackney.[2] Less than a year later, Tom and Fanny moved out to Bowers Gifford and Bea would have accompanied them to a newly built house in Pound Lane on the Clifton Road Estate, next door to her brother Herbert and his family. In 1902, Bea acted as a witness at the wedding of her brother Bertram at All Saints' Church, North Benfleet.[3]

Fig 76. This portrait perhaps marks Beatrice's coming of age in 1900.

Miss Beatrice Clark grew up in a family in which the arts played a prominent part. Her paternal relatives were musical and artistic. In her maternal family, classical music played a leading role. Her aunt, Jane Susannah Bailey, was a professor of music and a music teacher and her uncle by marriage was Josiah Fountain Meen, organist of Union Chapel, Islington, as well as an accompanist to many of the leading singers of the day. It is with music in mind and the likelihood that as an accomplished late Victorian young lady, Bea would also have learnt to play the piano, a skill essential if you were to live a respectable life in polite society.

It is not known how she came into the orbit of a certain young man named Edmund Henry George Palmer, but it seems clear that it was through music or musical instruments. Edmund Palmer, or Ted as he was known, was born in Dalston, London in 1880.[4] He later told his grandson, Peter Taylor-Wood, that he recalled the Ripper murders being announced in the Whitechapel area.

He could remember lying in bed hearing the "crier" shout outside his window, "ten o'clock and there has been another ghastly Ripper murder". He also took boxing lessons from one of the most infamous of the Palmer clan, one "Pedlar Palmer", who was one time champion of the world.

There is, however, no evidence that Pedlar Palmer was related to Ted. In April 1907 Thomas 'Pedlar' Palmer killed a man on a train from Epsom races and received a five year prison sentence for manslaughter. Although the start to his life was marked by historic events and characters, Ted Palmer followed traditional footsteps in his father's business. His father, also Edmund Palmer, managed a pianoforte shop in East London. Mr. Palmer senior was initiated into Freemasonry in 1895 and this is something that he had in common with Josiah F. Meen who, in addition to being a musician, was a member of the Grand Lodge.[5]

At the time of the 1901 census, Ted Palmer was living south of the river in Newington Butts; his occupation is listed as a music and instrument dealer, whilst his father is running the business as a piano salesman.[6] Ten years before, Edmund Palmer senior was a pianoforte manufacturer living in Shoreditch with his wife Louisa, their young family and Louisa's parents David and Jane Witton.[7] Mr. Witton also was a pianoforte manufacturer, perhaps indicating where the rise in the business occurred.

It is likely that Ted Palmer was introduced to Miss Clark through a family member. Possibly this could have been by her well-connected uncle Josiah Fountain Meen or merely by contact through the piano industry, or simply a requirement to tune a family piano.

The wedding of the only daughter in a family amongst five sons is always likely to be a cause for a big family gathering and excessive celebrations. Thus it was when the Clark family assembled on the Midsummer Day of Wednesday 22 June 1904, three years into the Edwardian era. The weather that month was rather disappointingly cloudy; sunshine in any quantity not arriving until the end of the month.[8]

Like her aunts before her, who had married in the 1870s and 1880s, Bea would have prepared for and assembled her wedding trousseau, paid for by her Papa, Tom. As a deft seamstress, she would make much of her trousseau including perhaps her own wedding dress evoking memories in the family of her aunt Matilda back in 1873.

Her three young nieces, the daughters of Herbert, perhaps filled the role of bridesmaids, Violet (9), Winnie (7) and Doris (4). Her uncle by marriage, Josiah Fountain Meen, perhaps played the organ in the small village church of St. Margaret of Antioch. Her Mama was happy to see her beautiful daughter married to a respectable tradesman working in the music industry who already felt like one of the family.

The family photograph was taken, almost certainly by her brother Herbert, as he is missing in the group. The party assembled in front of a hedgerow. The back row standing, the middle row, bride and groom centre, flanked by both of their mothers and Herbert's wife Edith on the side to break the symmetry. At the front, three giggling girls squat or sit in the long grass of the summer meadow, no doubt encouraged

Fig 77. St. Margaret of Antioch church, here pictured in 1905, was the setting for the wedding.

Bowers Gifford Church, Pitsea.

by their father Herbert in front of them and behind the camera (see Fig. No. 41).

Many of the family were keen to sign as a witness in the register on this great day.[9]

Bea and Ted began their married life back in the East of London. Their first child, Eileen, was born on 4 October the following year at 288 Green Street, Forest Gate, in the West Ham district.[10] Grace was born at the same address on 13 January 1909 and the family were still in residence at the time of the 1911 census.[11] Before the end of 1911, the Palmer's had another child, possibly a son, who then died very young.[12] The final child, Barbara, arrived on 7 July 1913.[13] Peter Taylor-Wood (Ted and Bea's grandson) later remarked that his grandfather's piano shop was very close to the old family home at 288 Green Street where his mother Barbara had been born.[14]

At the time of the 1911 census, Ted was working as a pianoforte showroom manager, the same as he was at his marriage. Family meant a great deal and at this time Bea's aunt, Alice Troup (née Clark), was staying with her and her family at 288 Green Street.[15] This bond with family existed on both sides to Ted's family too as Ted's parents, Edmund and Louisa Palmer, were staying as visitors on that same census night with Herbert and his family in Bowers Gifford – perhaps his services as a piano tuner had been called upon to work on Herbert's piano?[16]

Later on, the Palmer family moved to 74 Green Lane, Ilford. Her grandson, Peter, revealed that Beatrice ran a theatrical costumier business from 74 Green Lane and 234 Boleyn Road, Forest Gate.[17] The house would remain in the family until after Grace died in 1985, a much loved family home for three generations of the Palmer family.

Following her brother Herbert's move to the Norfolk village of Old Buckenham in the 1920s and subsequently Percy's a decade later, Beatrice and her family became regular visitors both before and after the War. A very happy time the two siblings had together and Bea was loved and appreciated by Herbert's daughter Marjorie too who found her aunt very gracious and was an admirer of her cousin's musical talent.

Fig 78. Beatrice with her daughters Grace on the left and Eileen (right) circa 1913.

Bea had a wonderful sense of humour and when she had a giggling attack, her whole body would convulse. She was a lady with a lovely, kind and gentle disposition in whose company one felt quite at ease and comfortable with and who was a delight to know and be in the presence of, were the abiding memories of Marjorie. *Later on in her life, Bea had a head of thick grey hair and had put on weight around the middle.*

Whilst at Old Buckenham, the family had musical soireés. Bea's three daughters were all musicians who had studied at the London Royal Academy of Music. They also were teachers of music, mostly to private clients; indeed, Grace met her husband Ian when he became a pupil.

Eileen sang and played piano, Grace, the violin and Barbara, the cello. It was unsurprising given the musical background on both sides of the family. Speaking of his mother and aunts, Peter described their musical talent as 'formidable' and he was 'most sad that he did not seize the opportunity to record them'.

Fig 79. Part of the 'The Palmer Trio' – Beatrice and Ted's daughters Barbara and Grace, (left and right flappers) captured performing with The Colleagues' Dance Band during the 1930s. Ted stands in the background.

Fig 80. Beatrice and Ted with members of the family at Ilford during the 1940s.

In Ilford, Barbara had married Maurice Wood in 1937. She was the only one of the three sisters to have a family. Her sons, Barrie and Peter, born in the 1940s, were thus the only grandchildren visiting 74 Green Lane. They were doted on by the family particularly their aunts, Eileen and Grace. Peter recalled spending a lot of his childhood at 74 and said it was nothing short of fantastic. 'Somehow life never measured up to what we experienced in that enchanted place, ordinary human beings are incredibly boring!' he reminisced.

One of the most magical things about our childhood was the loft at "74". "Well, all the wealth of that empire lay strewn about that amazing loft. There were full-sized dragons, a huge lion's suit with what I remember to be a 'real' lion's head, various military uniforms complete with real swords. As I remember it there were chests of jewels, jewel-studded crowns and clothes representing every nation on earth. No doubt in reality, it was a little more modest but I can honestly say not so much so.[18]

Fig 81. Beatrice at The Green, Old Buckenham, late 1940s.

It was a strange co-incidence that Herbert and Bea should die within a week of each other in 1955; brother and sister, close in life should share their time of death. Beatrice died on 14 March from a stroke – she was 76.[19] Bea's husband Ted, survived her by 14 years, dying in 1969.[20]

CONCLUSION

This story began with a man who rose from a seemingly obscure background. Ironically, even his likeness has eluded us throughout this project whilst images of his two wives live on in these pages. Although we know little about his father (also Thomas 1785-1853) and virtually nothing about his grandfather, William Clark (dates currently unknown), we know that his three sisters Ann, Hephzibah and Esther made good, if modest marriages, to men who did not achieve the same prestigious or lucrative heights. Perhaps he was just in the right place at the right time to reap the rewards of success. At just 20 years of age, he possessed confidence and clarity about who he was and where he was heading in life.

By the early 1870s he had reached the pinnacle of his career – the new purpose built large home in the suburbs with a couple of servants. He was, on the surface, the epitome of the respectable Victorian entrepreneur with 10 living children who viewed their Papa with some trepidation as someone moody, authoritarian and remote.

He lived through extraordinary and ambitious times being born the same year as Queen Victoria and accompanying her through the rise, and towards the fall, of the era when Britain's dominance as the leaders in world trade were coming to an end. He was a young man when photography was invented and he later faced the impact the epidemics of cholera, scarlet fever and typhoid had on his close family members. In an age when women were often invisible outside the home, he relied on his two wives to run his household and raise his family.

A pattern emerges of the family moving home after his promotion or demotion in fortunes and certainly in times of crisis. The move from Shenton Street, Old Kent Road, after the 1854 cholera epidemic having such a tragic outcome for him and his family and then after his first wife died in 1866, a hasty retreat from the country mansion of Crofton Hall to the exciting new London suburbs and finding a suitable new wife. The cholera outbreak of 1854 would have changed the course of history had more family members died.

His son Thomas was spared the burden of responsibilities and seems to have lacked a business drive. The wealth coming into the family, and his position as the oldest son amongst so many female siblings, enabled him to receive a good education as well as to find a creative outlet as a writer and poet. In addition he was able to indulge his personal interests focusing so heavily on religion and science – the two disciplines that were the hot topics of the age. By the time of the First World War, he was concerned by the advent of the secular world too.

The changes in family life in over just two generations can also be seen. Whilst Thomas Clark senior had 12 children, his son Tom and his wife Fanny had seven. The changing nature of fatherhood can also be seen – the son being more approachable, liked and appreciated by his sisters. He appears to have been a caring husband who spared his wife some of the rigours of life that his mother had endured and we know they had a happy marriage.

The third Clark generation grew up and many became self-made men running their own businesses, as they had neither their Papa nor their Grandpapa to help them towards achieving a successful life. In particular, Herbert and Bertie, no longer the middle men in a vast trading empire, forged lives by selling products direct to the public; they were at the end of the chain and formed relationships with lower middle-class and working-class people.

The size of family again decreased with the Clark siblings having three children each on average. Other changes in matrimony are also evident; the legal right for women to own property in their own right and later on divorce becoming more accessible. Three of the Clark siblings in this generation had failed marriages and their first wives showed strength and independence that would not have been possible just a generation before.

Above all, my research has exposed the links between generations cascading down to the present day which are still discernible in appearances, character traits and skills for example, such as writing, poetry and art. The wealth of material available has enabled me to pursue these lives in the modern age and to supplement the words of family members; some individuals that were born as long ago as the early 19th century and have voices that echo down the centuries. I am eternally privileged and grateful to be able to recall them all in this book.

APPENDIX ONE

———

VERBATIM COPY OF THE WILL OF THOMAS CLARK

———

(1819-1895)

I THOMAS CLARK of 6 Great Tower Street in the city of London Colonial Broker hereby revoke all wills and other testamentary dispositions heretofore made by me and declare this to be my last Will and Testament I bequeath to my daughter Mary Ann Esther Clark and my son-in-law Alfred Bawtree of Lloyds in the city of London Underwriter their executors and administrators all my household furniture plate plated articles china glass books linen prints pictures musical instruments and other articles of domestic use and ornament Upon trust to permit my wife Frances Clark during her widow hood and so long as she shall provide a home for my unmarried daughters for the time being who shall be willing to reside with her to possess use and enjoy the whole of such chattels and effects or such part thereof as my trustees or trustee may deem sufficient for the purpose of furnishing a suitable residence for my said wife and unmarried daughters but in case my said wife shall fail to provide a home for my unmarried daughters or such daughters shall decline to reside with her or all my daughters shall marry Then upon trust to permit my said wife during her widowhood to have the use and enjoyment of such portion of the said chattels and effects as my trustees or trustee in their his or her discretion may deem sufficient for her use alone And subject to the trusts hereinbefore declared all the said chattels and effects shall form part of my residuary personal estate and be disposed of accordingly I bequeath to my said wife the sum of fifty pounds to be paid to her within one calendar month after my death to enable her to provide mourning for herself and such of my daughters as at my death shall not be or have been married I devise all the messuages lands tenements hereditaments and real estate of every tenure of or to which I shall at my death be seized or entitled or over which I shall at my death have a general power of appointment or disposition by Will (except what I otherwise dispose of by this my Will or any codicil hereto) Unto and the use of the said Mary Ann Esther Clark and Alfred Bawtree their heirs executors and administrators respectively according to the tenure thereof respectively Upon trust that they the said Mary Ann Esther Clark and Alfred Bawtree or the survivor of them or the executors or administrators of such survivor shall sell the same either together or in parcels and either by Public Auction or Private contract and may make any stipulations as to title or evidence or commencement of title or otherwise which they he or she shall think fit And may buy in or rescind or vary any contract for sale and resell without being answerable for any loss occasioned thereby and may for the purposes aforesaid or any of them execute and do all such assurances and things as they he or she shall think fit I bequeath the Policies of Assurance numbered 2929 and 2930 in the Provident Clerks Mutual Benefit Association each for one hundred pounds payable on my death And all other Policies payable on my death and all the money securities for money goods chattels credits and personal estate of or to which I shall at my death be possessed or entitled or over which I shall at my death have a general power of appointment or disposition by Will (except chattels real included in the devise hereinbefore contained of real estate and except what else I otherwise dispose of by this my will or any codicil thereto) Unto the said Mary Ann Esther Clark and Alfred Bawtree their executors and administrators Upon trust that they the said Mary Ann Esther Clark and Alfred Bawtree or the survivor of them or the executors or administrators of such survivor shall call in sell and convert into money such part thereof as shall not consist of money And I hereby declare that the said Mary Ann Esther Clark and Alfred Bawtree and the survivor of them and the heirs executors and administrators respectively of such survivor shall out of the monies to arise from the sale of the said real estate hereinbefore devised in trust for sale and from the calling in sale and conversion into money of such parts of the said personal estate lastly hereinbefore bequeathed as shall not consist of money and out of the ready money of which I shall be possessed at my death pay my funeral and testamentary expenses and debts and the legacies (other than specific legacies) bequeathed by this my will or any codicil thereto And shall invest the residue of the same monies in the names or name or under the legal control of them the said trustees or trustee for the time being in any of the public stocks or funds or Government securities of the United Kingdom or India or upon freehold copyhold or leasehold securities in England or Wales or in or upon the debentures or debenture stocks or the preference preferred or guaranteed stocks or shales of any Company in the United Kingdom or India or upon the mortgages or securities of any Municipal Corporation or other Public body in the United Kingdom and may at any time vary or transpose such stocks funds shares or securities into or for others of the same or a like nature at their or his discretion And shall (subject as hereinafter mentioned) pay one equal third part of the interest dividends and income of the said residuary monies and the stocks funds shares and securities in or upon or for which the same or any part thereof may be invested or transposed to my said wife during her widowhood And subject thereto shall stand possessed of the said monies stocks funds shares and securities and the interest dividends and income thereof In trust for all my children who shall be living at my death and all such of the children then living of any child or children of mine who shall have died, in my lifetime as being male attain the age of twenty one years or being female attain that age or marry under that age in equal shares per stirpes so that my children who shall be objects of this trust shall take in equal shares and the children being objects of this trust or any child of mine who shall have died in my lifetime shall take equally between them the share which the parent would have taken had he or she survived me And I declare that the share to which every female child or grandchild shall become entitled under the trusts hereinbefore declared shall belong to her for her sole and separate use independently of her husband for the time being and her receipt shall be a discharge for the sale Provided always and I hereby declare that with respect to the share to which my daughter Eliza the wife of Frederick A Field will become entitled if she survive me it shall be lawful for the trustees or trustee for the time being of this my Will if they he or she shall in their his or her uncontrolled discretion think proper instead of paying or transferring the same share to her to retain the same in their her or his names or name and to pay the interest dividends and income thereof only to the said Eliza Field during the joint lives of herself and the said Frederick A Field for her sole and separate use but with power from time to time at the absolute discretion of the said trustees or trustee to pay to the said Eliza Field any part of the capital of her said share or to apply the whole thereof in any manner for her benefit And after the death of such one of them the said Eliza Field and Frederick A Field as shall first die the said trustees or trustee shall hold the capital of such share or so much thereof as shall not have been paid or applied under the power lastly hereinbefore contained upon the trusts following that is to say If the said Eliza Field shall survive the said Frederick A Field then in trust for the said Eliza Field her executors and administrators But if the said Frederick A Field shall survive the said Eliza Field then in trust for all the children or any the child of the said Eliza Field who being sons or a son shall attain the age of twenty one years or being daughters or a daughter shall attain that age or marry under that age and if more than one in equal shares Provided always and I hereby declare that all such sums of money as have already been advanced or given or shall hereafter be advanced or given by me to or for the benefit of any of my sons and which shall at my death appear in my current Account Book to be entered against such son shall be taken in or towards satisfaction of the share hereby provided for such son or (as to a son dying in my lifetime) for his children taking in the place of such son and shall be brought into hotchpot and accounted for accordingly But if if the sums so advanced and appearing in such Account book as aforesaid against any of my said sons shall exceed the amount of the share of my residuary estate of such son or his children (as the case may be) including his or their share of that part of my estate the income of which is payable to my said wife during her widowhood I direct my Executors to release such son or his estate (from so much of the sums so advanced as shall be in excess of such share Provided always and for the purpose of directing the mode in which the one third part whereof the income is to be paid to or received by my said wife as hereinbefore is mentioned is to be ascertained I hereby declare that the sums which by virtue of this my Will will have to be brought into hotchpot against the provision hereby made by me for any of my sons shall be included in the computation of the amount of my residuary estate the income of one third part whereof is to be paid to or received by my said wife as aforesaid and every sum which any of my said sons will have to bring into hotchpot as aforesaid shall in the first instance be brought into hotchpot against the two third parts devolving upon such son or his children (as the case may be) in the lifetime of my said wife of the share of such son or his children in such my residuary estate and if in excess of such two third parts shall to the extent of such excess be brought into hotchpot against the other third part of the share of such son or his children in such my residuary estate but as to any such excess as last aforesaid the income corresponding to such excess shall not be payable to my said wife or be accounted for by such son or his children and such excess shall for the purposes of this my will be deemed not to carry interest until the death or marriage of my said wife which shall first happen Provided always and I hereby further declare that it is my wish that my said wife shall provide a home for herself and such of my daughters as for the time being shall not be or have been married and that each of my daughters who shall reside with my said wife shall contribute a due proportion of the housekeeping expenses but not any part of the rent rates taxes or repairs of the house in which my wife may live And if my wife and my unmarried daughters or any of them shall not be able to agree as to the proportion of the housekeeping expenses which they or any of them ought to contribute the same shall be determined by the said Alfred Bawtree or other the trustee for the time being of this my Will who shall be substituted for him And in case my said wife shall fail to provide a home for my unmarried daughters or such daughters shall decline to residue with her or all my daughters shall marry then and in either of such cases the trustees or trustee of this my Will shall deduct the annual sum of forty pounds from the one third part of the income of my residuary estate hereinbefore directed to be paid to my said wife during her widowhood and shall hold such sum of forty pounds Upon trust for the persons under this my Will shall be entitled to the other two third parts of the income of my residuary estate in the same shares and manner as if the said sum of forty pounds formed part of such last mentioned two third parts of the income of my residuary estate Provided also and I hereby declare that after the expiration of three years from my death if my said wife shall be then living and not have married again it shall be lawful for the trustees or trustee for the time being instead of continuing to pay to my said wife one equal third part of the income of my residuary estate to secure for her an annual sum equal to the annual amount which on the average during the three years from the day of my death shall have been paid to my said wife on account of one third part of the income of my said residuary estate either by charging all or any part of my real estate if any which shall then remain unsold with such annual sum or by setting apart any part of my residuary estate the income of which will be in the opinion of the said trustees or trustee be sufficient to satisfy such annual sum as aforesaid and when such annual sum shall be so secured the residue of my residuary estate shall be discharged from all claims of my wife on account of her third part of the income thereof But in case the income of the property which shall be so charged or set apart shall at any time prove insufficient to satisfy such annual sum as aforesaid the deficiency shall from time to time be made good out of the capital or corpus of the same property Provided always that such annual sum as aforesaid shall be subject to the provision hereinbefore contained for the deduction in the events hereinbefore mentioned of the annual sum of forty pounds from the one third part of the income of my residuary estate Provided always and I hereby declare that it shall be lawful for the said Mary Ann Esther Clark and Alfred Bawtree and the survivor of them and the heirs executors and administrators respectively of such survivor to defer and postpone the sale conversion and collection of the whole or any part or parts of my said real and personal estate respectively so long as to such trustees or trustee shall in their his or her uncontrolled discretion seem proper but my real estate shall for the purpose of transmission be impressed with the quality of personality from the time of my death And I empower my said trustees or trustee during such interval of postponement to manage and let either on lease or from year to year my real and leasehold estates and to make out of the income or capital of my real and personal estate any outlay which such trustees or trustee may consider proper for the improvements repairs calls on shares premium on policies or otherwise for the benefit or in respect of my real or personal estate And I declare that the income produced from every or any part of my real or personal estate previously to the conversion or collection thereof pursuant to the trusts hereinbefore declared shall be applied in the same manner in all respects as if the same were income proceeding from such investments as are hereinbefore directed or authorised and that the whole of the income produced from my residuary estate (real or personal) in its actual condition or state of investment for the time being whether proceeding from property or investments of an authorised or an unauthorised description and whether of a permanent or a wasting character shall as well during the first year from my decease as at all times afterwards be applicable as income under the trusts of this my Will no part thereof being in any event liable to be retained as corpus or capital but no reversion or other property not actually producing income which shall form part of my estate shall under the doctrine of constructive conversion or otherwise be treated as producing income or as entitling any party to the receipt of income And I declare that the trustees or trustee for the time being of this my Will shall have the fullest powers of determining what articles of property pass under any specific bequest contained in this my Will or any codicil thereto and of apportioning blended trust funds and of determining whether any monies are to be treated as capital or income And generally of determining all matters as to which any doubt difficulty or question may arise under or in relation to the execution of the trusts of this my Will or any codicil hereto And I declare that every determination of the said trustees or trustee in relation to any of the matters aforesaid whether made upon a question formally or actually raised or implied in any of the acts or proceedings of the said trustees or trustee in relation to the premises shall bind all parties interested under this my Will and shall not be objected to or questioned upon any ground whatsoever And I hereby declare that notwithstanding the trusts hereinbefore declared it shall be lawful for the trustees or trustee for the time being (in case they he or she in their his or her uncontrolled discretion shall think fit) to continue for such a period or respective periods as they he or she shall think desirable any business or businesses in which I may be engaged at the time of my death and to engage and employ in any such business or businesses such part of my estate and effects not exceeding altogether the sum of five thousand pounds as such trustees or trustee shall think desirable and for the purposes aforesaid to appoint Managers and others to conduct or superintend the said businesses or any of them and to allow them such salaries either by way of commissions per centage or otherwise which they he or she shall deem expedient And I declare that when the said Trustees or Trustee shall determine to discontinue any such business and wind up the same they he or she may dispose thereof in such manner and make all such arrangements in relation thereto as they he or she may think proper And in particular may give time for payment of any sum or sums of money which shall be owing or which shall be agreed to be paid to my estate on account of any such business and that either with or without taking any security And generally may act in relation to the said businesses either as to carrying on or winding up the same as they he or she could do if they he or she were or was acting on their his or her own account It being my intention to vest in the said trustees or trustee for the time being the largest discretion and freedom from responsibility in order that they he or she may be induced to act in such manner with respect to such businesses as they he or she in their his or her judgment shall consider will be most advantageous to my estate And I declare that the net profits which the said trustees or trustee shall derive or receive from any such businesses as aforesaid shall for all the purposes of this my Will be considered annual income and shall be applied accordingly Provided always and I hereby declare that in case my son Thomas Clark the younger either alone or in conjunction with his Partner Gerald Fitz Gibbon shall in exercise of the power contained in an Agreement dated the second day of September one thousand eight hundred and seventy nine purchase the leasehold premises machinery and effects therein comprised and thereby agreed to be leased by me to the said Thomas Clark the younger and Gerald Fitz Gibbon or in case my son Frederick Henry Clark either alone or in conjunction with his Partner John Christie shall in exercise of the power contained in an Agreement dated the thirty first day of March one thousand eight hundred and eighty purchase the leasehold premises machinery and effects therein comprised and thereby agreed to be leased by me to the said Frederick Henry Clark and John Christie the trustees or trustee for the time being of this my Will may give to the person or persons exercising such powers such time for payment of the purchase monies for the said premises respectively and either with or without taking security for the same and generally upon such terms as to the said trustees or trustee shall seem proper without being accountable for any loss which may happen in consequence thereof Provided always and I hereby declare that if the said trustees hereby constituted or either of them shall die in my lifetime or if they or either of them or any trustee or trustees appointed as hereinafter provided shall after my death die or be abroad or desire to be discharged or refuse or become incapable to act then and in every such case it shall be lawful for the surviving or continuing trustee or trustee for the time being (and for this purpose every refusing or retiring trustee shall if willing to act in the execution of this power be considered a continuing trustee) or for the acting executors or executor administrators or administrator of the last surviving or continuing trustee to appoint a new trustee or new trustees in the place of the trustee or trustees so dying or being abroad or desiring to be discharged or refusing or becoming incapable to act as aforesaid And upon any or every such appointment as aforesaid the number of trustees may be augmented or reduced but not to less than two And upon every such appointment the trust property shall if and so far as the nature of the property and other circumstances shall require or admit be transferred so that the same may be vested in the trustees or trustee for the time being And every trustee so appointed as aforesaid may as well before as after such transfer of the said trust property act or assist in the execution of the trusts or powers of this my Will as fully and effectually as if I had hereby constituted him a trustee Provided always and I hereby declare that the trustees for the time being of this my Will shall be respectively chargeable only for such monies stocks funds shares and securities as they shall respectively actually receive notwithstanding their respectively signing any receipt for the sake of conformity and shall be answerable and accountable only for their own acts neglects and defaults respectively and not for those of each other nor for any Banker Broker Auctioneer or other person with whom or into whose hands any trust monies or securities may be deposited or come nor for dispensing wholly or partially with the investigation or production of the Lessors title on lending money on leasehold securities nor for otherwise lending on any security with less than a marketable title nor for the insufficiency or deficiency of any stocks funds shares or securities nor for any loss which may happen in carrying on any of my businesses or from acts of the Trustees or Trustee in relation thereto nor for any other loss unless the same shall happen through their own wilful default respectively And also that the said trustees or trustee for the time being may reimburse themselves himself and herself or pay and discharge out of the trust premises all expenses incurred in or about the execution of the trusts or powers of this my Will I devise and bequeath all the estates which at my death which shall be vested in me upon any trusts or by way of mortgage and of which I shall at my death have power to dispose by Will unto the said Mary Ann Esther Clark and Alfred Bawtree their heirs executors and administrators respectively according to the nature thereof respectively Upon the trusts and subject to the equity of redemption which at my death shall be subsisting or capable of taking effect therein respectively but the money secured on such mortgages shall be taken as part of my personal estate And I hereby appoint the said Mary Ann Esther Clark and Alfred Bawtree EXECUTRIX and EXECUTOR of this my Will and authorise and empower the acting Executors or Executor for the time being of this my Will to pay and satisfy or compromise or compound any debts owing or claimed to be owing by or from me or my estate and any liabilities to which I or my estate may be or may be alleged to be subject and to accept any composition or any security real or personal for any debts owing to me or my estate and to allow such time for the payment of any such debt or composition (either with or without taking security for the same) as to them him or her shall seem reasonable and to refer to arbitration and settle all debts accounts questions and things which shall be owing or claimed to be owing from or to me or my estate or be depending or arise between me or my Executors or Executor and any other person or persons and generally to act in relation to the premises in such manner as they he or she shall think expedient without being liable for any loss occasioned thereby IN WITNESS whereof I the said Thomas Clark have to this my last will and testament contained in nine sheets of paper set my hand this twelfth day of May one thousand eight hundred and eighty – THOMAS CLARK – SIGNED by the said Thomas Clark in the joint presence of us who in his presence and in the presence of each other subscribe our names as witnesses – W CARPENTER Solr 4 Brabant Court Philpot Lane London – THOs CARPENTER Solr 4 Brabant Court Philpot Lane London

On the 27th day of July 1895 Probate of this Will was granted to Mary Ann Esther Clark Spinster and Alfred Bawtree the Executors.

Explanation

Written in 1880, the will is a lengthy and complex document which reveals the strain of family relationships adapting to the presence of his second wife, Frances.

Following his demise he was keen that the needs of all his family, especially his wife and unmarried daughters, were catered for. At the time the will was written, there were only three of these unmarried daughters and all but one was married at his death – Mary Ann, the joint executor.

Most importantly in the aftermath, Frances is to have £50 paid within one calendar month following his death to provide her with mourning garments together with any of his unmarried daughters. Secondly, Frances is to be able to retain the chattels and effects deemed necessary by the trustees, which are considered sufficient to furnish a suitable residence for her and his unmarried daughters. However, if any daughters decline to live with her, she is to receive only a portion of these effects at the discretion of the executors.

If his daughters were to live with Frances, they shall contribute a due proportion of the housekeeping expenses but not any part of the rent, rates, taxes or repairs of the house. If there is a disagreement between his wife and his daughters as to the proportion of household expenses which they ought to contribute, the same should be determined by Alfred Bawtree, who probably was viewed as being more impartial and capable than anyone else in the family.

All of his family, whether married or unmarried, both children and grandchildren (in the case of parents who predeceased their father) are to be beneficiaries of his estate. The proceeds from the sale of both his Personal and Real estate and life insurance policies will firstly have paid his funeral and testamentary expenses and debts.

Following this his executors are given powers to use their own judgement as to whether to reinvest some of the money to allow any of his business interests in which he was engaged to flourish after his death and expressly five thousand pounds could be used to appoint managers, superintendents and permit salaries. They must act in such manner with respect to such businesses as they shall consider will be most advantageous to his estate. Net profits shall be considered and annual income and shall be applied accordingly. Such an arrangement could maximise funds for his extensive family to continue to live in comfort, as they had relied on his income during his lifetime.

Also, the trustees will have the ability to delay the sale, conversion or collection of the whole or part of the Personal and Real estate using their discretion. They are empowered if there is a postponement, to either manage or let either on lease or from year to year these estates, and to make out of the income or capital any outlay towards improvements, repairs, calls or shares, premiums on policies for the benefit of or in respect of the said estates. Out of the proceeds from the sale of the Personal and Real estates, and conversion of the personal estate, and following his funeral, the residue shall be invested under the legal control of the executors in any of the public stocks, funds, government securities of the United Kingdom or India.

One-third part of the interest dividends and Income from the residuary money invested will be paid to his wife Frances, during her widowhood whilst the remaining two-thirds will be held in trust, in equal shares, for all the children living at his death, or grandchildren (if a child of his has died in his lifetime) providing that grandchild is male and over 21 years. If the grandchild is female, she will need to have attained 21 years or marry under that age to benefit.

The share to which every female child or grandchild shall become entitled under the trusts, shall belong to her for her sole and separate use, independently of her husband and her receipt shall be a discharge for the same.

If any of his unmarried daughters shall decline to reside with Frances, his wife, the sum of forty pounds would be deducted annually from the one-third part of the Income of the residuary estate directed towards his wife Frances for the children who are entitled to share in the other two-thirds of the income and interest from the residuary estate.

However, after three years of widowhood, it would be lawful if the trustees stopped making the one-third of the income to Frances and instead, secured her with an annual income which was equal to the average payment during the last three years from the date of his death, as part of the income from the residual estate. This could be obtained from any real estate that remained unsold or by setting apart any of the residuary estate, if it was the opinion of the trustees that it was a sufficient amount. Thus his residuary estate should be discharged from all claim of his wife on account of her one-third part of the Income.

Perhaps he felt at the time that this outcome in the short term would support his wife sufficiently whilst at the same time, respecting or caring for his unmarried daughters and the rest of his family, who should, after all, still have many years ahead of them. He may have felt that this arrangement was necessary to keep the peace between the two parties.

Whatever his goals were, he was very keen to impress upon his family that he trusted in the ability and judgement of his executors to carry out his wishes. He states powerfully that every determination of the trustees in relation to any of the matters whether made upon a question formally or actually or implied in any of the sets or proceedings of the trustees in relation to the premises shall bind all parties interested in my will and shall not be objected to or questioned upon any ground whatsoever.

Regarding his daughter Eliza, different arrangements would be made which protected her from the man she had married five years before the writing of the will. Frederick Field was viewed with mistrust by her Papa. Instead of paying or transferring Eliza's share of the two-thirds residual estate income, the trustees are given the uncontrolled discretion to retain it in their names and pay the dividends/interest income only to Eliza during the joint lives of her and her husband Fred Field for her sole and separate use but with power at the absolute discretion of the trustees to pay Eliza any part of the capital of her said share or to apply the whole in any manner for her benefit. If one of them dies, the trustees will hold the capital of the share. If Eliza should survive Fred Field, then in trust for Eliza but if Eliza dies first, in trust for her children.

Regarding his sons, Thomas and Frederick, who were of course also colonial brokers, Fred was a beneficiary in the 1880 will but he had died in 1893. The position was in 1880, that apparently Papa had loaned (advanced) money to his sons for their benefit which appeared in his account book and any such money owing by them would be offset against their share of the interest from the two-thirds share of the residuary estate. However, if the amount owing should exceed the amount they were due under the residuary estate, and then considered payable to his wife, his executors were instructed to release such son (or his estate) from the sums so advanced which would be in excess of such share. However, any money owing would be included in the computation of the residuary estate, the income of which one-third to go to Frances.

APPENDIX 2

―――――

TIME LINE

―――――

1783-1927

Italics = family events

Year	Event
1783	William Pitt the younger becomes PM.
1785	*Thomas Clark born in Plumstead, Kent, son of William & Sarah*
1788	First edition of 'The Times' is published.
1789	Thames and Severn Canal opens.
1793	Britain goes to war with France.
1796	Edward Jenner successfully cures James Phipps of smallpox.
1805	Battle of Trafalgar, 21 October – Lord Horatio Nelson killed.
1811	George III's period of insanity, his son takes over as Prince Regent.
1813	Pride and Prejudice by Jane Austen is published.
1815	Battle of Waterloo, 18 June, ends the Napoleonic Wars.
1819	*Thomas Clark born 22 April at Webb Street, Bermondsey and baptised 5 May at St. Olave's, Southwark*

	Birth of Victoria, the future Queen, 24 May, at Kensington Palace.
	Peterloo Massacre in Manchester, 16 August.
1820	George IV becomes King.
1825	Stockton to Darlington Railway, the world's first public passenger railway opened.
1827	*Birth of Esther Clark, brother of Thomas Clark, date unknown – Tooley Street, Southwark.*
1828	Wellington is prime minster.
1829	Catholic Emancipation Act permits members of the Roman Catholic Church to sit in Parliament at Westminster.
	Police force founded in London.
	Stephenson's Rocket wins the competition on the Liverpool to Manchester line.
1830	William IV becomes King.
1832	First cholera epidemic in London.
	The Great Reform Act enfranchises the middle classes.
1833	Slavery Abolition Act abolishes slavery in parts of the Empire.
1834	Houses of Parliament destroyed by fire.
1837	Victoria ascends the throne, 20 June.
1838	Charles Dickens' Oliver Twist is published.
1839	*Thomas Clark marries Mary Ann Westfield on 16 December at St. Mary, Newington.*
1840	Victoria marries Prince Albert of Saxe-Coburg and Gotha, 10 February.
	First postage stamps issued – Penny Black.
	Fox Talbot patents a photographic process using a negative.
1841	First national census takes place, 6 June.
	Birth of the future Edward VII at Buckingham Palace, 9 November.
	Thomas Clark, son of Thomas and Mary Ann born at Victoria Terrace, Newington, 9 December.

1843–60	*Thomas Clark's 11 siblings are born between these years. All but two survive to adulthood.*
1844	Repeal of the Corn Laws.
	Brunel designs SS Great Britain, the first propeller driven steamship.
1847	Wuthering Heights by Emily Bronte published.
1848	Founding of the Pre-Raphaelite Brotherhood.
1850	*Esther Clark marries Thomas Try, 23 June.*
	Alfred Tennyson appointed Poet Laureate.
1851	The Great Exhibition, Crystal Palace, Hyde Park. Runs for six months – visited by six million people. Building later moved to Sydenham.
	Population of UK reaches 27,368,800.
	Thomas Clark and family resident at Shenton Street, Old Kent Road. Occupation – Commercial broker's clerk.
	Thomas Clark (b.1785) dies at East Street, Walworth of apoplexy, 17 October. His son-in-law Thomas Try is present at the death.
1853	Crimean War commences.
	Vaccination against smallpox compulsory for infants.
1854	*Ann Clark, mother of Thomas Clark, dies at Shenton Street from cholera – Wednesday 6 September.*
	Discovery that cholera is transmitted by drinking contaminated water not by miasma carried on the air during outbreak which included the Soho Broad Street water pump.
	Eliza Clark born Saturday 16 September – 10 days after her grandmother died.
1856	Invention of Bessemer converter permits mass production of steel.
1857	Matrimonial Causes Act passed – divorce is now more accessible (for the husband).
	Science Museum established at South Kensington.

1858	The Great Stink from the River Thames reaches its peak in August.
1858–60	*Thomas Clark involved in drainage dispute with neighbours and the local health board at Ordnance Terrace, Shooters' Hill.*
1859	Darwin publishes On the Origin of Species.
1861	Death of Prince Albert from typhoid.
1862–3	*Thomas Clark junior reaches his majority and publishes two books.*
1863	Prince Albert Edward (Bertie) marries Alexandra of Denmark at Windsor, 10 March.
	World's first underground station opens in London.
	Amelia Clark (age 6) dies of scarlet fever and typhoid at Ashmore House, Cudham, 21 June.
	The Clarks move to Crofton Hall, Orpington between July and September.
	Thomas Clark junior elopes to Kew with Miss Frances Charlotte Bailey age 17 and they secretly marry, 9 September.
1865	London drainage system designed by Bazelgette opens.
	Lewis Carroll's Alice in Wonderland is published.
	Thomas Clark now marries Miss Bailey legally at St. Giles, Camberwell, 9 September. She is 19 and has parental consent.
1866	*Mary Ann Clark (nee Westfield) dies on 23 October, age 50, in Sheffield.*
	Black Friday on London Stock Exchange.
	Thomas William Francis Clark, first son of Thomas and Frances, born at 5 Palace Road, Penge, 25 June.
1867	*Thomas Clark senior leaves Crofton Hall in February and moves to Sydenham with his family.*
	Second Parliamentary Reform Act passed – extends voting rights to urban working class males.
	Thomas Clark senior marries Miss Frances Colebatch at

	Stoke Newington, 23 November.
1868	Gladstone is PM
	Birth of Ernest Percival Frederick (Percy) at Clarendon House, Coburg Road, Camberwell (a second son) 5 March.
	St. Pancras station opens.
1869	Suez Canal opens – cuts journeys to and from Australia and the Far East.
1870	Death of Charles Dickens.
	Forster's Elementary Education Act set framework for schooling all children aged 5 to 12.
Circa 1870	*Thomas Clark junior and family move to Claremont House, Brighton Road, Sutton.*
1870/1	Franco-Prussian War, Camille Pissarro, the French painter, lives and works in Upper Norwood.
1871	*Birth of Herbert Lionel Alexander Clark, 4 December, at Claremont, Sutton*
1872/4	*Matilda Hephzibah Clark keeps a diary which illuminates family life.*
1873	*Matilda Clark marries Alfred Bawtree, 10 May, at South Dulwich.*
1873	*Birth of Sydney Clark at Sutton.*
1874	Benjamin Disraeli is prime minister.
1875	*Birth of Bertram Allan Leslie Clark, 29 June, at Claremont, Sutton.*
1876	*Sydney Clark dies at Hillside, Sutton, of diphtheria 24 March.*
1876	*Birth of Walter Vivian Harold Clark at Hill Side, 15 October.*
1877	Queen Victoria is Empress of India.
1877–9	Zulu War
1879	*Birth of Beatrice Frances Mary Clark at Tottenham, 29 April.*
1882	*Thomas Clark junior addresses the Metropolitan Anglo-*

Israel Association.

1882	Married Women's Property Act gives married women rights to own property in their own right.
1884	First London Underground train runs.
1885	*William Bailey dies (Frances Clark's father).*
1887	Victoria celebrates her Golden Jubilee.
1888–91	Jack the Ripper murders take place in Whitechapel.
1889	London Dock workers and match girls strike.
1891	*Annie Meen (née Bailey) dies age 49 in Islington.*
1893	Manchester ship canal completed.
1893	*Death of Frederick Henry Clark age 49.*
1893	*Herbert Clark marries Edith Reader, 4 September.*
1895	*Death of Thomas Clark, colonial broker, at his home, 20 March.*
1897	Queen Victoria celebrates her Diamond Jubilee.
1897	*Thomas Clark junior declared bankrupt in June.*
1898	Marie Curie discovers radium.
1899–1902	The Second Boer War.
1900	*Jane Bailey, Frances' mother dies in December.*
1901	Death of Queen Victoria – Edward VII accession.
1901	*Tom and Frances Clark move to Bowers Gifford, Essex.*
1904	*Beatrice Clark marries Edmund Palmer, 22nd June, at Bowers Gifford.*
1904	*Frances Clark, wife of Thomas, dies suddenly on 31 October.*
1905	*Thomas writes 'In Memoriam' poem in memory of his lost wife on the 1st anniversary.*
1909	*Death of brother-in-law, Josiah Fountain Meen, 11 October.*
1910	Death of King Edward VII, 6 May.
1914–1918	The Great War
1915+	*Thomas Clark reacts to War (Zeppelins and time changes).*
1917	*Death of sister Alice Troup at Bowers Gifford, 1 August.*

1917	Russian Revolution.
1900–1920	*Thomas Clark works as an artist and writer.*
1918	Enfranchisement of all men over 21 and women over 30.
c1923	*Thomas Clark's son Herbert moves to Norfolk following marriage breakdown.*
1926	The General Strike.
1927	*Thomas Clark dies on 31 January at Central Home, Leytonstone.*

APPENDIX 3

POETRY

IN MEMORIAM

Oh! my sweet, sweet dead darling one, tonight
I dedicate to thee a year of fears
No day has passed, throughout the dread sad year
Without my shedding bitter tears of grief
Each hour o'er shadowed by the direful loss
Of thy sweet presence, ever by my side
Each meal a torture by thy vacant chair:
And oft as I recall thy last sweet words,
"My darling love, my sweet one" and I feel
Thy fervent kisses on my trembling lips,
Methinks it seems disloyalty to thee
I should survive so long; so long endure
The absence of thy treasured love, and live.
My very being lies entombed with thee
Wedded to thy dead body, and the ring
I placed upon thy finger that glad day
When I espoused thee, and first called thee mine;
The ring, thou dids't so cherish and esteem,
As mad'st thy boast to never have removed

Remains with thee a silent testament
Of my enduring; my undying love,
Oh! when again, throughout the ceaseless years;
Shall meet our kindred spirits and renew
The deep devotion each to each did bear,
That every separation was a pain,
Almost beyond endurance and did prove
Our married life to be, through all its days
One long continued joyous honeymoon.
How then shall I now bear this bitter pang,
This final grievous parting; how endure
The aching void thy absence must need leave
Without a gleam of light or hope to cheer
This side the gloomy portals of the grave;
Nor can high Heaven contain a greater bliss
Than our reunion, on that joyous day,
In resurrection glory to appear,
Robed in the dear Lord's spotless righteousness
Oh! Come then death, in mercy bear me hence,
And close my eyes on this sad scene from whence
All joy, all hope has fled, and left my life
Naught but a weary blank, a living death,
Without my darling, my devoted wife.

T.C.W.
Thomas Clark Westfield
Bowers Gifford, Essex. 31ˢᵗ October 1905.

DEDICATED TO GRANDPA WESTFIELD

Dear Grandpa, you lived your life and died
Before my life had scarce begun
You lived way back in the "good old days" nay! Some

Would say they were bad,
When England was great, but many were poor
But there's just one thing of which I'm sure
And Oh! Grandpa it makes me sad
I didn't know you more.

I know what you looked like; I saw your
Portrait on the wall
You stood there, a young man, bearded not too tall,
Smartly dressed –
Of background details, I'm not aware,
Only of you, and how elegant you were standing there
There's truly one thing of which I'm sure
I wish I could have known you more.

And yet, Grandpa, I do know you, and know you well
For often I heard my dear Dad tell me many
Things and stories of you,
And I know what he said was surely true
Which makes me in my own mind sure
How I wish I could have known you more.

But you were a gentleman, gifted, learned and refined
You moved in a world so different to mine
I wonder what you would think of me
My husband and children dear?
Our way of life could not with yours compare.
Looking back you seem so grand, I wonder,
Would you understand us,
But one thing sure
I still would like to have known you more.

Many were the gifts you possessed,
You could write books and express

Yourself in prose, you could play the piano
And paint pictures too
I have one of a rural view.
I have your book called "Westfield's Essays"
So Grandfather in many ways
I would have been proud and privileged too
Just to have seen and known you.

And what of Grandma? How did she fare?
She was gentle and sweet, kind, a perfect dear.
And Grandpa loved her, there's no doubt
That when she died the light went out
Of his life; He wrote a lengthy poem
Bewailing his grief, and how alone
He felt in that first tragic dark year,
If only I could have been there,
There's one thing sure
'Twas a time I could have known him more.

And when he was old and ready to die 'twas
The saddest truth of all.
He was left with strangers, quite alone; his
Friends and loved ones, all of them gone
For it was Dad who told me I recall,
It was not his wish to leave him there, for I
Often heard him vow and declare
His fervent wish to have him home, but he was
Left to die alone
Oh! but I wish I could have been there
To hold his hand and whisper a prayer.

Dear Grandpa, at that time there were people
Known to say
That you were bad tempered, difficult, and better away.

But then it is true, there's few of us saints
And it's easy for people to make such complaints.
No matter your failures, I'm still quite sure
Of my wish and desire to have known you more.

M.D.W. 1974
Marjorie Doris Walshe

In Memory of my dear father who died March 1955

DAD

Memory goes back a long time; I recall the days
Spent with Dad
He died many years past, it's a sad
Truth, we never know a person's worth until they are gone
But God be praised! Memories linger on
Rendering him close and real each day
The way he looked, the things he would say
It all comes back to me fresh and clear
The many things which served to endear him to me.

Once more, I'm a child, beside him in the car
As he drove to places near and far;
To Norwich he would frequently go
And lunch at Lyons there,
Always boots upon his feet and trilby hat upon his head;
Around the market, we would be seen
Then home in the car to Buckenham Green
Calling at Cawstons on the way
For sweets, tobacco, so would end the day,
And always in the evenings, after work was done
I can both see and hear him; at the piano for hours he'd be

Playing so beautifully, Chopin, Beethoven
Or some simple melody
Oh! how I wish my children could also come
To memory lane and hear him play
So wondrously at the close of day.

I would go to bed and listen to him playing there
The lovely music moving me as I sometimes knelt in prayer;
And in Summer his sister, Beatrice, and her daughters three
Would come to stay and I'm sure you'd agree
What delightful music they would make together
Far into the night that summer weather.

Later in the year with roaring fire aglow
Mum and I sitting in the chair
I can see the piano now with photographs on top
In tune with music do a little rock;
As from its keys the notes would flow.
I can see him serving petrol holding
hat or mac in gusty wind
Or sitting in the chair discussing politics or
Worldly scene
And in the mornings not in bed asleep or waking
From a dream
But looking after car or wireless batteries
In garage or shed out back
Always busy, always active, never ever slack.

He couldn't bear to be disturbed or called
Away when he was working there
To others he would make this absolutely clear
"Petrol Dad" his reply "You'll have to go,
I'm much too busy, you should know."

He loved his dogs, his budgies too
He loved his music, this too was true,
He liked Brighton and took his holidays there
He liked Cromer, its quaintness and sea kissed air.
In later years he slighted fashion and smart dress
His workshop and garage were somewhat in a mess.

He was gifted and could turn his hand
To many a task
And would have a go at "aught", he was asked,
Building houses, mending clocks,
Putting together wireless sets, nothing could stop
Him from trying, electrical wiring
Car repairs, cycles too, always conspiring
How or what he could do, he could also
Paint a lovely view.

He had a habit of touching his ear
And moving his foot when cross legged in a chair
A great talker on any subject, be it politics,
Religion or Mars,
He could hold conversation for minutes or hours.
Oh! how I loved him, how I've missed him these years
And in remembering the silent tears will
Occasionally flow.

But I have a hope in a future day
That once again with Dad I will stay
And no more parting there will be
But life together eternally.

M.D.W. September 1975.

ABBREVIATIONS:

GRO: General Register Office
LMA: London Metropolitan Archives
TNA: The National Archives, Kew

BIBLIOGRAPHY

Balchin, W.G.V., ed., *The Country Life Book of the Living History of Britain* (London, Book Club Associates, 1981)

Blomfield, David, *St. Anne's Kew 1714-2014* (Much Wenlock, RJL Smith & Associates, 2014)

Cass, Deborah, *Writing Your Family History: A Practical Guide* (Ramsbury: The Crowood Press Ltd., 2004)

Clark Westfield, Thomas, *A Series of Seven Essays on Universal Science* (London: Robert Hardwicke, 1863)

Clark Westfield, Thomas, *England's Past, Present and Future in Connexion with Rome* (London: Protestant Evangelical Mission, 1866).

Clark Westfield, Thomas, *The Japanese: Their Manners and Customs; with an account of the general characteristics of the country, its manufactures and natural productions.*(London: Photographic News Office, 1862)

Clark Westfield, *Thomas, The Holy City: A Revelation or The Substance of Things Hoped For* (London: Robert Banks & Son, 1903)

Clements, Jonathan, *Darwin's Notebook: The Life, Times and Discoveries of Charles Robert Darwin* (Cheltenham, The History Press, 2009)

Clifford, Mrs. W.K., *A Flash of Summer: The Story of a Simple Woman's Life* (Amazon, reprint of a 1895 edition, undated)

Corbeau-Parsons, Caroline, ed., *Impressionists in London: French Artists in Exile 1870-1904* (London, Tate Enterprises Ltd, 2017)

Herber, Mark D., *Ancestral Trails* (Stroud: Sutton Publishing, 1997)

Hey, David, *The Oxford Companion to Local and Family History* (Oxford, Oxford University Press, 1996)

Hey, David, *The Oxford Guide to Family History* (Oxford, Oxford University Press, 1993)

Hicks, Carola, *Girl in a Green Gown: The History and Mystery of the Arnolfini Portrait* (London: Vintage, 2012)

Horn, Pamela, *Pleasures & Pastimes in Victorian Britain* (Stroud: Sutton Publishing Ltd, 1999)

Ikin, Caroline, *The Victorian Gardener* (Oxford, Shire Publications, 2014)

Jones, Jane E.M., *Pocket Images: Sutton* (Stroud, Nonsuch Publishing Ltd., 2006)

Leach, M., ed., *Aspects of the History of Ongar* (Ongar: Ongar Millennium History Project, 1999)

Levinsohn, Isaac,*The Russo-Polish Jew: A Narrative of the Conversion from the Darkness of Judaism to the Light and Liberty of the Gospel of Jesus Christ* (London, Robert Banks, 1878)

Loveday, John, *The Boy from Rod Alley: An Account of a 1930s Childhood* (Kibworth Beauchamp: Matador, 2019)

Picard, Liza, *Victorian London: The Life of a City 1840-1870* (London: Phoenix, 2005)

Probert, Rebecca, *Marriage Law for Genealogists: The Definitive Guide* (Kenilworth: Takeaway, 2012)

Pullen, Doris E., *Penge: From a hamlet, once part of Battersea in Surrey, to a London Suburb: A story of some of the people and the surrounding district* (Chislehurst, Lodgemark Press, 1978)

Sacks, Janet, *Victorian Childhood* (Oxford, Shire Publications, 2011)

Summerscale, Kate, *Mrs. Robinson's Disgrace: The Private Diary of a Victorian Lady* (London, Bloomsbury Publishing, 2012)

Titford, John, *The Titford Family 1547-1947* (Chichester: Phillimore & Co. Ltd, 1989)

Titford, John, *Writing up Your Family History: a do-it-yourself guide* (Newbury: Countryside Books, 2003)

Uglow, Jenny, *In These Times: Living in Britain through Napoleon's Wars 1793-1815* (London: Faber & Faber, 2014)

Weinreb, Ben, ed., *The London Encyclopaedia,* Third edition, (London: Macmillan, 2008)

Wilson, A.N., *The Victorians* (London: Arrow Books, 2003)

Wilson, J., *Our Israelitish Origin: Lectures on Ancient Israel and the fulness of the Gentiles* (London: James Nisbet and Co., 1865)

NOTES AND SOURCES

PART 1

Chapter 1 Thomas Clark – 'GENT'

1   Stephen Hart, *Website of Pascal Bonenfant, British weather from 1700 to 1849,* 2015 <https://www.pascalbonenfant.com/18c/geography/weather.html> [Accessed 11 February 2020].

2   In 1864 Monday was second only to Sunday as the most popular day for marriage. With the adoption of a standard working week, the old idea of 'Saint Monday' being a day (in rural areas) when the week's work had not really begun in earnest still held some sway. Rebecca Probert, *Marriage Law for Genealogists: The Definitive Guide* (Kenilworth: Takeaway, 2012) pp. 132-133

3   *Ibid.,* p.133. The Marriage Act of 1886 extended the hours of marriage up to 3 p.m., before this marriage had to take place between the hours of 8 a.m. and 12 noon as detailed in the Marriage Act of 1823. The parish register records that another wedding preceded that of Thomas Clark and Mary Ann Westfield's the same morning.

4   Wikipedia, *Newington, London,* 2019 <https://en.wikipedia.org/wiki/Newington,_London>
Wikipedia, *Newington Butts,* 2019 <https://en.wikipedia.org/wiki/Newington_Butts> [Accessed 22 February 2020].

5   "The Church of St Mary, Newington." *Survey of London: Volume 25, St George's Fields (The Parishes of St. George the Martyr Southwark and St. Mary Newington).* Ed. Ida Darlington. London: London County Council, 1955. 91-94. *British History Online.* Web. <https://www.british-history.ac.uk/survey-london/vol25/pp91-94> [accessed 11 February 2020].

6   It was illegal to marry under the age of 21 without parental consent until 1970. See Rebecca Probert, *Marriage Law for Genealogists: The Definitive Guide* (Kenilworth: Takeaway, 2012) p. 111.

7   One or both parties may not have been able to write more than their own name/s. It was usual practice for any one unable to write at all, to make a cross by the side of their name which was written by another hand.

8   Ann Clark's husband Frederick Thomas Aldridge's brother, George, emigrated to Australia in 1841 later becoming a prosperous hotelier in Adelaide. His daughter Rosa (1861-1922) was the mother of his grandson – Percy Aldridge Grainger, the composer.

9   Naming the father would result in the parish pursuing him for a form of child

maintenance known as a 'bastardy bond' so that the infant would not be reliant on the parish poor relief fund.

10 Thomas Clark's date of birth may well have gone unrecorded in the age before civil registration which started from 1837. However, it was included in a family tree drawn up for the Bawtree family of Sutton, Surrey in the late 19th/early 20th century. His daughter Matilda married Alfred Bawtree in 1873.

11 In the 1851 census, Thomas Clark meticulously records that he was born at Webb Street, Bermondsey Street, Borough. Ancestry.com: Class: HO107; Piece: 1581; Folio: 181; Page: 18.

12 Wikipedia, *Warehouseman*, 2019 <https://en.wikipedia.org/wiki/Warehouseman> [Accessed 22 February 2020].

13 Ancestry.com: *Parish Register*, St. Nicholas', Plumstead . LMA: Ref: 97/NIC/004

14 In the 1851 census, Ann Clark's birthplace is recorded as Bristol. Ancestry.com: Class: HO107; Piece: 1530; Folio: 201; Page: 24.

15 'Bermondsey Leather Market' and 'Bermondsey Street', *The London Encyclopaedia*, 3rd edn.ed. by John Hibbert, John Keay, Julia Keay and Ben Weinreb (London: Macmillan, 2008),p.62.

16 1871 Census, Esther Try (formerly Clark) Ancestry.com: Class: RG10; Piece: 731; Folio: 62; Page: 60.

17 Frederick Aldridge stated in the 1841 census that his occupation was a 'warehouseman'.

18 The average age for first marriages for grooms between 1800 and 1849 was 25.3. See Rebecca Probert, *Marriage Law for Genealogists: The Definitive Guide* (Kenilworth: Takeaway, 2012) p. 124.

19 Victorian Life Wiki, *Qualities of a Gentleman* <https://victorianlife.fandom.com/wiki/Qualities_of_a_gentleman> [Accessed 3 November 2020].

Chapter 2 –The Westfields 1788-1832

1 Parish register, St.Mary's, Portsea.

2 See Carola Hicks, *Girl in a Green Gown: The History and Mystery of the Arnolfini Portrait* (London: Vintage, 2012). Hicks suggests that some British soldiers delayed their return from France at the end of the Battle of Waterloo.

3 A bastardy bond was a form of child maintenance whereby the father would be named and compelled to make payments so that the responsibility would not fall on the parish poor relief fund. If the father was someone of lowly means, there would not be a case, as he would be unable to support his child.

4 St. Mary, Portsea marriage register records that Stephen Sims was of HMS *Brazen*.

5 Sloop is taken from the Dutch '*Sloep*' in turn from French *chaloupe*. The historical naval definition from this period is a small square rigged sailing warship with a single mast and a fore-and-aft. rig. It had only one head sail. Wikipedia, *Sloop*, 2020.<https://en.wikipedia.org/wiki/Sloop> [accessed 22 February 2020].

6 HMS *Brazen* had an interesting history having been launched during 1808, she then served during the Napoleonic Wars but it is not recorded that she took part in any combative action. However, she did participate in the war of 1812 between the United States and the United Kingdom. Subsequently, she was damaged in a hurricane near New Orleans and after local repair, returned to England for a maintenance survey. Wikipedia, HMS *Brazen* (1808), 2020 <https://en.wikipedia.org/wiki/HMS_Brazen_(1808)> [Accessed 22 February 2020].

7   Rotherhithe was historically the most north eastern settlement in the county of Surrey. Situated on the south bank of the Thames and part of the Docklands area, it adjoins Bermondsey on the west and Deptford to the south-east. It has a long history as a port with many shipyards from Elizabethan times. Rotherhithe is a Saxon name meaning 'mariner's landing place'.

8   Jenny Uglow, *In These Times: Living in Britain through Napoleon's Wars 1793-1815* (London: Faber & Faber, 2014) p. 132.

9   *Ibid.*

10   Circa 1805, for children, malnutrition and lack of clothing were persistent problems; the annual death rate of children under five was well above the national average in Portsmouth. *Portsmouth and its People 1800-1850* (2 July 2015) <http://www.hantsphere. org.uk/portsmouth-and-its-people-1800-1850> [Accessed 29 January 2019].

11   Jenny Uglow, *In These Times: Living in Britain through Napoleon's Wars 1793-1815* (London: Faber & Faber, 2014) p. 132.

12   Nelson was held in high regard by the people of Portsmouth, even if he expressed a loathing for the town. After his death, Nelson's body was returned to the port aboard *The Victory* on 2 December 1805 but he was not taken in at the port, instead he was taken up the Thames to London. *Portsmouth and its People 1800-1850* (2 July 2015) <http://www.hantsphere.org.uk/portsmouth-and-its-people-1800-1850> [Accessed 29 January 2019].

13   It is not possible to confirm if this Sarah Clark was a relative of Thomas Clark born in either 1785 or 1819; as Clark is a common name – it may just be coincidence.

14   An Edward Turner signed as a witness on the parish register of Thomas Clark and Mary Ann Westfield at their 1839 marriage. He is likely to be the same individual, but this is not confirmed.

15   In London, half the children died before the age of three in the late 18th century. The Westfield's probably gave some of their children the same names to ensure that one of them survived to carry on a family name. See Mark D. Herber, *Ancestral Trails* (Stroud: Sutton Publishing, 1997) p. 121.

16   Will of Edward Jenkins. Ancestry.com: Prerogative Court of Canterbury Wills, 1384-1858; The National Archives, Kew; Prerogative Court of Canterbury and Related Probate Jurisdictions: Will Registers; Class; PROB 11; Piece: 1841.

17   Baptism of Edward Jenkins Rice, 30 November 1834, St . Dunstan and All Saints, Stepney. Ancestry.com: Church of England Birth and Baptisms, 1813-1916; LMA; Board of Guardian Records, 1834-1906/Church of England Parish Registers, 1754-1906; Ref No: P93/DUN/017.

Chapter 3 –The Clerk – Newington – Milton – Peckham 1841–1856

1   Liza Picard, *Victorian London: The Life of a City 1840-1870* (London: Phoenix, 2005) p.117.

2   In the 1841 censes, the enumerator's instructions were to round down ages to the nearest five years so the couple should have been recorded as 20 year olds, had the enumerator followed orders.

3   Chloroform was not used as an anaesthetic for childbirth until January 1847.

4   The prevailing view was that babies needed to be baptised as soon as possible after birth, due to high infant mortality. If a baby died without the sacrament, its spirit would leave the earth without being cleansed of the stain of original sin, something that all mankind is born into. This was considered perilous to the immortal soul,

according to the established church.

5   Both Sarah Rice and Sarah Turner (formerly Westfield) may have died in the 1830s, according to burial records of the area but the details are unconfirmed.

6   1841 census Kitty Westfield and William Fowler. Ancestry.com: Class: HO107; Piece: 1047; Book 5; Civil Parish: St Mary Magdalen; Bermondsey; County: Surrey; Enumeration District: 15; Folio: 28; Page: 1; Line: 21.

7   Like most other Mary Anns of the time; the name Polly is a derivative of Molly and Molly is another form of Mary.

8   Weather Consultancy Services Limited, *Weather in History 1850 to 1899 AD,* 2020 <https://premium.weatherweb.net/weather-in-history-1850-to-1899-ad/> [Accessed 2 February 2021].

9   GRO death certificate for Alfred Clark, 23 February, 1850, Camberwell.

Chapter 4 – Old Kent Road, Peckham & Great Tower Street (City) 1850-1854

1   In 1840 about one child in six children died before the age of one, and about a third of children born died before the age of five. Iain Roberts,2010, Life Expectancy of 13? That's Victorian Values for You. Available from *Liberal Democrat Voice,* 31 January 2010, <https://www.libdemvoice.org/life-expectancy-of-13-thats-victoria-values-for-you17571.html> [Accessed 3 November 2020].

2   1851 census Shenton Street, Old Kent Road, Peckham, London. Ancestry.com: Class: HO107; Piece: 1581; Folio: 181; Page: 18.

3   Shenton Street, Old Kent Road is visible on an 1868 map of London but it had vanished from the area some years later.

4   Pamela Horn, *Pleasures and Pastimes in Victorian Britain,* (Stroud: Sutton Publishing Ltd, 1999) p.128.

5   'Indian Ivory Carvings for the Great Exhibition', *The Illustrated London News*, 26th April 1851.

6   Apoplexy – from ancient Greek meaning a 'striking away', up to the 19th century, it referred to any sudden death that began with a loss of consciousness, especially one where the victim died within a matter of seconds. Before the advent of medical science, physicians often had inadequate or inaccurate understandings and identifying a specific cause often proved difficult or impossible.

7   Personal correspondence from Southwark Regeneration, Cemeteries & Crematorium, Forest Hill, London dated 25th March 1999 confirms that records show there is a tomb type memorial sited on the grave.

8   Around the middle of the 19th century, overcrowded churchyards could no longer cope with burying the dead. During the first half of the century, London's population had risen from 1 million to 2.3 and in 1832 a bill was passed by Parliament to encourage the establishment of new private cemeteries outside of the city boundaries as Peckham then was. A ring of seven new cemeteries were built. Kensal Green was the first such cemetery to open in 1832 whilst All Saints' was consecrated in 1840 and was developed as a commercial enterprise by the London Cemetery Company.

9   Ancestry.com: *Freedom of the City Admission Papers, 1681-1930*; LMA: Ref No: COL/CHD/FR/02/1454-1459. Ancestry.com: *London Post Office Directory*, 1829. Lists Donald Gray, Broker, of Size Lane.

10   *The Public Ledger and Daily Advertiser* was a weekly trade magazine which was first published in 1760 and ran until 2017.

11   1851 Census: Donald Gray and family. Ancestry.com: Class: HO107; Piece: 1503; Folio: 84; Page: 25.

Chapter 5 – The River Thames – Cargoes and Cholera 1854

1   The London docks which were built by the late 1850s were The London Dock (1805) The East India Dock (1805) The Surrey Dock – on the south bank (1807) St. Katherine's Dock – near the Tower of London (1828) The West India South Dock (1829) were all built before the arrival of the railways. The Victoria Dock (1855) was the first dock designed for steam ships and provided hydraulic cranes and lifts for raising ships in a pontoon dock and was well served by rail links with the Great Eastern Line. See (Liza Picard, *Victorian London: The Life of a City 1840-1870* (London: Phoenix, 2005) pp. 25-26.

2   *Ibid.*, p. 25.

3   The London Commercial Sale Rooms opened in 1811 and were the model for traditional commodity trading. In 1834, when the East India Company ceased to be a commercial enterprise, and tea became a 'free trade' commodity, it gained fame for its tea auctions but it also sold other colonial produce. Mincing Lane – Tea merchants established offices in and around the street, earning it the name of Street of Tea. It was also the centre for spice trading and the opium business and other drugs in the 18th century. Businesses in the slave trade also were based here.

4   'Sales this day', *The Public Ledger and Daily Advertiser*, 6th September, 1854. p.1. Seahorse was in fact hippopotamus teeth (Greek for River Horse). The ivory was used to make false human teeth known as 'sea horse teeth'. Paul Kerley, BBC News Magazine, *The dentures made from the teeth of dead soldiers at Waterloo* (16 June 2015) <The dentures made from the teeth of dead soldiers at Waterloo – BBC News> [Accessed 31 October 2021].

5   The death certificate for Ann Clark stated that she had died of Asiatic cholera suffered for 18 hours and that her daughter-in-law had been present at her death. GRO death certificate for Ann Clark, 7 September, 1854, Camberwell.

6   Wikipedia, *1854 cholera outbreak* , 2020 <https://en.wikipedia.org/wiki/1854_Broad_Street_cholera_outbreak> [Accessed 13 March 2020].

7   Section of Epidemiology and State Medicine: *The History of Cholera in Great Britain* by E. Ashworth Underwood, M.A., B.Sc., M.D., D.P.H., F.L.S. [Online] <https://journals.sagepub.com/doi/pdf/10.1177/003591574804100309> [Accessed 10 May 2020].

Chapter 6 – Shooters' Hill 1855-1862

1   Len Reilly, *Old Ordnance Survey Maps: Shooters Hill 1866* (Gateshead: Alan Godfrey Maps, 1988). Shooters' Hill was even considered as a Georgian spa town with plans made in 1766 never coming to fruition due to a decline in popularity of spa towns after this time.

2   'Sales by Auction', *Kentish Mercury*, 19th January, 1867. p. 1.

3   'Woolwich, Plumstead & Shooter's Hill', *Woolwich Gazette*, 11 January, 1889. p.1.

4   'Hawkins v. Anderley', *Brighton Gazette*, 1 April, 1847.p.8.

5   Liza Picard, *Victorian London: The Life of a City 1840-1870* (London: Phoenix, 2005) p. 61.

6   Matilda Hephzibah Clark, *Diary 1872-1874.*

7   Ancestry.com: *Dictionary of National Biography Volumes 1-22: Gaspey, Thomas (1788-1871)*

8   Lucy Lane married the mathematician and philosopher William Kingdon Clifford in 1875 and then became known professionally as Mrs. W.F. Clifford. Her husband died

only four years after their marriage and she later became known for having a wide circle of literary friends including Henry James and Thomas Hardy.

9   Mrs. W.K. Clifford, *A Flash of Summer: The Story of a Simple Woman's Life* (Amazon, reprint of an 1895 edition) p. 4.

10   *Ibid.*, pp. 3-4.

11   'Local Board of Health – Tuesday: Letters, &c.', *Kentish Independent*, 6 March, 1858. p.4.

12   'Local Board of Health – Tuesday: Letters, &c.', *Kentish Independent*, 13 March, 1858. p.4.

13   'Woolwich: Board of Commissioners', *Kentish Mercury*, 16 November, 1850. p.3.

14   'Local Board of Health –Tuesday: Nuisances', *Kentish Independent*, 3 April, 1858. p.5.

15   'Local Board of Health – Tuesday: The Foul Ditch at Shooters' Hill', *Kentish Independent*, 22, May, 1858. p.4.

16   The Great Stink was the label bestowed on the stench of 1858, a combination of an unusually hot, dry summer and newly installed sewers which belched into the Thames. The problem resurged occasionally until the late 1860s when Joseph Bazelgette's drainage system came into operation. *The London Encyclopaedia*, 3rd edn. ed. by John Hibbert, John Keay, Julia Keay and Ben Weinreb (London: Macmillan, 2008), p.347.

17   'Local Board of Health – Tuesday: Letters', *Kentish Independent*, 2 July, 1859, p.5.

18   'District Board of Works – Wednesday: Shooters' Hill', *Kentish Independent*, 13 August, 1859. p.2.

19   'Local Board of Health – Tuesday: Shooters' Hill Drainage', *Kentish Independent*, 13 August, 1859. p.4.

20   'Shooters' Hill Drainage', *Kentish Independent*, 3 September, 1859 . p.5.

21   'Local Board of Health – Tuesday: Drainage at Shooters' Hill', *Kentish Independent,* 17 September, 1859. p.4.

22   'Local Board of Health – Tuesday: Shooters' Hill Drainage', *Kentish Independent*, 18 February, 1860. p.4.

23   'Woolwich: Local Board of Health, Tuesday February 14', *Kentish and Surrey Mercury and Home Counties Advertiser*, 18 February, 1860. p.5.

Chapter 7 – Cudham and Crofton, Kent 1862-1867

1   GRO death certificate for Donald Gray, 11 June, 1862, Brighton states that he died of chronic icterus (jaundice) and bronchitis. Donald Gray was very wealthy. His estate was valued at £60,000 in 1862. The equivalent value today would be £7,350,322 <https://www.bankofengland.co.uk/monetary-policy/inflation/inflation-calculator>

2   Luke Pocock died in 1829 at the age of 83 and was buried at Keston church. Frank Bamping, Kent Archaeological Society, *Keston* (13 October 2000) <https://www. kentarchaeology.org.uk/research/monumental-inscriptions/keston> [Accessed 6th November 2020].

3   Luke Pocock's daughter Belinda married the artist Thomas Landseer (1793/4-1880) on 1 September 1825 – Landseer came from the family of well-known artists; his youngest brother was Edwin Landseer, the renowned painter of horses, dogs and stags.

4   In 1851, Ashmore House was occupied by Sarah Evans, a widowed 38-year-old governess born in Enfield and two 'nieces' her charges Amy Mary Smithson and her sister Jane, 18 and 11 respectively, the girls had been born in Selby, Yorkshire the daughters of an iron founder. Also in residence was 19-year-old servant George James Borer born locally at Keston. In 1861, the only occupier was John Lassam a 56-year-old

agricultural labourer born in Hampshire who was probably keeping the estate active whilst new tenants were sought to take up residence in the house.

1851 census, Class: HO107; Piece: 1606; Folio: 1; Page: 287.

1861 census, Class: RG9; Piece: 462; Folio: 52; Page 20.

5   GRO death certificate for Amelia Seagrave Clark, 23 June, 1863, Bromley.

6   Bill Morton, *personal correspondence*, 10 August, 1995.

7   Bromley had been created Knight Commander of the Bath in 1858 following a long and successful career as a civil servant. One of his most recent achievements was on the outbreak of hostilities with Russia, when he was appointed accountant-general of the Navy. He retired from his office early in 1863 due to ill-health and this probably prompted the move from Crofton Hall to take up a new residence in Foots Cray, Kent. Bill Morton, *personal correspondence,* 17 August, 1995. Also see Ancestry.com: *Dictionary of National Biography Volumes 1-20, 22: Bromley, Sir Richard Madox (1813-1865)* p.149.

8   1861 census, Crofton Hall: Richard Madox Bromley, family and servants. Ancestry. com: Class: RG9; Piece 464; Folio: 171; Page 27.

9   'Sales by Auction', *Kentish Mercury*, 10 January, 1867. p. 1. The auction notice lists the farming stock and effects for sale at Crofton Hall.

10 *Ibid.* The advert stated that the lease had been disposed.

11 Matilda Hephzibah Clark, *Diary 1872-1874.*

12 Liza Picard, *Victorian London: The Life of a City 1840-1870* (London: Phoenix, 2005) p. 37.

13 *The Public Ledger and Daily Advertiser*, 2 and 3 May, 1864. p.1.

14 *The Public Ledger and Daily Advertiser*, 3 May, 1864. p.1.

15 'The City Courts: Brokers', *The City Press*, 22 July, 1865. p.2.

16 'Phillips, Mayor – The First Court', *The Morning Advertiser*, 15 November, 1865. p.1.

17 Matilda Hephzibah Clark, *Diary 1872-1874.*

18 Sheffield City Council: Picture Sheffield, y12065 *Advertisement for Chester Brothers, Cutlery manufacturers*, West End Cutlery Works, West Street. Image from Sheffield and Neighbourhood (page 111) (printed and published by Pawson and Brailsford, Sheffield, 1889 (Sheffield Local Studies Library: 914.274 S) <https://picturesheffield.com/frontend.php?keywords=Ref_No_increment;EQUALS;y12065&pos=3&action=zoom&id=120268>

19 John Chester's obituary described him as an upright, straightforward Christian man who was kind to the poor and charitable to hospitals whilst doing his charitable deeds in a quiet and unostentatious manner; throughout his career in Sheffield, he took little part in public affairs. In his lifetime, he gave largely to several public institutions in the city. He was described as an influential member of the congregation worshipping at Mount Zion Chapel. His native shrewdness and quiet humour ever present endeared him to very many either in his business life or his connection with cricket which had been a long time passion. One of the charities he supported was the Jessop Hospital for Women which he founded and some of the other charities which benefited from legacies bequeathed after his death included in the Sheffield Royal Hospital and the Royal Infirmary. 'The Death of Mr. John Chester: His Connection with Yorkshire Cricket', *The Sheffield Daily Telegraph*, 21 February, 1905. p.12.

    'The Late Mr. John Chester', *The Sheffield Daily Telegraph*, 24 February, 1905. p.4.

20 The name of John Chester in connection with the family was identified through the death certificate of Mary Ann Clark (née Westfield) on which he was named as present. GRO death certificate for Mary Ann Clark, 24 October 1866, Ecclesall Bierlow.

21 'Deaths', *The Sheffield Daily Telegraph*, 24 October, 1866. p.3.

Chapter 8 – Penge, Anerley, Sydenham

1   'Sales by Auction', *Kentish Mercury*, 10 January, 1867. p. 1.
2   Sales by Auction', *Kentish Mercury*, 19th January, 1867. p. 1.
3   GRO birth certificate for Thomas William Francis Clark, 11 August, 1866. Croydon. Supplies evidence that his eldest son Thomas and family were living at 5 Palace Road, Penge circa 1867.
4   Wikipedia**,** *The Crystal Palace* , 2021, <https://www/en.wikipedia.org/wiki/the_crystal_palace> [Accessed 15 January 2021].
5   1871 census, Thomas Clark and family, Anerley Road, Penge. Ancestry.com: Class: RG10; Piece: 849; Folio: 127, Page: 29.
6   Cassells Household Guide, New and Revised Edition (4 Vol.) c.1880s [no date] – *Death in the Household (4)* in Victorian London – Publications – Etiquette and Household Advice Manuals <https://www.victorianlondon.org/cassells/cassells-35.htm> [Accessed 22 May 2020]. See also Tracy Chevalier*, Victorian Mourning Etiquette* <https://www.tchevalier.com/fallingangels/bckgrnd/mourning/> [Accessed 22 May 2020].
    Angel.S, Victorian Era, *Death and Mourning: Mourning,* 1997, <http://www.avictorian.com/mourning.html> [Accessed 22 May 2020].
7   1861 census, Joseph and Frances Colebatch and family. Ancestry.com: Class: RG9; Piece: 141; Folio: 118; Page: 38.
8   LMA; London, England; Church of England Parish Registers, 1754-1931; Reference Number: P94/mry/015
9   1871 census, Isaac and Eliza Simon and family, Paradise Row, Stoke Newington. Ancestry.com: Class: RG10; Piece: 310; Folio: 6; Page: 6.
10 1871 census, Thomas and Frances Clark and family, Brighton Road, Sutton. Ancestry.com: Class: RG10; Piece: 796; Folio:92; Page: 24.
11 'Situations Wanted', *The Norwood News and Crystal Palace Chronicle,* 21 November, 1891. p. 2.

Chapter 9 – The Rocklands, Upper Norwood 1872-1873

1   Kate Summerscale, *Mrs. Robinson's Disgrace: The Private Diary of a Victorian Lady* (London: Bloomsbury Publishing, 2012) contains information about Victorian ladies who kept journals.
2   Ancestry.com: England & Wales, National Probate Calendar (Index of Wills and Administrations), 1858-1966 Colebatch, Frances 1872. Probate was granted on 12th April. The index states that Mrs. Colebatch died on 17 March 1872. Her effects were under £1,500.
3   *Ibid.*
4   Although wills of unmarried women and widows were fairly common, wills for married women before 1882 are very rare. Married women could not, by law, own property until The Married Women's Property Act 1882. See Mark D. Herber, *Ancestral Trails,* (Stroud: Sutton Publishing Limited, 1997) p. 174.
5   1872 was the wettest calendar year for England and Wales with May to September having above average rainfall. Summertime temperatures were also average or depressed. Weather Consultancy Services Limited, *Weather in History 1850 to 1899 AD,* 2020 <https://premium.weatherweb.net/weather-in-history-1850-to-1899-ad/> [Accessed 23 May, 2020].

6   'Penge and Anerley', *The Norwood News and Crystal Palace Chronicle*, 11 May, 1872. p.5.

7   Mr. Arbib was Eugenio Arbib (1847-1915) a spice and feather merchant working in London who was born in Tripoli, North Africa lending a very exotic atmosphere to family life. The National Archives, *Eugenio Joseph Arbib, Ref : 3075/32* https:// discovery.nationalarchives.gov.uk/details /r/810ebc3f-ffd4-436f-b8b4-99e0d6cc189e [Accessed 29 April 2021].

8   Marine Parade, Brighton was developed from 1790 eastwards from the Steine until about 1850 when Kemp Town had been reached and was protected against coastal erosion by a huge seawall constructed along the length of the cliff in 1830-8. With its magnificent setting, all the development was of a high-class nature and constituted much of the Regency architectural splendour of the town. Marine Parade is considered the country's most impressive marine façade. My Brighton and Hove, *History Notes: Marine Parade,* 22 March 2006, <https://www.mybrightonandhove.org.uk/places/ placestree/marine-parade/marine-parade> [Accessed 23 May 2020].

9   Will of Thomas Clark, Probate London 27 July 1895.

10   Goods and services costing between £80 – £100 in 1873 are equivalent to between £8,764 and £10,955 in 2019 – inflation averaged at 3.3% a year. These figures are approximate. Bank of England, *Inflation Calculator*, 2020, <https://www. bankofengland.co.uk/monetary-policy/inflation/inflation-calculator> [Accessed 6 June 2020].

11   W.G.V. Balchin, ed., *The Country Life Book of the Living History of Britain* (London: Book Club Associates, 1981).

12   Personal correspondence from Matilda's great-granddaughter, 11 January 1992.

13   Weather History, Netweather Community, *Winter 1872-73: The Long Wait*, 2011. <https://www.netweather.tv/forum/topic/72057-winter-1872-73-the-long-wait/> [Accessed 23 May 2020].

14   Henry Thornton Raw was born in Stoke Newington in 1852 into a privileged background. In the early 1870s he was training as a solicitor but in later life he fell on hard times and illness. Just before his death in 1909, he was working as a road sweeper.

15   In December 1871, Bertie went down with typhoid fever. It was the 10th anniversary of his father's death when he too nearly died. The illness temporarily restored the fortunes of the monarchy in the eyes of the press and public. A thanksgiving service was held in St. Paul's Cathedral on 27 February 1872. See A.N. Wilson, *The Victorians,* (London: Arrow Books, 2003) p.360.

Chapter 10 – Three daughters and four marriages 1873-1878

1   Mrs. Hall – it has not yet been possible to identify this person by using either civil registration records or will indexes.

2   Parish Register marriage of Eliza Clark and Frederick Albert Field. LMA: London, England; Church of England Parish Registers, 1754-1931; Reference Number: P86/ ctc1/008

3   Lizzie's daughter May Ingham (nee Field) and grand-daughter Irene Ingham never forgot their roots and corresponded with Thomas Clark's (1841-1927) son Herbert, daughter Beatrice and their families through the decades up to and beyond the 1960s. By this time, the name of Eliza or Lizzie was never mentioned and the link was only learned anew through research.

4   Civil Marriage of Melina Elizabeth Clark and Edmund Howe Lilley, Free BMD,

England & Wales, Civil Registration Marriage Index, 1837-1915

5   Parish Register Melina Elizabeth Clark and Edmund Howe Lilley. Ancestry.com: Church of England Marriages and Banns 1754-1935; City of Westminster Archives Centre; London, England; Westminster Church of England Parish Register; Reference: SSP/PR/3/2

6   1881 Census, Edmund Howe Lilley, '*Marlborough*', Shoeburyness, Essex. Ancestry. com: Class: RG11; Piece: 1755; Folio: 116; Page: 8.

Chapter 11: Brixton – Gipsy Hill 1879-1894

1   Parish Register Emma Ann Clark and Arthur William Hill. LMA; London, England; Church of England Parish Registers, 1754-1931; Reference Number: P85/jna2/011.

2   The Great Depression was an economic recession which begun in 1873 and ran through to 1896 – it subsequently became known as The Long Depression after the time of the Depression of the 1930s. It was during this time that the UK lost its large industrial lead over other Western European economies. The end of the Franco-Prussian War in 1871 resulted in the rise of an investment boom in Germany.

3   1881 Census, Thomas Clark and family, 12 Wiltshire Road, Brixton. Ancestry.com: Class: RG11; Piece: 618; Folio: 93; Page: 32.

4   *Ibid.*

5   "Brixton: The Angell estate." *Survey of London: Volume 26, Lambeth: Southern Area.* Ed. F H W Sheppard. London: London County Council, 1956. 125-131. *British History Online*. Web. 31 October 2020. <http://www.british-history.ac.uk/survey-london/vol26/pp125-131> [Accessed 31 October 2020].

6   *Ibid.*

7   Free BMD, England & Wales, Civil Registration Marriage Index, 1837-1915. Civil Marriage of Alice Mary Clark and Edward Alexander Troup

8   1891 Census, Thomas Clark and family, 'Oakleigh', 17 Alexandra Road, Gipsy Hill. Ancestry.com: The National Archives of the UK (TNA); Kew, Surrey, England; Class: RG12; Piece: 419; Folio: 63; Page: 37.

9   'Situations Wanted', *The Norwood News and Crystal Palace Chronicle,* 21 November, 1891. p.2. Maids-of-all-works were expected to start their working day around 6 a.m. hence the reference to 'an early riser'.

10 Emma and Arthur Hill, Blanchworth, Hendham Road, Wandsworth. Ancestry.com: The National Archives of the UK (TNA); Kew, Surrey, England; Census Returns of England and Wales; 1891; Class: RG12; Piece: 451; Folio: 33; Page: 14.

11 Thomas Clark's third son James mysteriously disappears from all official records after he appears in the 1871 census as a resident with the rest of the family. He is still around on 10 May 1873 as he is recorded at Matilda's wedding to Alfred Bawtree in which he participates in the wedding breakfast. There was a story that someone in the family perished after contracting anthrax as a result of handling imported animal skins. It is possible that this was James but no evidence has as yet come to light to support this.

12 Civil marriage of Florence Ada Clark and Thomas Alfred Page. Free BMD, England & Wales, Civil Registration Marriage Index, 1837-1915

13 Parish Register Florence Ada Clark and Thomas Alfred Page, Christ Church, Gypsy Hill, Lambeth. LMA; London, England; Church of England Parish Registers, 1754-1931; Reference Number: p85/ctc1/007

Chapter 12 – 1895 Gipsy Hill

1 'Local Intelligence: Sudden Death at Gipsy Hill', *The Norwood Review and Crystal Palace Reporter,* 23 March, 1895.
2 'Upper Norwood: Sudden Death', *Norwood News and Crystal Palace Chronicle*, 23 March, 1895. p.6. The doctors cited in the newspaper reports were traced using the 1891 and 1901 census.
3 GRO death certificate for Thomas Clark, 22 March, 1895, Lambeth. Definition of cause of death: syncope – fainting, loss of consciousness and muscle strength caused by decreased blood flow to the brain typically from low blood pressure.
4 'Deaths: CLARK, Thomas', *Norwood News and Crystal Palace Chronicle*, 30 March, 1895. p.1.
5 Personal correspondence from Southwark Regeneration, Cemeteries & Crematorium, Forest Hill, London dated 25 March 1999.
6 Personal correspondence from one of Matilda's great-granddaughters.
7 Ancestry.com, England & Wales, National Probate Calendar (Index of Wills and Administrations), 1858-1966. *Clark, Thomas 1895.*
8 Goods and services costing £8286 are equivalent to £1,097,702 in 2019 – inflation averaged at 4% a year. These figures are approximate. Bank of England, *Inflation Calculator*, 2020, <https://www.bankofengland.co.uk/monetary-policy/inflation/inflation-calculator> [Accessed 6 June 2020].
9 1901 Census, Frances Clark, 35 South Street, Greenwich. Ancestry.com: Class: RG13; Piece: 537; Folio: 12; Page: 15.
10 1911 Census, Frances Clark, 93 Park Lane, Stoke Newington. Ancestry.com: Class: RG14; Piece: 1017; No. on schedule: 374
11 Ancestry.com: LMA; London, England; Ref. No: ISBG/283/097, London, England, Workhouse Admission and Discharge Records, 1764-1930.
12 Ancestry.com: LMA; London, England; Ref. No: ISBG/290/05, London, England, Church of England Deaths and Burials, 1813-2003 [database online].

PART TWO

Chapter 1 – Crofton Hall 1863-1865 – Scientia Potentia Est

1 'Publications – *The Japanese: their Manner and Customs*', *London Evening Standard*, 10 May, 1862. p.8.
2 The Marylebone Literary and Scientific Institute existed from the 1830s to 1860s. It was situated in one of the richest and most fashionable parts of London and was the middle and upper class equivalent of the working-class mechanics institutes. From the start it had an emphasis on science, experimentation and discovery. It attracted high-quality speakers but its decline was caused by financial problems and attracted low membership from the early 1860s. This lead to reorganisation in 1864 under new management as the 'Marylebone Literary Institute and Club' but it only provided a few years more of life. UCL, Survey of London, *Marylebone Literary and Scientific Institution*, 1 November 2019, <https://blogs.ucl.ac.uk/survey-of-london/2019/11/01/marylebone-literary-and-scientific-institution/> [Accessed 14 January 2021].
3 Thomas Clark Westfield, *The Japanese: Manners and Customs; with an account of the general characteristics of the country, its manufactures and natural productions* (British Library, Historical print editions) reprint of the 1862 edition. Preface.

4   Prince Albert was the president of the Society of Arts up to his death in 1861 after which time his son the Prince of Wales (Bertie) assumed the role. Meetings of the annual 'sessions' were held on Wednesdays from November through to the following June. Candidates for membership had to be proposed by three members of the Society and afterwards balloted for. Annual subscriptions were two guineas. Members enjoyed the following privileges: to be present and vote at all general meetings; attend the Wednesday evening meetings; attend the courses or lectures and to give orders admitting one visitor to each lecture; to have personal free admission to all exhibitions held by the Society; to be present at the Society's *conversazioni* ; to receive a copy of the weekly journal; to use the library and reading room. Urquhart, David. "Journal of the Society for Arts, Vol. 10, No. 484." *The Journal of the Society of Arts*, vol. 10, no. 484, 1862, pp. 217–236. *JSTOR*, <www.jstor.org/stable/41334952> [Accessed 30 June 2020]. LE NEVE FOSTER, P., et al. "Journal of the Society for Arts, Vol. 10, No. 486." *The Journal of the Society of Arts*, vol. 10, no. 486, 1862, pp. 259–274. *JSTOR*, <www.jstor.org/stable/41334548> [Accessed 30 June 2020].
     Thomas Clark's membership seems to have lapsed after the 1866/7 session as his name is then absent from the annual register. No doubt, this was due to his marriage and family life taking priority by this time.
5   Wikipedia, 1862 International Exhibition, See <1862 International Exhibition – Wikipedia> 2020 [Accessed 14 January 2021].
6   Pierre Rossier was in Japan by 1859 producing photographs in Nagasaki, Kanagawa, Yokohama and Edo (later Tokyo) being the first professional photographer to work in the country. His photographs of Japan were advertised twice in 1860 but not published until October/November 1861 by Negretti and Zambra. Five of his views appeared earlier that year in George Smith's book, *Ten Weeks in Japan*. It is unknown how Thomas Clark Westfield obtained the images for inclusion in his work of 1862 but they are attributed to Negretti and Zambra throughout. Monovisions, Black & White Photography Magazine, *Biography: 19th century Swiss photographer Pierre Rossier*, 14 February 2018, <https://monovisions.com/pierre-rossier-biography-19th-century-swiss-photographer/> [Accessed 10 July 2020]
7   Negretti and Zambra were a company active 1850–circa 1999.They produced scientific (philosophical) and optical instruments and also operated a photographic studio based in London. The founding partners were Henry Negretti and Joseph Zambra. Wikipedia, *Negretti and Zambra,* 2020, <https://en.wikipedia.org/wiki/Negretti_and_Zambra> [Accessed 10 July 2020].
8   Thomas Clark Westfield, *The Japanese: Manners and Customs; with an account of the general characteristics of the country, its manufactures and natural productions* (British Library, Historical print editions) reprint of the 1862 edition. p.2.
9   Wikipedia, *Laurence Oliphant*, 2020, <https://en.m.wikipedia.org/wiki/Laurence_Oliphant_(author)> [Accessed 7th November 2020]
     Wikipedia, Rutherford Alcock, 2020, <https://en.wikipedia.org/wiki/Rutherford_Alcock> [Accessed 7th November 2020]
10   Thomas Clark Westfield, *The Japanese: Manners and Customs; with an account of the general characteristics of the country, its manufactures and natural productions* (British Library, Historical print editions) reprint of the 1862 edition. pp. 20-21.
11   *Ibid*, p. 22.
12   James McNeil Whistler was an American artist who worked in London from 1859. He was acquainted with the Pre-Raphelite artists and influenced by some of their art, started using Japanese costumes and accessories as props to his works in the early 1860s. *Battersea Reach from Lindsey Houses 1864-1871* shows a setting by the River

Thames but one girl of the three in the painting stands out as she wears a kimono and holds a parasol.

13 1861 Census, William Bailey and family, 2 Clarendon Place, Camberwell Ancestry. com: Class: RG9; Piece: 387; Folio: 165; Page: 21.

14 Parish register, William Bailey and Jane Muir, 18 December 1839. LMA: London, England; Reference Number: P69/GIS/A/01/Ms6422/1

15 GRO birth certificate, Frances Charlotte Bailey, 1865, Camberwell. FreeBMD: England & Wales, Civil Registration Birth Index, 1837-1915

16 1851 Census, William Bailey and family, Albany Road, Camberwell. Ancestry.com: Class: HO107; Piece: 1582; Folio: Page: 15.

17 Jane was living in the household of William (a music seller) and Caroline Brunt and her occupation is stated as 'Professor of Music'. This family were almost certainly known to William Bailey's brother-in-law Charles Vizer who hailed from Bristol and was living with the Bailey's at the time of the 1861 census. 1861 Census, Jane Bailey, 6 St. Augustine's Parade, Bristol, Ancestry.com: Class: RG9; Piece: 1723; Folio: 95; Page: 2.

18 Thomas Clark Westfield, A *Series of Seven Essays on Universal Science*: (London, Robert Hardwicke, 1863)

19 Parish Register, St. Anne's, Kew Green, 9 September 1863. Ancestry.com; Surrey, England. Church of England Marriages, 1754-1937.

20 Percy Wemyss Phillips Nott was born in Manchester in 1838 and was a student at Trinity College, Cambridge in 1861. Shortly graduating with an MA, he became curate of St. Anne's Church, Kew Green. At the young age of 28 in 1869 he succeeded as Vicar following the death of the former incumbent Revd. Richard Byam. Nott was a bachelor who lived at 5 Cumberland Gate along the Richmond Road, Kew sharing a house with his parents. He died relatively young in 1885 at Kew. See David Blomfield, *St. Anne's Kew 1714-2014* (Much Wenlock, RJL Smith & Associates, 2014) p. 53.

21 There is a Jane Bass in the 1861 census, a 56 year-old resident of Kew living in a cottage at the back of the Green with her husband Edward, a gardener at The Royal Botanic Gardens. This is evidence that this same person who acted as a witness was a parishioner and unknown to the couple. Ancestry.com: Class: *RG 9*; Piece: *460*; Folio: *51*; Page: *26*.

22 Thomas Clark Westfield , '*In Memoriam*', 31 October 1905.

Chapter 2 – Westfield's Essays on Universal Science

1 'Literature: A Series of Seven Essays On Universal Science', *The Sun*, 28 October, 1863.

2 'Books of Popular Science: A Series of Seven Essays on Universal Science', *The Examiner*, 12 December, 1863. p.6.

3 'Literature: Seven Essays on Universal Science', *The Globe and Traveller*, 31 December, 1863.

4 *The Spectator*, 19 December, 1863.

5 Thomas Clark Westfield, A *Series of Seven Essays on Universal Science*: (London, Robert Hardwicke, 1863) Preface.

6 *Ibid*., Preface, IV.

7 *Ibid*.

8 *Ibid*., p. 45.

9 *Ibid*., p. 44.

10   *Ibid.*

11   *Ibid.*, p. 60.

12   *Ibid.*, p. 78.

13   Wikipedia, *Isabelle Wright Duncan*,<https://en.wikipedia.org/wiki/Isabelle_Wright_ Duncan> 13 December 2020 [Accessed 21   December 2020].

14   Thomas Clark Westfield, *A Series of Seven Essays on Universal Science*: (London, Robert Hardwicke, 1863) pp. 132-133.

15   *Ibid.*, p.133.

16   *Ibid.*, p. 168.

17   *Ibid.*, pp. 206-7.

Chapter 3 – Penge – Camberwell – Sutton 1865-1876

1   'The City Courts: Court of Aldermen – Brokers', *The City Press,* 22 July 1865. p. 2.

2   Parish Register, St. Giles, Camberwell, 9th September 1865. LMA; London, England; Church of England Parish Registers 1754-1931; Ref. No. P73/GIS/030.

3   GRO birth certificate for Thomas William Francis Clark, 11 August 1866, Croydon.

4   For more information about the presence and art work of Camille Pissarro in Penge and Sydenham from 1870-1 see The Norwood Society, *Pissarro and Norwood* <https://www. norwoodsociety.co.uk/articles/74-pissarro-and-norwood.html> [accessed 10 July 2020}.

5   Demolition in Palace Road, Penge during 1977 revealed the anatomy of the houses. See Doris E. Pullen, *Penge: From a hamlet, once part of Battersea in Surrey, to a London suburb. A story of some of the people and the surrounding district* (Chislehurst, Lodgemark Press Ltd, 1978) p.32.

6   GRO birth certificate for Ernest Percival Frederick Clark, 15 April 1868, Camberwell.

7   'Partnerships dissolved: Clark T., T., jun. & F.H., Great Tower Street, produce brokers (so far as regards Frederick Henry Clark)', *The Public Ledger*, 10 July 1869, p.6.

8   Claremont House, Brighton Road, Sutton was demolished in the 1960s to make way for a block of flats.

9   1871 Census, Thomas Clark and family, Brighton Road, Sutton. Ancestry.com: Class: RG10; Piece 796;Folio: 92; Page: 24.

10   Matilda Hephzibah Clark, diary entry, 22 June 1873.

11   GRO birth certificate for Herbert Lionel Alexander Clark, 15 January 1872, Epsom.

12   In Derby Week 1865, 70,000 people travelled on the new Epsom Downs line which ran behind Brighton Road. Jane E.M. Jones, *Pocket Images: Sutton* (Stroud, Nonsuch Publishing Ltd, 2006) p.10.

13   Will of William Bailey, 1885 states he was formerly of Claremont House, Sutton in the County of Surrey. Ancestry.com: England & Wales, National Probate Calendar (Index of Wills and Administrations), 1858-1966.

14   GRO birth certificate for Bertram Allan Leslie Clark, 10 August 1875, Epsom.

15   GRO death certificate for Sydney James Douglas Clark, 1876, Epsom.

16   Personal correspondence from Southwark Regeneration, Cemeteries & Crematorium, Forest Hill, London dated 2nd November 1998 confirms that records show there is a pedestal type memorial situated on the grave and that Sydney J.D. Clark was interred on 31st March 1876.

17   Birth certificate of Walter Vivian Harold Clark, 1876 FreeBMD: England &Wales, Civil Registration Birth Index, 1837-1915

18   A copy of the programme for the Lord Mayor's Banquet 13 October 1876 has survived in the family's possession.

Chapter 4 – Tottenham – Leyton 1879-1891

1   GRO Birth certificate of Beatrice Frances Mary Clark, 9 June, 1879, Edmonton.
2   1881 Census, William and Jane Bailey & Thomas Clark and family, 2 Lansdowne Road, Tottenham Ancestry.com: Class RG11; Piece: 1382; Folio: 36; Page: 64-65.
3   1881 Census, Grammar School, High Street, Chipping Ongar, Essex. Ancestry.com: Class RG11; Piece: 1741; Folio: 56. Page: 39.
4   In his unpublished memoirs, Fountain Meen recalls his interactions with famous composers and singers of his day.
5   North London regional press is littered with advertisements for, or reviews of, concerts in which Fountain Meen performed most of which took place at Union Chapel Islington or other north London venues. However, he has been found in provincial press too; he performed at the inaugural event for the new Masonic Hall at Sudbury, Suffolk. The concert was reported in the Bury Free Press.
6   Inscribed 'T. Clark Westfield from the author's son 15/11/22' in the front page to Our Israelitish Origin: Lectures on Ancient Israel, and the fulness of the Gentiles by J. Wilson.
7   Roger Carswell, *Isaac Levinsohn – The Story of a Russian/Polish Jew's Search for Forgiveness*, 2018, Evangelical Times <https://www.evangelical-times.org/41284/isaac-levinsohn-the-story-of-a-russian-polish-jews-search-for-forgiveness/> [Accessed 15 August 2020].
8   'The Court – The May Meetings: Meeting of the Metropolitan Anglo-Israel Association', *The Daily News*, 19 May, 1882. p.6.
9   For more information on Pyramidology and Charles Piazzi Smyth see <https://en.wikipedia.org/wiki/pyramidology> [Accessed 21 December 2020]. <https://en.wikipedia.org/wiki/Charles_Piazzi_Smyth> [Accessed 21 December 2020].
10   'Correspondence: The Great Pyramid', *Hastings and St. Leonards Observer*, 17 May, 1879. p.7.
11   Verbal testimony (Marjorie Walshe nee Westfield).
12   Will of William Bailey, 1885. Ancestry.com: England & Wales, National Probate Calendar (Index of Wills and Administrations), 1858-1966
13   Personal correspondence (Robert Randell Clark) 21 June 1994.
14   1891 Census, Thomas Clark and family, 'Devonia', Queen's Road, Leyton. Ancestry.com: Class: RG12; Piece: 1346; Folio: 98; Page: 20.
15   Hidden London: *Leyton, Waltham Forest*, 2020 <https://hidden-london.com/gazetteer/leyton/> [Accessed 14 August 2020}.
16   1891 Census, Maria Harris and family, 'Clifton Villa', Queen's Road, Leyton. Ancestry.com: Class RG12; Piece: 1346; Folio: 99; Page: 21.

Chapter 5 – Leyton – Upper Clapton – Bowers Gifford 1891-1901

1   1881 Census, Dennis Reader and family, No. 1 Thomas Cottage, Leyton. Ancestry.com: Class: RG11; Piece: 1727; Folio: 80; Page:30.
2   1891 Census, Edith Reader, general servant Ancestry.com: Class: RG12; Piece: 1350; Folio: 34; Page 15.
3   Free BMD, England & Wales, Civil Registration Marriage Index, 1837-1915, Civil marriage of Herbert Clark and Edith Reader, 4 September, 1893.
4   Free BMD, England & Wales, Civil Registration Marriage Index, 1837-1915 Civil marriage of Thomas Clark and Rose Carter, 31 August, 1895.

5   Stays are a term for boned undergarments more commonly called corsets in the 19th century.

6   Will of Thomas Clark, Probate London 27 July 1895.

7   Thomas Clark bankruptcy notice, *The Gazette*, 1897.

8   A photograph of an interior bears the address stamp of '27 Springfield, Upper Clapton', with 'W. Westfield, fine art dealers' also stamped onto the reverse.

9   Parish Register, St. Botolph without Bishopgate, London, 14th August 1900. LMA; London, England; Reference Number: *P69/BOT4/A/01/Ms 4520/23*

10 1901 Census, Thomas Clark and family, 27 Springfield, Upper Clapton. Ancestry.com: Class: RG13; Piece: 211; Folio: 10/11; Page: 12-13.

11 1901 Census, Walter Clark-Westfield, Ancestry.com: Class: RG13; Piece 1667; Folio: 23; Page: 5.

12 'Furniture', *Hackney and Kingsland Gazette*, 20 September, 1901. p.4.

13 'Sales by Auction: By the order of the owner W.T.Clarke, Esq', *Hackney and Kingsland Gazette*, 4 November, 1901. p.4. The earliest 'refrigerators' were nothing more than wooden cabinets with ice slowly melting in the top.

Chapter 6 – Bowers Gifford – 1901-1920

1   'Situations Wanted: Clerk used to ledger…', *Southend Standard and Essex Weekly Advertiser*, 1 and 8 May, 1902. p.4.

2   Parish Register Bertram Allan Leslie Clark and Ethel Maud Lamerton, July 1902. Ancestry.com: Essex Record Office; Chelmsford, Essex, England; Church of England Parish Registers, Church of England Marriages 1754-1935.

3   Thomas Clark Westfield, *The Holy City: A Revelation or The Substance of Things Hoped For* (London: Robert Banks & Son, 1903)

4   GRO marriage certificate, Beatrice Frances Mary Clark and Edmund Henry George Palmer, 22nd June, 1904. Billericay.

5   1901 Census, Edmund Palmer, 51 Newington Butts, Newington. Ancestry.com: Class: RG13; Piece: 384; Folio: 80; Page: 55.

6   Verbal testimony (Marjorie Walshe nee Westfield).

7   GRO Death certificate for Frances Charlotte Clark, 2 November 1904, Billericay. This states that she suffered a cerebral haemorrhage five days earlier.

8   Personal correspondence from Southwark Regeneration, Cemeteries & Crematorium, Forest Hill, London dated 2 November 1998 confirms that records show there is a pedestal type memorial situated on the grave and that Frances Charlotte Clark was interred on 5 November 1904.

9   'Death of Mr. Fountain Meen: A Distinguished Musician', *Islington Daily Gazette*, 14 October 1909. p.4.

10 1911 Census, Thomas Clark and Thomas Clark junior, Edith Cottage, Clifton Road. Ancestry.com: 1911 England Census [database Online], Class: RG14; Piece: 10019; Schedule No. 4.

11 Malcolm Hill and Edmund Arthur Howe Lilley (known as Jack). Ancestry.com: UK Commonwealth War Graves Commission, 1914-1921 Graves Registers

12 Verbal testimony (Eunice Bridge nee Croisette).

13 Verbal testimony (Marjorie Walshe nee Westfield).

14 Alice Mary Troup, North Benfleet 1917. Ancestry.com: Essex Record Office, Chelmsford, Essex, Church of England Parish Registers

Chapter 7 – The final years – What to do with Pa?

1   Personal correspondence (Maurice Wood) 7 March 1990.
2   Personal correspondence (Patricia Cowley) 13 January 1992.
3   Verbal testimony (Marjorie Walshe née Westfield)
4   Verbal testimony (Marjorie Walshe née Westfield)
5   GRO death certificate for Thomas Clark, 31 January 1927, West Ham.
6   Personal correspondence from Southwark Regeneration, Cemeteries & Crematorium, Forest Hill, London dated 2 November 1998 confirms that records show there is a pedestal type memorial situated on the grave and that Thomas Clark was interred on 4 February 1927.
7   'In Memoriam', Thomas Clark Westfield, 31 October, 1905.

PART THREE

Chapter 1 – Thomas William Francis Clark

1   GRO birth certificate for Thomas William Francis Clark, 11 August, 1866. Croydon.
2   1871 census, Thomas and Frances Clark and family, Brighton Road, Sutton. Ancestry. com: Class: RG10; Piece: 796; Folio: 92; Page: 24.
3   Matilda Hephzibah Clark, *Diary 1872-1874*
4   Annie Clark, born in 1868, was the daughter of Frederick Henry Clark, the younger brother of Thomas Clark.
5   1881 Census, Grammar School, High Street, Chipping Ongar, Essex. Ancestry.com: Class RG11; Piece: 1741; Folio: 56. Page: 39.
6   Ongar Millennium History Group, *Aspects of the History of Ongar: The History of Ongar Grammar School Part two: 1860-1940* (Ongar, Ongar Millennium History Project, 1999). p.162.
7   *Ibid.*, p.159.
8   *Ibid.*
9   *Ibid.*, p.166.
10 *Ibid.*, p.161.
11 *Ibid.*
12 1881 Census, Grammar School, High Street, Chipping Ongar, Essex. Ancestry.com: Class RG11; Piece: 1741; Folio: 56. Page: 39.
13 Ongar Millennium History Group, *Op.cit* ., pp. 160-161.
14 1881 Census, Grammar School, High Street, Chipping Ongar, Essex. Ancestry.com: Class RG11; Piece: 1741; Folio: 56. Page: 39.
15 Ongar Millennium History Group, *Op.cit* .,p. 165.
16 *Ibid.*, p. 166.
17 *Ibid.*, p. 161.
18 1881 Census, Grammar School, High Street, Chipping Ongar, Essex. Ancestry.com: Class RG11; Piece: 1741; Folio: 56. Page: 39.
19 Ongar Millennium History Group, *Op.cit.*,p. 165.
20 *Ibid.*, p. 166.
21 *Ibid.*, p. 162.
22 *Ibid.*, pp. 164-165.
23 1891 Census, Thomas Clark and family, 'Devonia', Queen's Road, Leyton. Ancestry. com: Class: RG12; Piece: 1346; Folio: 98; Page: 20.

24 GRO Marriage Certificate for Thomas William Francis Clark and Rose Eveline Clara Carter, 31 August 1895. Edmonton Register Office.

25 Ancestry.com: FreeBMD, England & Wales, Civil Registration Birth Index, 1837-1915. Thomas John W. Clark: Qtr. Dec, 1895; Reg. Dist: Edmonton; Vol. 3a; Page: 333.

26 GRO birth certificate, Mabel Eveline Janet Clark, 2 January 1897. Edmonton.

27 Ancestry.com: FreeBMD, England & Wales, Civil Registration Birth Index, 1837-1915 Leonard Albert S. Clark: Qtr. Sep, 1898; Reg. Dist: West Ham; Vol: 4a; Page: 243.

28 1901 census Rose Clark and family, 108 Leigh Road, Walthamstow. Ancestry.com: 1901 England Census Class: RG13; Piece: 1629; Folio: 41; Page: 12.

29 1911 Census, Thomas Clark and Thomas Clark junior, Edith Cottage, Clifton Road. Ancestry.com: 1911 England Census [database Online], Class: RG14; Piece: 10019; Schedule No. 4.

30 1911 census Rose and Alfred Moss and family, 25 Ashford Road, Walthamstow. Ancestry.com: 1911 England Census [Database Online], Class: RG14; Piece: 9686; Schedule Number: 277.

31 Ancestry.com: FreeBMD England & Wales, Civil Registration Marriage Index, 1837-1901. Rose E.C. Clark and Moss: Qtr: Jun,1914; Reg. Dist: West Ham; Vol: 4a; Page: 569.

32 Personal correspondence (Maurice Wood) 7 March 1990.

33 Personal correspondence (Eunice Bridge née Croisette) 6 May 1995.

34 GRO death certificate Thomas William Francis Clark, 29 April, 1947. Rochford.

35 Ancestry.com: Essex, England, Church of England Deaths and Burials, 1813-1994; Essex Record Office; Chelmsford, Essex; Essex Church of England Parish Registers.

Chapter 2 – Ernest Percival Frederick Clark

1 GRO birth certificate, Ernest Percival Frederick Clark, 15 April 1868, Camberwell.

2 1861 Census, Charles H. Vizer and family, Clarendon House, Camberwell. Ancestry. com: Class: RG9; Piece: 1387; Folio: 165; Page: 21.

3 1871 Census, Thomas and Frances Clark and family, Brighton Road, Sutton. Ancestry. com: Class: RG10; Piece: 796; Folio: 92; Page: 24.

4 Matilda Hephzibah Clark, *diary*, 1872-1874

5 Personal correspondence, Robert Randell Clark, 20th August 1994.

6 Ongar Millennium History Group, *Aspects of the History of Ongar: The History of Ongar Grammar School Part two: 1860-1940* (Ongar, Ongar Millennium History Project, 1999). p.163.

7 *Ibid.*, p.166.

8 1891 Census, Thomas Clark and family, 'Devonia', Queen's Road, Leyton. Ancestry. com: Class: RG12; Piece: 1346; Folio: 98; Page: 20.

9 Parish Register Ernest Percival Frederick Clark and Gertrude Susie Clarke, 15 August 1900, St. Botolph Bishopsgate, city of London.

10 1901 Census, Ernest and Susie Clark, Pevensey, Churchgate, Cheshunt. Ancestry.com: Class: RG13; Piece: 1278; Folio: 75; Page: 1.

11 *Ibid.*

12 GRO Birth Certificate, Maurice Randell Clark, 2 June 1904, Edmonton.

13 Ancestry.com: LMA; London, City Directories, 1736-1943.

14 Edith's Streets – *Local London History, Albury Ride* (14 January 2012) <https://edithsstreets.blogspot.com/search?q=Albury+Ride> [Accessed 13th November 2020].

15 1911 census, Ernest and Susie Clark, Vista, Albury Ride, Cheshunt. Ancestry.com: 1911 England Census [database Online], Class: RG14; Piece: 7455; Schedule No. 153.

16 Personal correspondence, (Robert Randell Clark) 14 October 2019.

17 Robinson was awarded the Victoria Cross for his action but he did not live long; he died in the Spanish influenza epidemic at the end of 1918. The German men were given a military funeral at Potters Bar cemetery and they were reinterred at Cannock Chase German Cemetery in 1962.

18 The Worcestershire Regiment: Captain William Leefe Robinson, V.C. – Shoots down SL11 Zeppelin (no date) <http://www.worcestershireregiment.com/wr.php?main=inc/vc_w_l_robinson_page6#:> [Accessed 13 November 2020] This website contains a comprehensive account of the life and times of Leefe Robinson.

19 Percy's London address, 22 Shirehall Park, Hendon. Ancestry.com: LMA; London: Electoral Registers 1832-1965.

20 Stella Gedge was born on 19 March 1922 and married Henry Moule in 1943. She died in 1992 in Norfolk.

21 Personal correspondence (Maurice Wood) 7 March 1990.

22 Verbal testimony (Marjorie Walshe née Westfield)

23 Will of Ernest Percival Frederick Clark. Ancestry.com; England and Wales, National Probate Calender (Index of Wills and Administrations), 1858-1966.

Chapter 3 – Hebert Lionel Alexander Clark

1 GRO Certificate, Herbert Lionel Alexander Clark, 15 January 1872, Epsom.

2 1891 Census, Thomas Clark and family, 'Devonia', Queen's Road, Leyton. Ancestry.com: Class: RG12; Piece: 1346; Folio: 98; Page: 20.

3 Herbert's daughter Marjorie recalled being taken to the theatre in Norwich during the 1930s to see a musical hall artiste. Possibly this was Vesta Victoria (1873-1951) who was active until 1938 performing during these end days of the music hall era.

4 Baptism of Violet Frances Dorothy Clark. Ancestry.com: Essex, England, Church of England births and baptisms, 1813-1918; Essex Record Office; Chelmsford, Essex, Church of England Parish Registers.

5 Ancestry.com: 1939 England and Wales Register, The National Archives, Kew. Ref: RG10/1473C.

6 1901 Census, Herbert Clark and family, Clifton Road, Bowers Gifford. Ancestry.com: 1901 England census. Class: RG13; Piece 1667; Folio: 23; Page: 5.

7 The 1911 census forms required the householder to state how many rooms they had in their dwelling.

8 Chelmsford Record Office; Log Book: North Benfleet Church of England Primary School; 1891-1905 Ref E/ML 176/1 and 1905-1921 Ref E/ML 176/2.

9 1908 trade directory. Ancestry.com:London, City Directories, 1736-1943; LMA, London.

10 1910 Kelly's Directory. Ancestry.com: UK, City and County Directories, 1766-1946.

11 Verbal testimony (Eunice Bridge née Croisette).

12 1911 Census, Herbert Clark and family, Clifton Road, Bowers Gifford. Ancestry.com: 1911 England Census [database Online], Class: RG14; Piece: 10019; Schedule No. 5.

13 1911 census, Violet Clark. Ancestry.com: 1911 England Census [Database Online], Class: RG14; Piece: 9619; Schedule Number: 40.

14 Verbal testimony (Marjorie Walshe née Westfield).

15 Parish Register Violet Frances Dorothy Clark-Westfield and Harold Alexander Rand, 1 July July 1916. Ancestry.com: Essex Record Office; Chelmsford, Essex, England; Church of England Parish Registers, Church of England Marriages 1754-1935.

16 Verbal testimony (Lawrence Rand).

17 Parish Register, Winifred Edith Clark-Westfield and Alfred Marc Croisette, October 1916, South Benfleet, St. Mary the Virgin. Ancestry.com: Essex Record Office; Chelmsford, Essex, England; Church of England Parish Registers, Church of England Marriages 1754-1935.

18 Kelly's Directory of Essex, 1922.

19 Ancestry.com: Free BMD; England and Wales: Civil Registration Birth Index, 1837-1915.

20 'Attleborough Petty Sessions – Monday', *Diss Express and Norfolk and Suffolk Journal*, October 5, 1923. p. 8.

21 Divorce Papers, Edith Mary Clark and Herbert Lionel Clark PRO J77/2276

22 Verbal testimony (Marjorie Walshe née Westfield).

23 Weather reports state that the end of the year of 1925 brought heavy snowfall whilst there was a late August heatwave in 1926.

24 John Loveday, *The Boy from Rod Alley: An Account of a 1930s Childhood* (Kibworth Beauchamp, Matador, 2019) p. 124.

25 Herbert's father Thomas Clark perhaps followed the theories of William Paley (1743-1805) who used the 'Watchmaker argument' for creation as a teleological one which stated by way of analogy, that a design implies a designer. The existence of an intelligent creator deity was used to support the existence of God and intelligent design.

26 Master Joe Petersen was actually a Scottish female named Mary O'Rourke (1913-1964) who dressed as a boy. During the 1930s boy sopranos (contraltos) were very popular. Recording from 1933 onwards her last record was released in 1942. She lived a sad life and died relatively young an alcoholic.

27 The Legend of Sister Beatrix (La Legende de Souer Beatrix) was a 1923 French silent film starring Sandra Milovanoff (1892-1957).

28 This book although not known or named by Marjorie was almost certainly 'Christ, the Life of the Soul' by Columba Marmion OSB which was published in 1917. It was an overwhelming success in the Catholic world and was revolutionary for the church.

29 Herbert was incorrect because this actually referred to the old religion of Rome under the emperors, rather than the later concept of the papacy.

Chapter 4 – Bertram Allan Leslie Clark

1 Personal correspondence (Patricia Cowley) 13 January 1992.

2 1891 Census, Thomas Clark and family, 'Devonia', Queen's Road, Leyton. Ancestry.com: Class: RG12; Piece: 1346; Folio: 98; Page: 20. This states that Bertram Clark was a 15-year-old scholar.

3 1901 Census, Thomas Clark and family, 27 Springfield, Upper Clapton. Ancestry.com: Class: RG13; Piece: 211; Folio: 10/11; Page: 12-13.

4 Birth certificate of Ethel Maud Mary Lamerton, 1879. FreeBMD: England &Wales, Civil Registration Birth Index, 1837-1915

5 Walter E. Lamerton and family, Rectory House, Whaddon, Gloucester. Ancestry.com: The National Archives of the UK (TNA); Kew, Surrey, England; Census Returns of

England and Wales, 1891; Class: RG12; Piece: 2015; Folio: 27; Page: 2.

6   1901 Census, Walter E. Lamerton and family, 63 Dartmouth Park Hill, St. Pancras. Ancestry.com: Class: RG13; Piece: 156; Folio: 39; Page: 2.

7   Parish Register Bertram Allan Leslie Clark and Ethel Maud Lamerton, July 1902. Ancestry.com: Essex Record Office; Chelmsford, Essex, England; Church of England Parish Registers, Church of England Marriages 1754-1935. All Saints' Church, North Benfleet is now a Greek Orthodox Church having been made redundant in 1996, it was returned to regular use in 2013.

8   Ancestry.com: 1939 England and Wales Register, The National Archives, Kew. Ref: RG101/5656I.

9   Ancestry.com: Church of England Births and Baptisms 1813-1916; LMA; London, England; Board of Guardian Records, 1834-1906/Church of England Parish Registers, 1754-1906; Ref. No: dro/020/a/01/026.

10   GRO birth certificate of Muriel Lamerton Clark, 8 August 1908, Kensington.

11   Ancestry.com: UK Lunacy Patients Admission Registers, 1846-1912; The National Archives, Kew, Surrey, England; Class: MH94; Piece: 44.

12   GRO death certificate, Ethel Maud Mary Clark, 8 March 1909, Barnet.

13   Ancestry.com: Church of England Deaths and Burials, 1813-2003; LMA, London, England; Reference Number: P90/pan1/209.

14   The living arrangement of Rita and Muriel Clark were provided by Muriel's daughter Pat. However, at the time of the 1911 census, six-year-old Rita Clark was staying with her uncle Herbert, his wife, Edith and her cousins at Bowers Gifford.

15   Bertram revealed in a letter to his local newspaper in January 1921 that during 1909 he invented a flaming bullet which he claimed preceded a similar incendiary device developed in Coventry during WWI.

16   1891 Census, George Steer and family, 9d Horn Lane, Greenwich. Ancestry.com: Class: RG12; Piece: 513; Folio: 110; Page: 26.

17   1901 Census, George Steer and family, Southend Road, Vange, Essex. Ancestry.com: Class: RG13; Piece: 1668; Folio: 46; Page: 12/13.

18   'Vange Post Office Destroyed by Fire: Appeal by the Rector on behalf of the Postmaster', *The Newsman*, 8 March, 1902. p.3.

19   1911 Census, George Steer and family, Post Office, Vange, Essex. Ancestry.com: 1911 England Census [database Online], Class: RG14; Piece: 10028; Schedule No. 19.

20   Parish Register marriage Bertram Allan Leslie Clark and Emily Steer, October 1911. Ancestry.com: Essex Record Office; Chelmsford, Essex, England; Church of England Parish Registers, Church of England Marriages 1754-1935.

21   Personal correspondence (Patricia Cowley) 13 January 1992.

22   George and Bertram Clark, 1914. Ancestry.com: FreeBMD: England & Wales, Civil Registration Birth Index, 1837-1915
Ancestry.com: FreeBMD: England & Wales, Civil Registration Death Index, 1837-1915 Baby Bertram's death entry states that he was premature. It was later mistakenly recalled by Roy's wife Edna (nee Patchett) that the twins died in the influenza pandemic of 1918/19.

23   See Jenny Waddingham, 2018, World War One: How Coventry Fed the Allied War Machine Available from *Coventry Live*, 6 November <Coventry was centre of munitions production during World War One – CoventryLive (coventrytelegraph. net)> [Accessed 14 January 2021]. For the duration of the war, the War Department spent more than £40 million on contracts with Coventry companies – the equivalent of over £1 billion today.

24   'The Incendiary Bullet', *The Midland Daily Telegraph*, 28 January, 1921. p.2.

25 Ancestry.com: 1939 England and Wales Register, The National Archives, Kew. Ref: RG101/5647B.

26 Verbal testimony of Roy's daughter, January 2020.

27 Personal correspondence (Patricia Cowley) 13 January 1992.

28 'Fighting the Zepps – An Incendiary Bullet: Government Reward Coventry Inventor', *The Midland Daily Telegraph, 26 January, 1921. p.2.

29 'The Incendiary Bullet', *The Midland Daily Telegraph*, 28 January, 1921. p.2.

30 Personal correspondence (Patricia Cowley) 13 January 1992.

31 Personal correspondence (Ron Brookes) December 1991. The houses in Broad Street were demolished in the mid-1970s after being empty for some time and unfit for habitation.

32 'Sales by Auction – George Loveitt & Sons: Broad Street', *The Coventry Herald,* 26 January, 1923. p.6.
    'Sales by Auction – George Loveitt & Sons: Broad Street', *The Coventry Herald*, February 2 and 3, 1923. p.6.
    'Property Market: Coventry Properties', *The Coventry Herald*, March 23 and 24, 1923. p.12

33 Personal correspondence (Constance Leigh, nee Hirons) 14 October 1997.

34 Personal correspondence (Vincent Ball) 13 December 1991.

35 Matilda Clark mentioned in her diary in 1873 that her brother Tom had given her some strawberry plants.

36 Personal correspondence, (Constance Leigh, née Hirons) 14 October 1997.

37 Personal correspondence (Patricia Cowley) 13 January 1992.

38 Verbal testimony of Roy's daughter, January 2020.

39 Personal correspondence (Patricia Cowley) 13 January 1992.

40 Verbal testimony (Marjorie Walshe, née Westfield).

41 'Letters to the Editor: Guns Before Butter', *The Coventry Evening Telegraph*, 3 February, 1942. p.4.

42 Personal correspondence (Patricia Cowley) 13 January 1992.

43 Personal correspondence (Ron Brookes) December 1991.

44 'Gardening Specialities – Cactus and Succulent Plants for sale', *The Coventry Evening Telegraph*, 22 May, 1942. p.7.

45 Personal correspondence (Ron Brookes) December 1991.

46 GRO death certificate, Bertram Allan Leslie Clark, 28 August, 1944, Nuneaton.

47 'Births, Marriages, Deaths and In Memoriam Notices – Deaths: CLARK', *The Coventry Evening Telegraph*, 29 August, 1944. p.4.

48 *Ibid.*

Chapter 5 – Walter Vivian Harold Clark

1 Ancestry.com: FreeBMD; England & Wales, Civil Registration Birth Index, 1837-1915

2 1891 Census, Thomas Clark and family, 'Devonia', Queen's Road, Leyton. Ancestry.com: Class: RG12; Piece: 1346; Folio: 98; Page: 20.

3 Ancestry.com: Church of England birth and baptisms 1813-1916 LMA; London, England; Reference Number P79/mtw/003.

4 1901 Census, Thomas Clark and family, 27 Springfield, Upper Clapton. Ancestry.com: Class: RG13; Piece: 211; Folio: 10/11; Page: 12-13.

5 'Music', *Lloyd's Weekly Newspaper*, June 29, 1902. p.8.

6 Ancestry.com: Essex Record Office; Chelmsford, Essex, England; Church of England

Parish Registers, Church of England Marriages 1754-1935.

7   1901 Census, William Dennis and family, 636a Romford Road, East Ham. Ancestry.
     com: RG13; Piece: 1600; Folio: 105; Page 1.
8   1911 census, Walter and Gertrude Clark-Westfield, 1 Brancaster Road, Manor Park.
     Ancestry.com: RG14; Piece 9583; Schedule No: 363.
9   Ancestry.com: FreeBMD; England & Wales, Civil Registration Birth Index, 1837-1915
10   Verbal testimony (Marjorie Walshe née Westfield).
11   Will of Ernest Percival Frederick Clark. Ancestry.com; England and Wales, National
     Probate Calender (Index of Wills and Administrations), 1858-1966.
12   Ancestry:com: 1939 England and Wales Register; The National Archives, Kew,
     London; Ref. RG101/1026E.
13   1945 marriage of Don Lamble to Gladys Drinkwater. Ancestry.com: Civil Marriage
     Registration Index, 1916-2005; GRO, UK; Volume 8a; Page 1648.
14   Personal correspondence (Maurice Wood) 3 June 1991.
15   Personal correspondence (Peter Taylor-Wood) summer 1991.
16   GRO death certificate, Walter Clark Westfield, 7 November, 1957. Ilford.
17   Personal correspondence (Maurice Wood) 7 March 1991.

Chapter 6 – Beatrice Frances Mary Clark

1   GRO birth certificate, Beatrice Frances Mary Clark, 9 June, 1879, Edmonton.
2   1901 Census, Thomas Clark and family, 27 Springfield, Upper Clapton. Ancestry.com:
     Class: RG13; Piece: 211; Folio: 10/11; Page: 12-13.
3   Parish Register Bertram Allan Leslie Clark and Ethel Maud Lamerton, July 1902.
     Ancestry.com: Essex Record Office; Chelmsford, Essex, England; Church of England
     Parish Registers, Church of England Marriages 1754-1935.
4   Birth of Edmund Palmer, 1880. Ancestry.com: FreeBMD: England & Wales, Civil
     Registration Birth Index, 1837-1915
5   Ancestry.com: United Grand Lodge of England Freemason Membership Registers,
     1751-1921. Library and Museum of Freemasonry; London, England; Freemasonry
     Membership Registers, London F1541-1679 to London G1681-1922; Reel Number: 4.
6   1901 census Edmund Palmer and family, 51 Newington Butts, Newington. Ancestry.
     com: RG13; Piece: 384; Folio: 80; Page: 35.
7   1891 census David Witton and family, 58 Queen's Road, Shoreditch. Ancestry.com: The
     National Archives of the UK (TNA); Kew, Surrey, England; Class: RG12; Piece: 255;
     Folio: 55; Page: 1.
8   London Weather : *1904 rather dry and cool. A chilly autumn.* 2014, <http://www.
     london-weather.eu/article.44.html> [Accessed 18 November 2020].
9   GRO marriage certificate, Beatrice Frances Mary Clark and Edmund Henry George
     Palmer, 22nd June, 1904. Billericay.
10   Ancestry.com: FreeBMD, England & Wales, Civil Registration Birth Index, 1837-1915
11   1911 census, Edmund Palmer and family, 288 Green Street, Forest Gate. Ancestry.com:
     1911 England Census [Database Online], Class: RG14; Piece: 9374; Schedule No: 195.
12   In the 1911 census, the family disclose that they have two living children and one
     which had died. It is remembered that a son had been mentioned before but no details
     can be confirmed.
13   Ancestry.com: FreeBMD, England & Wales, Civil Registration Birth Index, 1837-1915
14   Personal correspondence (Peter Taylor-Wood) summer 1991.

15   1911 census, Edmund Palmer and family, 288 Green Street, Forest Gate. Ancestry.com:
     1911 England Census [Database Online], Class: RG14; Piece: 9374; Schedule No: 195.
16   1911 Census, Herbert Clark and family, Clifton Road, Bowers Gifford. Ancestry.com:
     1911 England Census [database Online], Class: RG14; Piece: 10019; Schedule No. 5.
17   Personal correspondence (Peter Taylor-Wood) summer 1991.
18   *Ibid*.
19   Ancestry.com: England and Wales Civil Registration Death Index, 1916-2007.
20   *Ibid*.